THE STATE OF FOOD AND AGRICULTURE 1993

FAO Agriculture Series

No. 26

ISSN 0081-4539

THE STATE OF FOOD AND AGRICULTURE 1993

FOOD AND AGRICULTURE ORGANIZATION OF THE UNITED NATIONS

Rome, 1993

The statistical material in this publication has been prepared from the information available to FAO up to August 1993.

The designations employed and the presentation do not imply the expression of any opinion whatsoever on the part of the Food and Agriculture Organization of the United Nations concerning the legal status of any country, territory, city or area, or of its authorities, or concerning the delimitation of its frontiers or boundaries. In some tables, the designations "developed" and "developing" economies are intended for statistical convenience and do not necessarily express a judgement about the stage reached by a particular country or area in the development process.

FAO, Rome (Italy)
The state of food and agriculture 1993.
(FAO Agriculture Series, no. 26)
ISBN 92-5-103360-9

1. Agriculture.   2. Food production.   3. Trade

I. Title   II. Series

FAO code: 70   AGRIS: E16 E70

Foreword

The world has changed in remarkable ways since, as the newly elected Director-General of FAO, I first prepared the foreword to *The State of Food and Agriculture 1975*. On that occasion, and for each of the 17 issues that were to follow, we focused on the current outlook, pointing out important improvements and highlighting the many alarming aspects of the world's situation – food insecurity, poverty and environmental degradation, to name a few. In this foreword, I wish to break with that tradition and share some reflections and thoughts about the past.

As an international civil servant who has served FAO for well over 30 years, I recall the heady and optimistic days of the early 1960s when colonial empires were dissolving and new nations were springing to life in every part of the world. Humankind seemed then to be on the verge of a technological and scientific breakthrough, with formidable progress being achieved in the fields of space exploration, data processing, telecommunications and – most important for agriculture – the green revolution which was under way in Asia.

It was a time when the Cold War was also at its height, but great faith was being put on multilateral action to promote development and economic growth and to maintain peace. I decided to join FAO not only because the United Nations system was being called on as the major conduit of high-quality technical and material assistance to developing countries, but mainly because FAO was the first expression of that postwar idealism that was soon to be embodied in the UN Charter as a global response to the cry for social justice for the underprivileged, the poor and the hungry.

During my early years with FAO – in fact, throughout the 1960s – economic growth and improved living standards in the developing countries were the rule, not the exception. Primary product prices were relatively stable, official development assistance was increasing in real terms over time and the presence of large stocks of cereals was taken for granted.

This relatively stable era for most developing countries came to an end with the oil price increases of 1972-73 and the fall in grain production in the main producing areas in 1972. Import needs rose, and grain surpluses disappeared almost overnight. A buying panic ensued, with cereal prices more than tripling and fertilizer prices more than quadrupling. Oil-importing developing countries turned to official and private financial markets to pay for imports and fill current account gaps. In 1975 when I was first elected Director-General, the world was in the midst of a major food crisis and a rapidly emerging debt crisis.

As the world recession unfolded in the early 1980s, the debt crisis matured. Economic recession and rising protectionism sharply reduced import demand. The terms of trade collapsed as oil and oil-based energy prices initially soared and prices of other commodities fell. The eagerness of the commercial banks to grant loans turned to an eagerness for repayment, and interest rates increased sharply, resulting in burgeoning debt-service payments. Developing countries faced a profoundly different world economic environment where repaying loans dominated both discussions and decisions on how economic adjustment should proceed during the 1980s.

After three postwar decades that involved grappling with economic expansion, the international development agencies, policy-makers and theoreticians had become accustomed to taking growth for granted and to debating how it could be optimized in terms of its rate and distribution. It was not expected that most developing countries would be implementing austerity programmes amid severe policy constraints caused by debt-service burdens, fiscal imbalances and balance-of-payments problems, to say nothing of civil strife.

Thus, the 1980s introduced a grimmer period of declining per caput incomes in most developing countries. Development assistance gradually shifted away from projects and the direct creation of infrastructure, and moved instead towards conditional lending that required changes in economic policy and management as well as institutional reforms. During the 1980s, these "stabilization" and "structural adjustment" programmes became commonplace. Ironically, while the developing countries came under heavy external pressure to adopt adjustment policies (devaluation, fiscal and monetary restraint, market and trade liberalization), most of the OECD countries became increasingly protectionist and pursued unsustainable financial policies.

For many developing countries, the 1980s was certainly a period of frustration. For others, including the most populous ones, the decade saw periods of remarkable progress. But all of us entered the 1990s with a renewed awareness that development should first and foremost emphasize its human dimensions. This renewed emphasis has had a number of important implications. First, recognition dawned of the need to "adjust adjustment" in such a way as to attenuate its recessive effects and to alleviate acute disparities and social hardship. Second, the importance of people's knowledge, skills and aptitudes, together with the strengthening of appropriate institutions and mechanisms that would enable them to participate in the development process, was recognized. Third, the need to enhance food security and nutrition policies and programmes became apparent, with the recognition that food access often has more to do with incomes than with supply. Finally, we began to focus collectively on improving the sustainability of agriculture and rural development.

Although we are no longer haunted by the imminent risk of nuclear conflagration, sadly, many regions of the world are as turbulent today as they were in 1975. Furthermore, many industrial countries are grappling with crucial political choices regarding national and regional issues. West European countries are pursuing efforts aimed at closer integration despite mounting and unforeseen political and economic difficulties. Market-oriented transformations are continuing in Eastern Europe and the former USSR in the context of grave economic and social disruptions, plummeting agricultural and industrial production; and ethnic and political tensions which, in former Yugoslavia, SFR, have degenerated into a devastating armed conflict.

These events have taken place in an overall climate of economic malaise. The much-awaited and repeatedly predicted revival of economic growth in the industrial countries has remained elusive. Instead, rising unemployment, unstable financial and foreign exchange markets and severe budgetary difficulties in several industrial countries have continued to exert their destabilizing influence worldwide.

Yet, there are many reasons to be optimistic when drawing lessons from past experiences. Despite the recent and dramatic changes in the political and economic environment, the rivalries among power blocs and the rhetorical exchanges of accusations across ideological divides have ceased and have been replaced by a renewed confidence in the ability of the UN system to find mutually agreed solutions to global problems.

On the whole, developing countries have much to be proud of with respect to their substantial progress in life expectancy, child mortality and educational attainment. Likewise, FAO can take pride in its efforts to help the developing countries improve their agricultural sectors and enhance rural welfare. Even though the world has about 1.5 billion more inhabitants than when I took office, the global community has proved its ability to provide sufficient food and to avert food crises brought about by natural disasters. We have achieved substantial increases in per caput food supplies worldwide and many of today's developing countries now cover a significant proportion of their populations' food needs.

Today we are producing more cereals on less land than we did in 1975 – rice and wheat yields have increased by nearly 50 percent, maize yields by more than 35 percent and pulses by 30 percent. Similar gains have been made in livestock, forestry and fisheries. Aquaculture, for instance, was only an infant industry 20 years ago but, today, it provides food, jobs and income for millions.

These significant achievements have meant that world food production has outpaced population growth and that per caput calorie consumption is approximately 10 percent above what it was in the mid-1970s.

Our changing world is always producing surprises, both good and bad. And while we may not be entirely able to determine the course of events, it remains my conviction that we can at least have a hand in influencing it. Indeed, in some instances, our action can make the difference between survival and death, welfare and destitution and progress and frustration for millions of people. This is true for Africa, as it is for other developing country regions around the world.

Perhaps the most critical issues today are the paucity of financial resources to fuel the development process and the consequent need to generate the necessary political commitment for increasing and channelling these resources so as to improve the well-being of the poor relative to the rich. The widely documented gap between the poor and the rich continues to grow in almost every nation of the world – a situation that can only lead to even greater tensions and turmoil.

Not long ago it was hoped that a substantial share of the so-called peace dividend would be allocated for development. Instead, it has been absorbed by peacemaking, peace-keeping, emergency relief, unification, domestic programmes, reductions in fiscal imbalances on national accounts, and other uses. The key to relief from these demands, and the major ingredient for avoiding further social disintegration and violence, is an acceleration in the development process and, in the poorer countries of the world, sustainable agriculture and rural development.

It is my hope that the international community will recognize that equitable and sustainable development is the only way to avoid massive outlays for peacemaking, peace-keeping and relief, and that it will consequently rise to the challenge presented by the current situation.

Edouard Saouma
DIRECTOR-GENERAL

Contents

PART II
REGIONAL REVIEW

EXHIBITS

BOXES

TABLES

FIGURES

Acknowledgements

The State of Food and Agriculture 1993 *has been prepared by a team from the Policy Analysis Division led by F.L. Zegarra and comprising P.L. Iacoacci, G.E. Rossmiller, J. Skoet, K. Stamoulis and R. Stringer. Secretarial support was provided by S. Di Lorenzo and P. Di Santo; computer and statistical support was provided by T. Sadek, G. Arena and Z. Pinna.*

Background papers for the World review were prepared by I.J. Bourke, P. D'Angelo, D.J. Doulman, G.V. Everett, R. Grainger, J. Greenfield, V. Menza, E.B. Riordan, R.B. Singh, S. Teodosijevic, P.A. Wardle.

Background papers for the Regional review were prepared by M. Burfisher, A. Buainain, O. Cismondi, N.J. Cochrane, D. Phiri, S. Pollack, P. Mudbhary, R. Kennedy, and K.E. Wädekin.

The special chapter, Water policies and agriculture, was prepared by R. Stringer, with contributions from I.H. Carruthers and R. Young.

The State of Food and Agriculture 1993 *was edited by R. Tucker, the graphics were prepared by M. Cappucci and the layout by M. Criscuolo with C. Ciarlantini. The cover and illustrations were produced by Studio Page.*

Glossary

AAF-SAP
African Alternative Framework to Structural Adjustment Programmes for Socio-Economic Transformation
ACDESS
African Centre for Development and Strategic Studies
AFB
River Basin Financial Agency
AfDB
African Development Bank
AFTA
ASEAN Free Trade Area
AKKOR
Association of Peasant Farms and Cooperatives of Russia
AMC
Agricultural Marketing Corporation
ARP
Acreage Reduction Program
AsDB
Asian Development Bank
ASEAN
Association of Southeast Asian Nations

BADC
Bangladesh Agricultural Development Corporation
BANRURAL
Banco Nacional de Crédito Rural
BCA
Benefit-cost analysis

CAP
Common Agricultural Policy
CCC
Commodity Credit Corporation
CDS
Conservation-based development strategy
CEC
Commission of the European Communities
CGIAR
Consultative Group on International Agricultural Research

c.i.f.
Cost, insurance and freight
CIS
Commonwealth of Independent States
CMEA
Council for Mutual Economic Assistance
CPI
Consumer price index
CRP
Conservation Reserve Program

DRS
Debtor Reporting System

EAP
Economically active population
ECA
Economic Commission for Africa
ECLAC
Economic Commission for Latin America and the Caribbean
ECU
European Currency Unit
EDAEs
Economies highly dependent on agricultural exports
EEC
European Economic Community
EEP
Export Enhancement Program
EEZ
Exclusive economic zone
ERM
Exchange rate mechanism
ERSAP
Economic reform and structural adjustment programme

FACT
Food, Agriculture, Conservation and Trade Act
FFP
Food for Progress

FIRA
Fideicomiso Instituído en Relación con
la Agricultura
f.o.b.
Free on board
FOCIR
Fund for Rural Investment and Capitalization
FOR
Farmer-Owned Reserve
FSWR
Food Security Wheat Reserve
FY
Fiscal year

GATT
General Agreement on Tariffs and Trade
GDP
Gross domestic product
GEMS
Global Environment Monitoring System
GNP
Gross national product
GTZ
German Agency for Technical Cooperation

HYV
High-yielding variety

IAP-WASAD
International Action Programme on
Water and Sustainable Agricultural
Development
ICCO
International Cocoa Organization
ICN
International Conference on Nutrition
ICO
International Coffee Organization
ICSU
International Council of Scientific
Unions
ICWE
International Conference on Water and
the Environment
IDA
International Development Association
IEFR
International Emergency Food Reserve

IFAD
International Fund for Agricultural
Development
IFPRI
International Food Policy Research Institute
IIMI
International Irrigation Management
Institute
IMF
International Monetary Fund
IPR
Intellectual property rights
ISA
International Sugar Agreement
ITTO
International Tropical Timber
Organization

LDCs
Least-developed countries
LIFDCs
Low-income food-deficit countries
LPCs
Low-potential cropping areas

MERCOSUR
Southern Common Market
MTNs
Multilateral trade negotiations

NAFINSA
Nacional Financiera
NAFTA
North American Free Trade Association
NGO
Non-governmental organization
NIA
National Irrigation Administration
NMP
Net material product

OAU
Organization of African Unity
ODA
Official Development Assistance
OECD
Organisation for Economic Cooperation
and Development

PAEC
Pan-African Economic Community
PAP
Poverty Alleviation Plan
PA
Peasant association
PECE
Pact for Economic Stabilization and Growth
PEM
Protein-energy malnutrition
PRONASOL
National Solidarity Programme
PSE
Producer subsidy equivalent
PTA
Preferential Trade Area for Eastern and
Southern African States

RBC
River Basin Committee

SAARC
South Asian Association for Regional
Cooperation
SADC
Southern African Development
Community
SADCC
Southern African Development Coordination
Conference
SAFTA
South Asian Free Trade Area
SAHR
Secretariat of State for Agriculture and Water
Resources
SAM
Mexican Food System
SICA
Central American Integration System
SM
Suspended particulate matter

TGE
Transitional Government of Ethiopia
TNC
Trade Negotiations Committee
TRQ
Tariff-rate quota

UN
United Nations
UNCED
United Nations Conference on Environment
and Development
UNCTAD
United Nations Conference on Trade and
Development
UNDP
United Nations Development Programme
UNEP
United Nations Environment Programme
Unesco
United Nations Educational, Scientific and
Cultural Organization
UNICEF
United Nations Children's Fund
UNIDO
United Nations Industrial Development
Organization
UNSO
United Nations Sudano-Sahelian Office
USAID
United States Agency for International
Development

VMR
Voluntary marketed rice

WFP
World Food Programme
WHO
World Health Organization
WMO
World Meteorological Organization
WRI
World Resources Institute

ZEN-NOH
National Federation of Agricultural
Cooperative Associations
ZENCHU
Central Union of Agricultural Cooperatives

Explanatory note

The following symbols are used in the tables:

-	=	none or negligible
...	=	not available
1991/92	=	a crop, marketing or fiscal year running from one calendar year to the next
1990-92	=	average for three calendar years

Figures in statistical tables may not add up because of rounding. Annual changes and rates of change have been calculated from unrounded figures. Unless otherwise indicated, the metric system is used throughout.

The dollar sign ($) refers to US dollars. "Billion", used throughout, is equal to 1 000 million.

Production index numbers
FAO index numbers have *1979-81* as the base period. The production data refer to primary commodities (e.g. sugar cane and sugar beet instead of sugar) and national average producer prices are used as weights. The indices for food products exclude tobacco, coffee, tea, inedible oil seeds, animal and vegetable fibres and rubber. They are based on production data presented on a calendar-year basis.[1]

Trade index numbers
The indices of trade in agricultural products also are based on *1979-81*. They include all the commodities and countries shown in the *FAO Trade Yearbook*. Indices of total food products include those edible products generally classified as "food".

All indices represent changes in current values of exports (f.o.b.) and imports (c.i.f.), all expressed in US dollars. When countries report imports valued at f.o.b. (free on board), these are adjusted to approximate c.i.f. (cost, insurance, freight) values. This method of estimation shows a discrepancy whenever the trend of insurance and freight diverges from that of the commodity unit values.

Volumes and unit value indices represent the changes in the price-weighted sum of quantities and of the quantity-weighted unit values of products traded between countries. The weights are, respectively, the price and quantity averages of 1979-81, which is the base reference period used for all the index number series currently computed by FAO. The Laspeyres formula is used in the construction of the index numbers.[2]

Definitions of "narrow" and "broad"
The OECD definitions of agriculture are generally used in reporting on external assistance to agriculture. The *narrow* definition of agriculture, now referred to as "directly to the sector" includes the following items:
- Appraisal of natural resources
- Development and management of natural resources
- Research
- Supply of production inputs
- Fertilizers
- Agricultural services
- Training and extension
- Crop production
- Livestock development
- Fisheries
- Agriculture (subsector unallocated)

---

[1] For full details, see *FAO Production Yearbook 1992*.

[2] For full details, see *FAO Trade Yearbook 1991*.

The *broad* definition includes, in addition to the above items, activities that are defined as "indirectly to the sector". These activities are:

- Forestry
- Manufacturing of inputs
- Agro-industries
- Rural infrastructure
- Rural development
- Regional development
- River development

Regional coverage

Developing countries include: Africa, Latin America and the Caribbean, the Near East[3] and the Far East.[4]

Developed countries include:[5] North America, Western Europe (including former Yugoslavia, SFR), Oceania, Bulgaria, former Czechoslovakia, Hungary, Israel, Japan, Poland, Romania, South Africa and the former USSR. Albania is omitted in this report because of insufficient data.

Country designations used in this publication remain those current during the period in which the data were prepared.

---

[3] The *Near East* includes: Afghanistan, Bahrain, Cyprus, Egypt, Islamic Republic of Iran, Iraq, Jordan, Kuwait, Lebanon, Libyan Arab Jamahiriya, Oman, Qatar, Kingdom of Saudi Arabia, Sudan, Syrian Arab Republic, Turkey, United Arab Emirates and Yemen.

[4] The *Far East* includes the former Asian centrally planned economies: Cambodia, China, Democratic People's Republic of Korea, Mongolia and Viet Nam.

[5] Note that "industrial countries", as defined by the IMF, include: Australia, Austria, Belgium, Canada, Denmark, Finland, France, Germany, Greece, Iceland, Ireland, Italy, Japan, Luxembourg, the Netherlands, New Zealand, Norway, Portugal, Spain, Sweden, Switzerland, United Kingdom and United States.

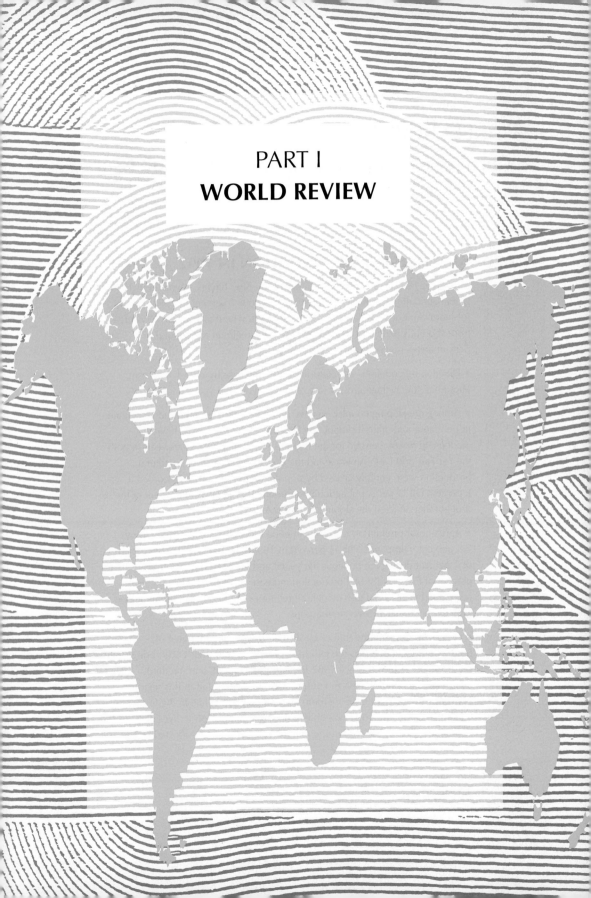

PART I
WORLD REVIEW

WORLD REVIEW

I. Current agricultural situation – facts and figures

1. CROP AND LIVESTOCK PRODUCTION IN 1992

• Overall, 1992 was a poor agricultural year. After having stagnated in 1991, global agricultural production only rose by about 1 percent in 1992. Except for North America, Oceania and the Near East, where production recovered from shortfalls experienced the previous year, regional agricultural performances ranged from mediocre to weak.

• Developing countries' agricultural production rose by only 1.7 percent, about half the average growth rate of the previous ten years.

• Among developing country regions, only the Near East achieved some gain in per caput agricultural production (1.6 percent), which was, however, inadequate to compensate for the region's losses of the previous year. In both the Far East and Latin America and the Caribbean, gains in agricultural production were entirely eroded by population growth. Africa recorded a 6 percent fall in per caput agricultural production, largely on account of the drought that affected developing southern Africa.

• Agricultural production in North America recovered significantly (up by 7.5 percent, compared with -1 percent in 1991 and a yearly average growth of 1 percent during the previous ten years) and accounted for more than 80 percent of the world's total production increase in 1992. Production also rebounded in Oceania (3.6 percent, three times the trend rate) but remained virtually unchanged in Western Europe.

• Eastern Europe and the former USSR recorded yet another year of production decline: it was the fifth in six years in the former USSR, bringing the cumulative decline since 1987 to nearly 15 percent, and the third consecutive decline in Eastern Europe, with the overall fall in this region between 1989 and 1991 being more than 18 percent. While in the former USSR the shortfall in 1992 was chiefly due to a contraction in livestock production, that in Eastern Europe mainly reflected drought-affected crops.

Exhibit 1

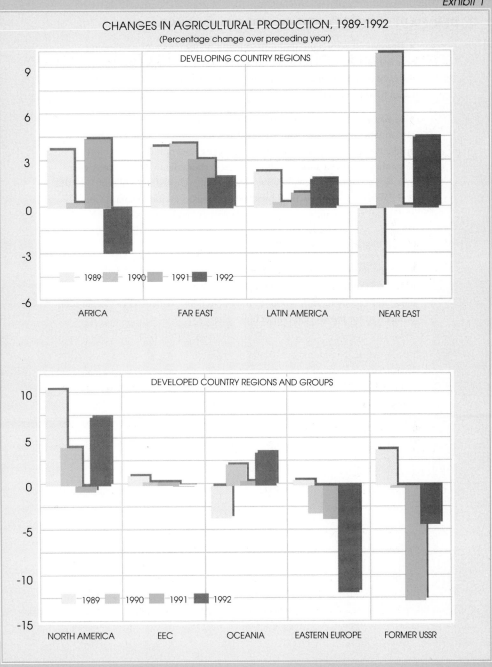

CHANGES IN AGRICULTURAL PRODUCTION, 1989-1992
(Percentage change over preceding year)

DEVELOPING COUNTRY REGIONS

1989   1990   1991   1992

AFRICA   FAR EAST   LATIN AMERICA   NEAR EAST

DEVELOPED COUNTRY REGIONS AND GROUPS

1989   1990   1991   1992

NORTH AMERICA   EEC   OCEANIA   EASTERN EUROPE   FORMER USSR

Source: FAO

2. PER CAPUT FOOD PRODUCTION IN 1992

• The overall poor agricultural production performance of developing country regions was also reflected at the country level. No less than two-thirds of all developing countries recorded stagnant or declining levels of per caput food production.

• As has so often been the case in the past, the highest concentration of poor performances was in Africa, where all but six countries suffered per caput production losses. In some cases these were catastrophic, all the more so since they followed similarly dramatic crop shortfalls in the previous year. This was the case of Mozambique, Somalia, the United Republic of Tanzania and Zimbabwe. The few bright spots in the region included Chad, Ghana and, more significantly – given the population involved – Nigeria. These countries achieved sizeable gains in per caput food production for the second consecutive year.

• Among densely populated countries in other regions, Brazil, China and Indonesia continued to expand food production significantly, while Egypt, India and Turkey recorded poor to mediocre performances in per caput food production for the second consecutive year.

Exhibit 2

RATES OF CHANGE IN PER CAPUT FOOD PRODUCTION BY COUNTRY, 1991-1992
(Percentage rate of change)

Percentage rate of change	Developing countries				Developed countries
	Africa	Asia and Pacific	Latin America and Caribbean	Near East	
More than 5	Chad	Laos	Ecuador	Cyprus	Australia
	Nigeria	Vanuatu	El Salvador	Iraq	Ireland
		Viet Nam	Guadeloupe	Sudan	United States
			Uruguay	Syrian Arab Rep.	
				Yemen	
3.01 to 5	Congo		Brazil	Libyan Arab Jamahiriya	France
			Jamaica		
			Paraguay		
0.1 to 3	Ghana	Bhutan	Argentina	Islamic Rep. of Iran	Belgium/ Luxembourg
	Mauritius	China	Guyana	Jordan	Greece
		Fiji	Panama		Iceland
		Indonesia	Puerto Rico		Japan
		Korea, Rep.			Malta
		Malaysia			New Zealand
		Myanmar			Spain
		Papua New Guinea			Switzerland
		Solomon Islands			
		Tonga			

(cont.)

Source: FAO

Exhibit 2

RATES OF CHANGE IN PER CAPUT FOOD PRODUCTION BY COUNTRY, 1991-1992
(Percentage rate of change)

Percentage rate of change	Africa	Asia and Pacific	Latin America and Caribbean	Near East	Developed countries
		Developing countries			
0 to -3	Algeria	Brunei Darussalam	Belize	Egypt	Israel
	Angola	India	Chile	Turkey	Italy
	Burkina Faso	Korea, Dem. People's Rep.	Guatemala		United Kingdom
	Burundi	Maldives	Honduras		
	Central African Rep.	Pakistan	Martinique		
	Ethiopia	Philippines	Mexico		
	Gabon	Sri Lanka	Nicaragua		
	Guinea-Bissau		Venezuela		
	Madagascar				
	Namibia				
	Niger				
	Reunion				
	Sierra Leone				
	Togo				
	Uganda				
	Zaire				
-3.01 to -5	Cameroon	Bangladesh	Colombia		Austria
	Cape Verde	Samoa	Dominican Rep.		Former USSR
	Comoros	Thailand	Trinidad and Tobago		
	Liberia				
	Rwanda				

(cont.)

Source: FAO

Exhibit 2

RATES OF CHANGE IN PER CAPUT FOOD PRODUCTION BY COUNTRY, 1991-1992
(Percentage rate of change)

Percentage rate of change	Developing countries				Developed countries
	Africa	Asia and Pacific	Latin America and Caribbean	Near East	
-5.01 to -10	Benin	Cambodia	Barbados	Lebanon	Albania
	Côte d'Ivoire		Bolivia	Saudi Arabia, Kingdom	Bulgaria
	Guinea		Costa Rica		Canada
	Kenya		Peru		Former Czechoslovakia
	Mali				Denmark
	Mauritania				Netherlands
	Sao Tome and Principe				Norway
	Senegal				Portugal
	Swaziland				
	Tanzania, United Rep.				
More than -10	Botswana	Mongolia	Cuba	Afghanistan	Finland
	Gambia	Nepal	Haiti		Hungary
	Lesotho	Singapore	Suriname		Poland
	Malawi				Romania
	Morocco				South Africa, Rep.
	Mozambique				Sweden
	Somalia				Former Yugoslavia, SFR
	Tunisia				
	Zambia				
	Zimbabwe				

Source: FAO

3. AGRICULTURAL PRODUCTION BY MAJOR COMMODITIES

• World *cereal* production in 1992 increased by 4.2 percent to 1 959.3 million tonnes following the decline recorded in 1991. Most of the expansion occurred in developed countries, where production rose by 6.6 percent to 890.7 million tonnes. The bulk of this increase was accounted for by a significant recovery in production in the United States and a partial recovery in the former USSR after the major contraction experienced by both in 1991. In the United States, production increased by 73 million tonnes (26 percent), while the increase in the former USSR amounted to 33 million tonnes (22 percent). Production in developing countries, on the other hand, increased by only 2.3 percent to 1 069 million tonnes.

• World *cassava* production rose significantly in 1992, especially in Asia and Africa. The outlook for 1993 is for continuing growth in global production. Some increase was reported in world production of *pulses*. A decline of more than 3 percent in the developing countries was offset by a sharp increase in the developed countries.

• World production of *fats and oils* increased by 3.2 percent in 1992 to 84.9 million tonnes, a marked improvement over the sluggish growth of the previous year. Output in the developed countries rose to 39.5 million tonnes, led by an increase in the production of all oilseeds in the United States and of rapeseed in Canada. There was also a significant recovery in olive oil production in the EEC, while production of cottonseed, sunflowerseed and butter fell sharply in the former USSR. For the developing countries, output increased to 45.4 million tonnes, largely as a result of the sizeable recovery in soybean production in Brazil and the continued growth of palm oil production in Indonesia. Total output of fats and oils increased modestly in both India and China while palm oil production in Malaysia was stagnant for the second consecutive year. On the other hand, declines in output occurred in soybean and sunflowerseed production in Argentina and in coconut oil production in the Philippines.

• World production of *centrifugal sugar* (raw value) in 1992/93 declined to its lowest level since 1989/90. A lower output was registered in all major cane sugar-producing countries, except Brazil and Australia, mainly because of poor weather. Cuba's harvest is estimated to be only 4.5 million tonnes, against 7 million tonnes in 1991/92, the lowest level since 1963.

• *Meat* production increased slightly in 1992, as a larger poultry and pork output outweighed the reduced output in bovine and ovine meat. The outlook for 1993 is for a continued growth in world meat production and trade. There is still considerable uncertainty about the impact of policies in major exporting countries, notably connected with the mid-1993 implementation of the Common Agricultural Policy (CAP) reform in the EEC.

Exhibit 3

AGRICULTURAL PRODUCTION BY MAJOR COMMODITIES, 1991-1992

Commodity	Developed countries			Developing countries			World		
	1991	1992	1991-1992 Change	1991	1992	1991-1992 Change	1991	1992	1991-1992 Change
	(... million tonnes ...)		(%)	(... million tonnes ...)		(%)	(... million tonnes ...)		(%)
Total cereals	835.7	890.7	6.6	1 044.5	1 068.6	2.3	1 880.2	1 959.3	4.2
–Wheat	305.0	320.5	5.1	241.5	245.0	1.4	546.5	565.5	3.5
–Rice, paddy	24.2	26.6	9.9	495.9	501.2	1.1	520.1	527.8	1.5
–Coarse grains	506.5	543.6	7.3	307.1	322.4	5.0	813.6	866.0	6.4
Root crops	179.8	187.5	4.3	386.7	398.6	3.1	566.6	586.1	3.4
Total pulses	17.2	19.3	12.2	39.5	38.2	-3.3	56.7	57.5	1.4
Fats and oils	38.2	39.5	3.4	44.1	45.4	2.9	82.3	84.9	3.2
Sugar, centrifugal (raw)[1]	42.5	41.4	-2.6	74.1	68.7	-7.3	115.6	110.0	-4.8
Total meat	103.2	100.9	-2.2	76.0	80.0	5.3	179.2	180.9	0.9
Total milk	366.4	349.3	-4.7	160.1	163.8	2.3	526.5	513.1	-2.5
Hen eggs	18.9	18.5	-2.1	17.0	17.6	3.5	35.8	36.1	0.8
Cocoa beans	-	-	-	2.3	2.4	4.3	2.3	2.4	4.3
Coffee, green	-	-	-	6.0	5.7	-5.0	6.0	5.7	-5.0
Tea	0.222	0.208	-6.3	2.4	2.3	-4.2	2.6	2.5	-3.8
Vegetable fibres	7.6	7.0	-7.9	19.1	16.9	-11.5	26.7	23.9	-10.5
–Cotton lint	7.0	6.4	-8.6	13.7	12.0	-12.4	20.7	18.4	-11.1
–Jute + jute-like fibres	-	-	-	3.6	3.1	-13.9	3.6	3.1	-13.9
Tobacco	1.9	1.9	0.0	5.7	5.9	3.5	7.6	7.8	2.6
Natural rubber	-	-	-	5.4	5.6	3.7	5.4	5.6	3.7

[1] Crop year beginning in the year shown.

Source: FAO

• World *milk* production decreased by 2.5 percent in 1992, following a similar decline in the previous year. Production dropped in Europe and the former USSR, while it increased in North America, Oceania and Japan. In the developing countries, drought severely curtailed production in the southern countries of Africa, but production increased in Latin America and Asia.

• At 5.7 million tonnes in 1992/93, *coffee* output recorded a 5 percent decline from the previous year's level. Falling prices, which during the first nine months of 1992 fell to the lowest level in more than 20 years, caused a reduction in the use of agricultural inputs, a neglect of crop husbandry and a decrease in yields. Sharp reductions of output were recorded in Brazil, Guatemala and Mexico while a new record crop was achieved in Colombia, mainly because of temporary price support from the National Coffee Fund. Smaller crops were reported in major African producer countries except Côte d'Ivoire.

• In 1992/93, *cocoa* output recovered by more than 4 percent to 2.4 million tonnes. Increases in Africa and the Far East offset a slight decline in Latin America. In Côte d'Ivoire, the world's major producer, output remained roughly unchanged from the previous year. Ghana's production was 17 percent above the previous season's level but below the peak of 1988/89. Good weather conditions favoured a recovery in Nigeria's output.

• World *tea* production fell by about 4 percent to 2.5 million tonnes. Smaller harvests were reported in India, Sri Lanka, Indonesia and Kenya and other countries of East Africa. In Sri Lanka, severe drought conditions and serious damage to tea bushes in several parts of the country resulted in smaller harvests and could even affect the 1993 crop. Drought also affected eastern countries of Africa, including Kenya, Malawi, Uganda and Zimbabwe. The only major producer country where an increase was reported in 1992 was Bangladesh, mainly because of new plantings coming into production.

• World *cotton* output declined by more than 11 percent to 18.4 million tonnes, more in the developing (-12.4 percent) than in the developed countries (-8.6 percent). The decline was due to the response of producers to considerably lower prices, which were down from the high prices of 1989 and 1990. China's unusually high production levels in 1991 could not be expected to be sustained. The former USSR continues to face market disruption as well as environmental problems in cotton areas.

• World production of *jute, kenaf and allied fibres* fell sharply to the smallest crop since the mid-1970s: 3.1 million tonnes. This was less than half of the previous peak of 6.5 million tonnes in 1985/86. Severe droughts in Bangladesh and India were the main cause of the sharp decline.

• World output of *rubber* increased by 3.7 percent to 5.6 million tonnes, with output expanding in all major producer countries except Malaysia. Thailand continued to show the fastest growth (12 percent) among the major producer countries. In Africa output also rose strongly, especially in Liberia. By contrast, output in Malaysia declined further because of unfavourable weather, depressed prices and high labour costs.

4. FOOD SHORTAGES AND EMERGENCIES

• Africa is still the continent most seriously affected by food shortages requiring exceptional and/or emergency assistance. Fourteen countries in the region are currently facing exceptional food emergencies and, significantly, half of these countries are also being affected by civil strife.

• In *Somalia*, the distribution of relief supplies to parts of Mogadishu has been severely disrupted. Despite prospects of an improved main-season crop, hundreds of thousands of people continue to face acute difficulties in meeting their basic food requirements.

• In *Angola*, the civil war has had disastrous consequences for national food security. Fighting has disrupted and paralysed marketing. Only international support for relief food distribution will prevent widespread suffering.

• Aggregate cereal production rose in southern Africa but several countries harvested below-average crops. Despite a larger crop than last year, the food supply situation will remain serious in *Mozambique* as there are several million displaced persons and returnees whose consumption needs can only be met by relief food. Below-average crops in *Lesotho* and *Swaziland* point to continuing food supply difficulties in both countries.

• Serious difficulties are still reported from the southern *Sudan*, where recent population displacements have exacerbated the situation. Food problems continue in *Rwanda* where the uncertain security situation has prevented displaced persons from returning to their homes. In *Kenya*, given the uncertain crop prospects, substantial food aid may be needed in 1993/94.

• Other African countries requiring exceptional or emergency assistance include: *Eritrea, Ethiopia, Liberia, Mauritania, Sierra Leone* and *Zaire*.

• In *Iraq*, the food supply situation has substantially deteriorated. A recent FAO/WFP mission found that, despite some recovery in cereal harvests, a vast majority of the Iraqi population, suffer from persistent deprivation, chronic hunger and endemic malnutrition. The low-cost food rations distributed by the government are inadequate, while food prices on the open market are well beyond the purchasing power of most of the population.

• In Europe, *Bosnia and Herzegovina* continues to face serious food shortages. As commercial deliveries of essential supplies have been curtailed, there is almost total dependence on UN relief convoys, and the food situation remains extremely tight owing to distribution problems. Food shortages requiring exceptional assistance have also been reported in *Albania* and the *Former Yugoslav Republic of Macedonia*.

• Numerous other countries are facing shortfalls in food supplies requiring exceptional or emergency assistance. These include: *Afghanistan, Armenia, Cambodia, Georgia, Haiti, Laos, Lebanon, Mongolia, Peru* and *Vanuatu*.

Exhibit 4

FOOD SUPPLY SHORTFALLS* REQUIRING EXCEPTIONAL ASSISTANCE

Source: FAO, Global Information and Early Warning System, July 1993

* In current marketing year

5. CURRENT CEREAL SUPPLY, UTILIZATION AND STOCKS

• World *cereal production in 1992* is estimated to have increased by 4.2 percent, reaching 1 959 million tonnes. With rice converted from paddy to milled basis, this corresponds to 1 779 million tonnes, as shown in Exhibit 5.

• World *cereal utilization in 1992/93* increased by an estimated 2.3 percent, remaining below 1992 production. This resulted in a buildup of global cereal stocks in 1993 following the drawdown over 1991/92.

• World *cereal carryover stocks* at the close of crop years ending in 1993 is estimated to be 351 million tonnes, 24 million tonnes or 7 percent above the level of 1992. Most of the increase occurred in developed countries (from 170 million tonnes in 1992 to an estimated 193 million tonnes in 1993). In the United States alone, cereal carryover stocks increased by 31 million tonnes, to 78 million tonnes, as a result of the major pickup mainly in coarse grain production in 1992. Stocks in developing countries are estimated to have expanded by approximately half a percentage point.

• The estimated level of global cereal carryover stocks in 1993 corresponds to 20 percent of the forecast trend utilization in 1993/94.

• *Cereal output in 1993* is forecast to be 1 929 million tonnes, about 1.5 percent below the good harvest in 1992. All of the contraction is expected in developed countries, where production is forecast to decline by 30 million tonnes to 861 million tonnes. Developing country cereal production would remain stable at a forecast 1 068 million tonnes.

• Most of the projected contraction in cereal production in 1993 is expected to be in coarse grain production, about -3 percent, while wheat production should contract by about 1.5 percent. Paddy production is tentatively set to increase by slightly less than 1 percent.

• As a consequence of the forecast contraction in cereal production in 1993, global supply and demand for cereals is projected to be more closely balanced in 1993/94 than in the previous marketing year, and world cereal carryover stocks may again have to be drawn down in order to meet expected cereal utilization in 1993/94. Thus, carryover stocks at the end of the 1993/94 marketing year may decline by a projected 19 million tonnes to 332 million tonnes. This corresponds to 18 percent of the projected trend utilization.

Exhibit 5

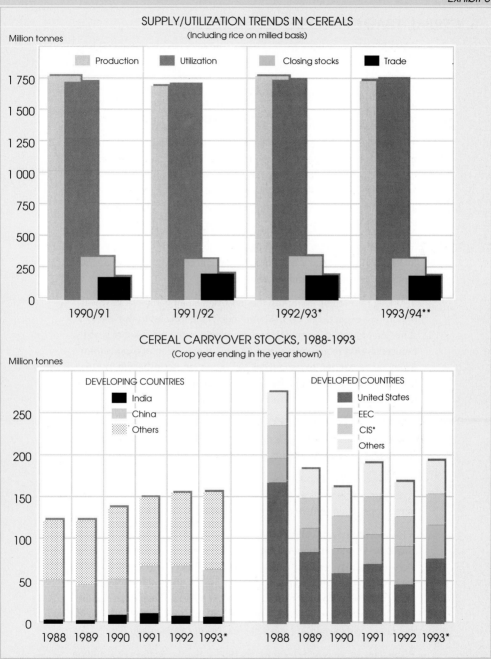

SUPPLY/UTILIZATION TRENDS IN CEREALS
(Including rice on milled basis)

Million tonnes

Production   Utilization   Closing stocks   Trade

CEREAL CARRYOVER STOCKS, 1988-1993
(Crop year ending in the year shown)

Million tonnes

DEVELOPING COUNTRIES
India
China
Others

DEVELOPED COUNTRIES
United States
EEC
CIS*
Others

Source: FAO   * Estimate   ** Forecast

6. CEREAL TRADE PROSPECTS FOR 1993/94

• World *trade in cereals* in 1993/94 is forecast to be 201 million tonnes, almost equal to the estimated volume in 1992/93.

• Developing countries' imports are forecast to increase by 1 million tonnes to 125 million tonnes, while their exports should increase by 1.5 million tonnes, leaving their net imports almost unvaried at 85 million tonnes.

• World *trade in wheat and wheat flour* (in wheat equivalent) is forecast to increase by an estimated 2 million tonnes to 100 million tonnes. Imports by the developed countries are expected to rise by 1.5 million tonnes to nearly 33 million tonnes, while aggregate shipments by the developing countries are forecast to rise only marginally, to more than 67 million tonnes.

• Among the developed countries, wheat shipments to the CIS are forecast to rise from an estimated 15 million tonnes in 1992/93 to 17 million tonnes in 1993/94, while total wheat imports into Europe are forecast to decline by 1 million tonnes, to 5.8 million tonnes.

• Among developing countries, the most significant variations in wheat imports are expected in Asia, where imports are forecast to decline by 2 million tonnes, to 33 million tonnes, mainly as the net result of sharply reduced import requirements in India and an expansion of exports from China. An expansion of imports by 1 million tonnes is expected in Africa, mainly reflecting larger purchases by Morocco, while total shipments to Latin America are forecast to rise only slightly.

• World trade in *coarse grains* is forecast to fall by 2 million tonnes to 88 million tonnes, reflecting a decline in developed country imports of 2.5 million tonnes. Developing country imports should rise only slightly.

• Among developed countries, an expected 2 million tonne increase in coarse grain shipments to the CIS will be more than offset by smaller imports into Europe, North America and South Africa.

• Developing country imports of coarse grains are expected to increase marginally to 47 million tonnes. Unfavourable weather conditions in parts of North Africa may result in larger imports into Algeria and Morocco, while the return to more normal production levels in southern Africa should lead to smaller coarse grain imports into sub-Saharan Africa. Total coarse grain imports into Asia are forecast to remain near the level of 1992/93. Significant increases are expected in Latin America, mainly Mexico and Brazil.

• The forecast for world rice trade in 1993 (calendar year) is 12.7 million tonnes, as compared with 13.8 million tonnes in 1992. Developing country imports should contract from 11.1 million tonnes in 1992 to 10.2 million tonnes in 1993, while those of developed countries should fall slightly from 2.7 million tonnes in 1992 to 2.5 million tonnes in 1993.

Exhibit 6

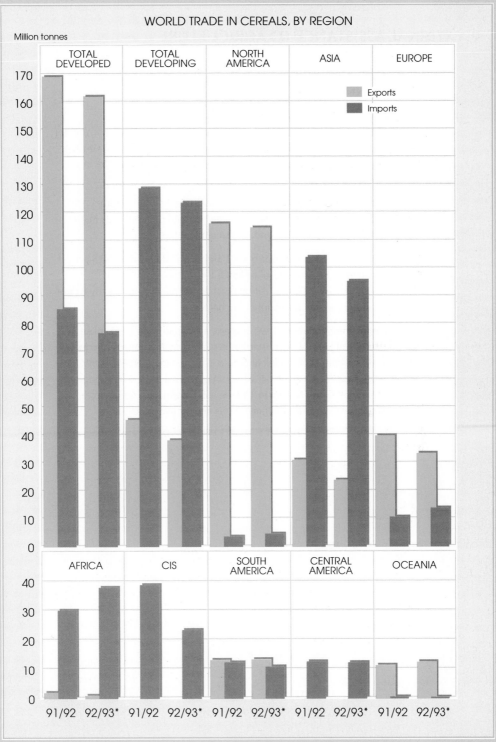

WORLD TRADE IN CEREALS, BY REGION

Source: FAO

* Estimate

7. EXTERNAL ASSISTANCE TO AGRICULTURE

• External assistance flows to agriculture have tended to decline in real terms in recent years, despite a moderate upsurge in 1991. This applies both to commitments and the much lower figures of actual disbursements – the latter following the former with a lag of several years.

• Commitments of external assistance to agriculture in 1991 (the last year for which complete information is available) reached $14.3 billion. At constant 1985 prices this represented $9.1 billion, only slightly more than the low amount committed in 1990.

• The concessional component of external assistance to agriculture continued to decline, representing 70 percent of total commitments in 1991, down from 75 percent in 1990 and 76 percent in 1988.

• Bilateral commitments in 1991 totalled $4 billion (at constant 1985 prices), nearly 11 percent above the level of 1990. By contrast, multilateral commitments declined slightly. All bilateral commitments, and nearly half of multilateral ones, were concessional in character.

• Preliminary information for 1992 suggests a sharp decline in multilateral commitments (19 percent at constant prices). The decline reflected reduced commitments by the World Bank and, to a lesser extent, UNDP/FAO/CGIAR. By contrast, regional development banks were estimated to have expanded their commitments with respect to 1991 levels. Information for bilateral commitments and disbursements in 1992 is not yet available.

Exhibit 7

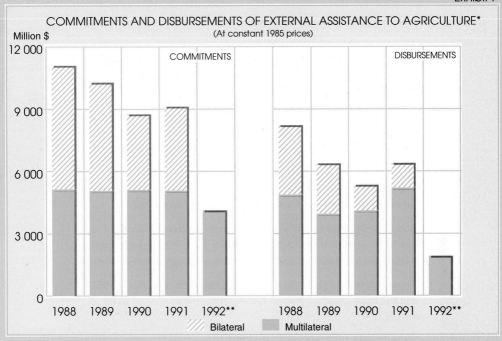

COMMITMENTS AND DISBURSEMENTS OF EXTERNAL ASSISTANCE TO AGRICULTURE*
(At constant 1985 prices)

Source: FAO and OECD

* Broad definition   ** Preliminary data

8. FOOD AID FLOWS IN 1992/93

• Shipments of food aid in cereals during 1992/93 (July/June) are estimated to be 12.8 million tonnes (5 percent below the previous year's level of 13.5 million tonnes), representing 0.8 percent of world cereal production and 6.4 percent of world cereal imports.

• Of the total cereal food aid in 1992/93, 11.1 million tonnes were destined for developing countries, compared with 11.9 million tonnes in 1991/92. Deliveries to developing countries still remain significantly less than the 13.5 million tonnes delivered in 1987/88.

• Food aid to developing countries in 1992/93 represented 1.2 percent of their cereal production and 8.9 percent of their cereal imports.

• Sub-Saharan Africa continues to be the major recipient of food aid. As much as 60 percent of food aid to this region is intended to meet emergency needs of refugees and displaced persons and of drought-affected countries.

• Shipments of food aid to the CIS and East European countries in 1992/93 is estimated to be about 1.7 million tonnes, about the same level as the previous year.

• As of 24 May 1993, pledges to the 1993 International Emergency Food Reserve (IEFR) amounted to 562 496 tonnes of food commodities, of which 501 641 tonnes were in the form of cereals and 60 855 tonnes in the form of other foodstuffs.

• In addition to IEFR contributions, 650 904 tonnes of cereals and 78 550 tonnes of other food commodities had been pledged under the subset of WFP regular resources for meeting the requirements of Protracted Refugee Operations.

• As of May 1993, total pledges to WFP's regular resources for the biennium 1993-94 stood at $618 million, representing 41 percent of the pledging target of $1.5 billion.

Exhibit 8

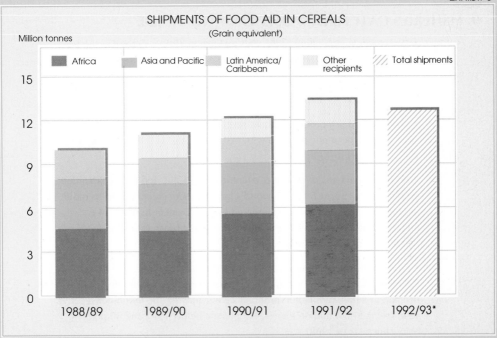

SHIPMENTS OF FOOD AID IN CEREALS
(Grain equivalent)

Million tonnes

Legend: Africa | Asia and Pacific | Latin America/Caribbean | Other recipients | Total shipments

1988/89 1989/90 1990/91 1991/92 1992/93*

Source: FAO   *Note:* Years refer to the 12-month period July/June   * Projection

9. FISHERIES CATCH, DISPOSITION AND TRADE

• World *catch and culture* of fish and shellfish in 1992 stabilized at the level of 1991, i.e. 96.9 million tonnes, following declines both in 1990 and 1991.

• World marine fish production declined for the third consecutive year to 81.5 million tonnes, although the decline was a marginal 0.4 percent.

• World inland fish production continued to grow, increasing in 1992 by an estimated 2.1 percent compared with expansion rates of 3.8 percent in 1991 and 5.7 percent in 1990.

• Among the five major producer countries, only Chile and China expanded production in 1992. China, the world's largest producer, continued its rapid production expansion, which increased by 11.2 percent to reach 14.6 million tonnes, while Chile's production increased by an estimated 6.1 percent to reach 6.4 million tonnes.

• Production in the former USSR contracted by an estimated 16.8 percent to 7.7 million tonnes. This brought the cumulative decline since 1989 to 32 percent. In Japan, production dropped significantly for the fourth consecutive year, falling to 8.4 million tonnes, 9.7 percent below 1991 and 30 percent below the peak of 1988.

• Estimates of the *disposition of world catch* in 1992 record a marginal decline of 0.3 percent in fish for human consumption, following declines of 0.9 percent in 1991 and 1.1 percent in 1990.

• In 1991, international *trade in fishery products* grew less in terms of value than volume because of lower prices for some commodities, including shrimp and salmon. Exports in 1991 reached $38.5 billion, up from $35.8 billion in 1990.

• Estimates for 1992 are for an increase in the value of fish traded to more than $40 billion, a trend which is expected to continue in 1993. The share of developing countries in world exports of fishery products is estimated to remain stable at around 46 percent.

• Developing country exports in 1991 represented 34 percent of their total catch as compared with 43 percent for developed countries. In spite of this, developing countries as a group recorded an increasingly positive trade balance in fish products, which reached $11.3 billion in 1991; while the developed countries' position as net importers of fish products continued to accentuate strongly, with their exports only accounting for about 60 percent of their imports in 1991.

Exhibit 9

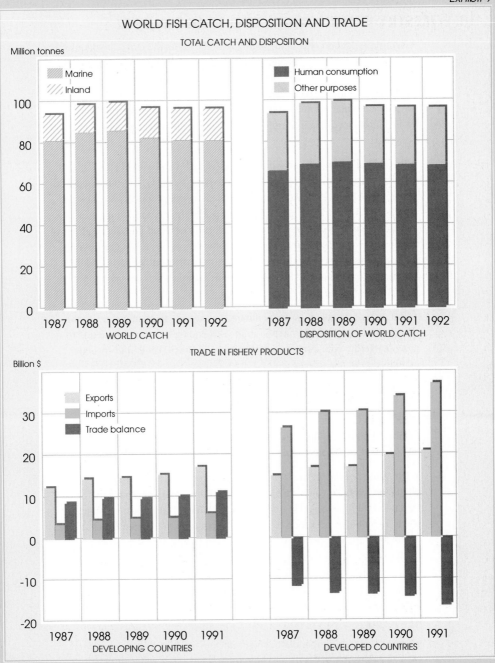

WORLD FISH CATCH, DISPOSITION AND TRADE

TOTAL CATCH AND DISPOSITION

Million tonnes

Marine
Inland

Human consumption
Other purposes

WORLD CATCH

DISPOSITION OF WORLD CATCH

TRADE IN FISHERY PRODUCTS

Billion $

Exports
Imports
Trade balance

DEVELOPING COUNTRIES

DEVELOPED COUNTRIES

Source: FAO

10. FORESTRY PRODUCTION AND TRADE IN 1992

• World production of *roundwood* increased marginally above the depressed level of 1991, mainly reflecting the continuing fuelwood production growth in the developing countries and the recovery of industrial roundwood markets in North America. Demand for industrial roundwood and mechanical wood products in Japan and Western Europe remained weak while it continued to fall sharply in the former USSR and some East European countries.

• Production of *sawnwood* and *wood-based panels* increased in the developed countries, led by the North American recovery, but remained well below the level of 1990. Some major tropical timber producers are facing increasing environmental problems in the use of their natural forest resources, which is constraining their production of wood products both for the domestic and export markets. Environmental concerns are also limiting log supply from the old growth natural forests of the northwestern United States, thus favouring the use of the recently established, cultivated forests of the southeastern region.

• The *pulp and paper* industry continued to expand, albeit at a slower rate than in the late 1980s. Production in the developing countries continued to grow markedly, with dynamic performances in Brazil, Chile and several countries in Southeast Asia.

• Lower utilization of capacity, low prices and poor profitability characterized the pulp and paper markets. The increasing trend in the use of waste paper continued, backed by legislative and policy measures in a number of countries, and this may have contributed to the reduced utilization of wood pulp capacity.

• The value of *trade* in forest products recovered after two years of stagnation. Notable gains were recorded by Canadian coniferous sawnwood exporters who increased their exports to the United States by 15 percent to reach 31 million m³. Exports of coniferous logs from the United States continued to be hampered by the reduced log supply from the Pacific northwestern region, caused by the set-aside of timber land for environmental reasons. These exports, mainly directed to Asian countries, dropped by a further 13 percent, causing a steep price increase for coniferous logs and sawnwood in international markets during the first part of 1993.

• Trade in tropical timber continued to decline in 1992, as major exporters, such as Peninsular Malaysia and Indonesia, deliberately reduced their exports of logs, sawnwood and plywood through the imposition of limits, quotas or levies. This policy aims at increasing exports of processed products such as mouldings, furniture and furniture parts.

Exhibit 10

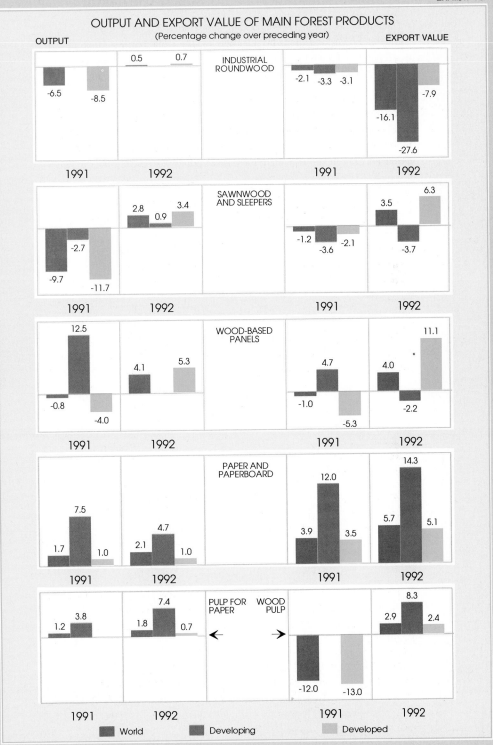

OUTPUT AND EXPORT VALUE OF MAIN FOREST PRODUCTS
(Percentage change over preceding year)

• Trade in paper products continued to expand in 1992, reflecting in particular increasing exports from Europe and the United States. Trade in wood pulp continued to stagnate, as prices for major grades remained depressed because of increased competition from recycled fibres and excessive capacity.

• In early 1993, the Malaysian state of Sabah temporarily suspended its log exports while, in the state of Sarawak, logging in tropical forests has been severely curtailed since 1992. Lower timber supply from the main Asian producers contributed to a sharp increase in prices of tropical timber in the first part of 1993.

WORLD REVIEW

II. Overall economic environment and agriculture

ECONOMIC OVERVIEW

The global economic downturn that started in 1990 has continued into 1993 and prospects for recovery in the near term appear particularly uncertain. After having virtually stagnated in 1991, world economic activity is estimated to have increased by only 1.7 percent in 1992 while forecasts for 1993 point to a 2.2 percent growth rate.[1]

The General Agreement on Tariffs and Trade (GATT) estimates world merchandise trade in 1992 to have expanded by 5.5 percent in value and 4.5 percent in volume, the first acceleration in growth since 1988. Current forecasts for 1993 are for trade growth of more than 4.5 percent in volume, although a downside risk is recognized for trade performance.[2] In any event, the relatively brisk expansion in world trade is seen as a bright spot in an economic environment that is otherwise characterized by depressed growth and uncertain prospects. Economic growth in the industrial countries, which account for three-quarters of world output, is currently estimated by the Organisation for Economic Cooperation and Development (OECD) to be a mere 1.2 percent in 1993, below the already depressed growth levels of the previous year.

European countries are facing a particularly difficult situation: economic recession (oddly combined with high real interest rates); high and rising levels of unemployment; widening fiscal deficits; and financial and currency instability which is seriously straining the exchange rate mechanism (ERM) of the EEC and adding to the difficulties of achieving Maastricht objectives.

Japan's growth expectations for 1993 are barely of the order of 1 percent, but recent indications suggest that stimulative fiscal and monetary measures may help recovery to take hold in 1994. With

---

[1] Unless otherwise indicated, estimates and forecasts in this section are from IMF. *World Economic Outlook,* April 1993.

[2] GATT world trade estimates are somewhat different from those of the IMF.. According to the IMF, the volume of world trade in 1992 expanded by 4.2 percent and forecasts for 1993 point to a 5.2 percent growth.

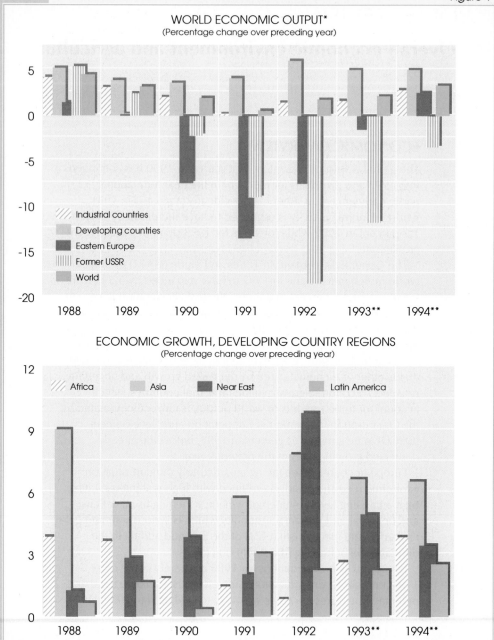

Figure 1

WORLD ECONOMIC OUTPUT*
(Percentage change over preceding year)

Industrial countries
Developing countries
Eastern Europe
Former USSR
World

1988 1989 1990 1991 1992 1993** 1994**

ECONOMIC GROWTH, DEVELOPING COUNTRY REGIONS
(Percentage change over preceding year)

Africa   Asia   Near East   Latin America

1988 1989 1990 1991 1992 1993** 1994**

Source: IMF   * Real GDP or real NMP   ** Projections

Western Europe and Japan loosing momentum as global growth poles, the United States appears to offer the best prospects for stimulating the world economy in the short and medium term. United States economic growth in 1993 was forecast by the OECD to be 2.6 percent, below previous expectations but still more than twice the average growth for the OECD area. Recovery appears to be gaining momentum although major uncertainties remain, particularly with regard to the large federal budget deficit and the effectiveness of measures to reduce it.

Among the former centrally planned economies, the Czech Republic, Poland and Hungary are showing signs of recovery and reduced inflationary pressure, but they still face difficulties in containing fiscal deficits. The Baltic states are also showing encouraging progress in growth and stabilization.

On the other hand, the process of economic restructuring is encountering major obstacles in most other countries in the former USSR. After catastrophic output losses in the previous two years, real GDP in the former USSR is expected to decline sharply again in 1993. Underlying these dismal performances are extremely high rates of inflation, a collapse of trade flows within and outside the area, inability to compress the fiscal deficit and uncertainties over the process of transformation itself.

Figure 2

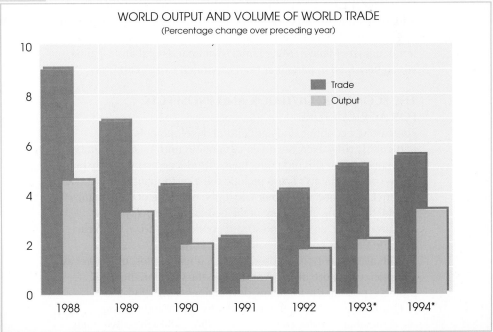

WORLD OUTPUT AND VOLUME OF WORLD TRADE
(Percentage change over preceding year)

Source: IMF

* Projections

In marked contrast with the depressed economic performances of developed countries and economies in transition, developing countries as a whole showed robust growth in 1992 (about 6 percent) and are expected to continue growing at a relatively fast, although somewhat slower, rate in 1993. There were wide regional differences, however, and the overall strong growth of developing countries mainly reflected the performances of relatively few dynamic economies. The best performers were again Far East countries, particularly those in eastern Asia. China emerged as possibly the fastest-growing economy in the world, with its production, investment and exports shooting up in 1992 and 1993 – but with growing concern about inflationary pressure. Economic activity also remained reasonably buoyant in Latin America and the Caribbean, a major exception being the Brazilian economy which is crippled by stagflation and a budget deficit representing 40 percent of GDP. Finally, Africa was badly affected by conflicts, drought in southern countries and depressed prices for several of the region's main export products in 1992; an improvement in terms of trade and return to normal weather conditions in southern Africa are expected to strengthen growth somewhat in 1993 (see Part II, Regional review, Sub-Saharan Africa). The darkest side of the global economic picture is the large number of poor countries that continue to see their situation worsen. According to the United Nations Conference on Trade and Development (UNCTAD) the 47 least-developed countries (LDCs) are expected to record a fourth straight year of economic decline in 1993. Only a few of these countries will have avoided the negative trend, namely Malawi, Mauritania, Myanmar, Nepal and Uganda, which benefited in particular from expanded export earnings.

THE ECONOMIC OUTLOOK AND PROSPECTS FOR AGRICULTURE

Forecasting economic and agricultural developments is a particularly risky exercise, given current circumstances. A number of events that are still unfolding have introduced an unusually high degree of uncertainty. These include the transformation process in Eastern Europe and the former USSR; the outcome of the Uruguay Round; the timing and extent of the economic recovery in the industrial world; and the unresolved conflicts in Africa, the Near East, the Balkans and other parts of the world.

With all the caution imposed by such uncertainties, most forecasts – in particular those of the World Bank, the IMF and the LINK project – point to the following developments for 1994-95:

• Economic activity in the industrial world should recover somewhat in 1994 and further in 1995, although growth rates

will probably remain below 3 percent. The United States is likely
to be the main driving force in the recovery.

- Central Europe's economies in transition may resume positive
growth in 1994; those in the former USSR are unlikely to do so
before 1995 or even later.
- Economic growth in the developing countries as a whole should
continue outpacing that in the industrial world, at rates between
5 and 6 percent. The fastest-growing economies should continue
to be in East Asia (6 to 7 percent), with China gradually
emerging as a "fourth pole" of world growth. Several adjusting
countries in Latin America and the Caribbean should
consolidate recovery, bringing the region's growth to 5 to 6
percent. At 3 to 4 percent, Africa's economic growth should
show some pickup; however, this growth would remain well
below the developing country mean and gains would be meagre
in per caput terms. Growth in the Near East would slow from the
very high rates of 1992, although growth would continue to
exceed the rate of past trends.

One remarkable feature in these forecasts is that developing
countries would continue outpacing the developed countries in
growth. It may be generally observed, however, that: *i)* the
dynamism of developing countries' economies would be narrowly
based, being chiefly accounted for by East Asian countries (mainly
China) and liberalizing countries at an early and still uncertain
stage of recovery, mainly in Latin America and the Caribbean;
ii) although the growth rate differentials imply some narrowing in
the economic gap between industrial and developing countries, the
gap remains vast. Average per caput income levels in OECD
countries are currently about three times higher than those of the
richest developing countries. Even the highest-income and fastest-
growing developing countries still have to make up a large
difference in per caput income levels[3] and, in order to do so, in
factor productivity; *iii)* the North/South growth differential must be
seen as a transitory phenomenon rather than a sign of lesser
economic interdependence. Indeed, the recent home-based
recovery of many developing countries is unlikely to be sustained in
the absence of more trade and investment impulses from the
industrial world.

---

[3] The World Bank estimates that, should China's economy continue growing in the
7 to 8 percent range throughout the 1990s, the size of its GDP by 2002 would be
approaching that of the United States. However, China's per caput income would
remain about one-fifth that of the United States.

BOX 1
EXTERNAL DEBT OF DEVELOPING COUNTRIES

The total external debt of the 116 developing countries reporting to the World Bank's Debtor Reporting System (DRS), estimated to be $1 418 billion at end-1991, was projected to reach $1 510 billion in 1992.

For all DRS countries, the *debt-to-exports ratio* in 1992 was estimated to be 178 percent, about the same as the previous year but much higher than in 1990, when it stood at 167 percent. Yet, from 21 percent in 1991, the ratio of *debt service-to-exports* is projected to decline slightly to 19 percent in 1992. The *debt-to-GNP ratio* is expected to remain almost unchanged in 1992 at 37 percent.

Regional debt indicators varied widely, as shown in Figure 3. The debt situation in sub-Saharan Africa and Latin America and the Caribbean are discussed in the Regional review of this report. For the group of severely indebted low-income countries, the debt-to-GNP ratio stood at an estimated 113 percent in 1992, down from 117 percent in the previous year. The debt service-to-exports ratio was estimated to be 22 percent, the same level as in 1991.

Developing countries' external *debt originated from agriculture-related projects* was estimated to be $72.2 billion in 1991, representing approximately 6 percent of these countries' total external debt. Overall, this share has remained fairly constant in past years, although variations between regions were significant. These ranged from 4 percent in Latin America and the Caribbean to 8 to 10 percent in the Near East, sub-Saharan Africa and East Asia and 15 percent in South Asia. The low share of agriculture in total debt reflects the fact that external finance to the sector, chiefly provided by official sources, is highly concessional.

Net transfers (net flows minus interest payments) related to all debts, which reached a negative $16 billion in 1991, are projected to decrease to negative $3.6 billion in 1992. The long-term component of such transfers, which were a negative $23 billion in 1991, were expected to turn slightly positive in 1992, with negative net transfers to private creditors falling from $27 billion in 1991 to $7 billion in 1992. This was partly due to larger disbursements by private creditors, which rose from $70 billion in 1991 to $84 billion in 1992.

Debt reduction operations were estimated to have reduced the debt of all developing countries by $13 billion in 1992, against $9 billion in 1991. Official debt forgiveness accounted for about $6.5 billion. The reduction in private debt was done mainly through officially sponsored operations. Those under the Brady Plan reduced debt by $4.7 billion, market buy-back by $7.9 billion and debt-equity swaps by $1 billion. The *Paris Club* of developed creditor countries negotiated special agreements under the Houston terms[1] with

---

[1] The Houston terms are longer terms of repayment granted by the Paris Club for countries that have a strong adjustment programme and have performed well under previous Paris agreements. These were decided as a follow-up to the July 1990 Houston economic summit.

severely indebted lower-middle-income countries, consolidating more than $5 billion in 1992. Conventional restructuring agreements amounting to $13 billion were also negotiated. Twelve severely indebted low-income countries obtained special concessions under the new *"enhanced Toronto terms"*[2] and, during 1992, consolidated more than $2.5 billion. In 1992, only seven countries benefited from debt reduction operations under the "IDA only" World Bank Debt Reduction Facility. Such reduced use of the Facility was due to difficulties experienced by debtor countries in carrying out adjustment programmes.

An important financial development in 1992 was the *increase in private capital flows* to developing countries and the shift from debt to equity financing, particularly through foreign direct investment (FDI) and portfolio equity investment. This development affected more particularly Latin America and the Caribbean and is discussed in the Regional review of this document. Only a few low-income countries have benefited from the increased FDI flows. This group of countries received an estimated $9 billion in 1992, of which $5 billion were invested in China alone.

---

[2] The enhanced Toronto terms, agreed by the Paris Club in December 1991, provide for a new menu of enhanced concessions for the countries designated by the World Bank as "IDA-only" borrowers, i.e. eligible for concessional assistance from the International Development Association.

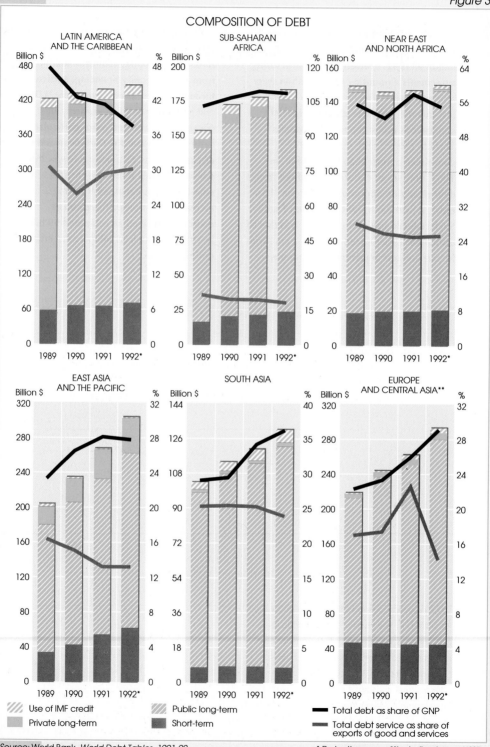

Figure 3

COMPOSITION OF DEBT

Source: World Bank. *World Debt Tables, 1991-92*   * Projections   **Including former USSR

TABLE 1

Projected growth in agricultural value added, exports and imports for developing regions

Region	Agricultural value added		Agricultural exports		Agricultural imports	
	1993	1994	1993	1994	1993	1994
	(... % ....)					
Sub-Saharan Africa	2.34	2.99	0.50	8.22	6.64	8.89
Latin America and Caribbean	2.58	3.54	4.50	6.81	4.44	4.65
Far East and Pacific	4.98	4.20	10.29	9.10	8.22	12.29
Near East and North Africa	3.64	4.03	5.33	7.12	6.69	7.20

Source: LINK Project.

Prospects for developing countries' agriculture

Short-term forecasts for developing countries' agricultural output and trade are shown in Table 1. The projections suggest that:
• The increase in agricultural value added in 1993-94 would be broadly in line with the average trend values of the 1980s, except in Latin America and the Caribbean where projected growth rates would significantly exceed past trends. Growth in agricultural value added would accelerate in 1994 in all regions except Asia and the Pacific, although agricultural growth in this region would remain strong.
• Agricultural exports and imports would expand well above the 1980s and more recent trends. For sub-Saharan Africa, 1994 would be a year of strong recovery for agricultural exports. However, imports would expand at an even faster rate, causing the agricultural trade deficit recorded in this region to reach $12 billion in 1994 – nearly twice the deficit recorded in 1991. The agricultural trade deficit record would also increase in the Near East (to $15 billion in 1994, up from $12 billion in 1991).
• The agricultural trade surplus in Latin America and the Caribbean would expand moderately from $24 billion in 1991 to $26 billion in 1994, but that of Asia and the Pacific would fall from $4.9 billion to $2.5 billion during the same period.

Two factors will crucially determine developing countries' growth and trade prospects for the sector: i) the extent of the overall economic recovery, which will affect domestic and international demand for agricultural products as well as agricultural supply through its impact on input costs and capital flows; and *ii)* largely related to the above, the future behaviour of commodity prices – with agricultural commodities accounting for about 10 percent of world trade but a far greater proportion of the export earnings of many developing countries.

As regards the first factor, the current uncertainty regarding the timing and strength of the global recovery makes it hard to assess the impact it will have on agriculture. Bearing in mind the past record of oversanguine forecasts of global recovery, it may be interesting to explore what might happen if, for instance, the recovery does not materialize in the near future. For a specific region, what would be the impact on agricultural exports, imports and total GDP of zero growth in the rest of the world? A simulation exercise can at least attempt to appraise the magnitude of such impacts, given these hypothetical scenarios. In this type of simulation exercise, of which the results for sub-Saharan Africa are summarized in Table 2, such impacts are estimated as percentage deviations from "baseline" projections.[4]

The figures indicate that regional agricultural exports in 1993 would expand by 0.5 percentage points less than the "baseline" growth estimate for that year; and by 1.5 percentage points less in 1994, assuming a second year of zero growth in the rest of the world.

In other words, using the baseline projections shown in Table 1, sub-Saharan Africa's agricultural exports would stagnate instead of growing by 0.5 percent in 1993 and would increase by 6.6 percent instead of 8.2 percent in 1994 – the difference between the latter two being about $1.41 billion in actual value terms. This amount is considerable in the African context. Converted at 1992 prices it would represent over 10 percent of sub-Saharan Africa's repayments on all debts, or roughly the total value of estimated FDI into the region that year.

Global economic stagnation would also affect the region's economic activity, which would grow by about 2.9 percent in 1994 instead of the 3.1 percent currently forecast by LINK. While such a loss does not appear dramatic, it represents the difference between catching up with population growth – currently 3.1 percent annually – and recording yet another decline in per caput output for the region.

As regards *commodity prices*, most forecasts point to a firming of

---

[4] This simulation is based on an econometric model elaborated for FAO by Prof. George P. Zanias, Agricultural University of Athens.

TABLE 2

Sub-Saharan Africa:[1] simulated effects of zero GDP growth on the rest of the world

Year	Agricultural exports	Non-agricultural exports	Agricultural imports	Non-agricultural imports	GDP
	(.............................. % changes over baseline projections ....)				
1993	-0.50	-0.64	-0.01	-0.04	-0.05
1994	-1.51	-2.06	-0.06	-0.13	-0.17

[1] Excluding Nigeria.
Source: FAO.

international quotations from their current, deeply depressed levels, reflecting some increase in demand as global recovery proceeds as well as reductions in supply caused by shifts away from primary production. Thus, the World Bank baseline forecasts predict some increase in food and beverage prices and a continuing long-term decline in the production of perennial crops, especially coffee and cocoa, where production costs often exceed world prices and new plantings have fallen.[5]

Project LINK projections for 1994-95 indicate a strong upsurge in coffee and, to a lesser extent, cocoa prices, although this would be insufficient to offset the declines of the previous two years. On the other hand, prices of other commodities, including sugar, banana, beef, cotton and hard fibres, are expected to increase only slightly or, in some cases, even decline. Grain prices are likely to be depressed through and beyond 1993 while, according to FAO projections, a tightening of the global market is not likely until the mid- to late 1990s.

Note must be taken, however, of the high risks involved in commodity forecasting – as well known to market analysts as they are to speculators. Furthermore, while there appears to be a degree of consensus on the general price trends for several commodities, there is disagreement among analysts on the magnitude, and even direction, of forecast changes for several others.

Prospects for economies heavily dependent on agricultural trade
Pursuing the approach introduced in *The State of Food and Agriculture 1992*, this section reviews the economic and agricultural

---

[5] World Bank. 1993. *Global Economic Prospects and the Developing Countries.*

TABLE 3A

LIFDCs with the lowest capacity to finance food imports

Sub-Saharan Africa	Latin America and Caribbean	Far East and Pacific	Near East and North Africa
Cape Verde	Haiti	Samoa	Egypt
Gambia	Nicaragua	Bangladesh	Yemen
Lesotho	Dominican Rep.	Cambodia	Sudan
Djibouti		Afghanistan	
Mozambique		Nepal	
Guinea-Bissau		Laos	
Somalia		Sri Lanka	
Comoros		Maldives	
Sierra Leone			
Ethiopia			
Burkina Faso			
Togo			
Senegal			
Benin			
Rwanda			
Mali			
Mauritania			

Note: The criteria for the definition of these groups are explained in *The State of Food and Agriculture 1992*, p. 11-12.

prospects for two groups of selected developing countries: *i)* low-income food-deficit countries (LIFDCs) with the lowest capacity to finance food imports; and *ii)* economies highly dependent on agricultural exports (EDAEs). The countries classed in these groups are shown in Table 3A and 3B.

The analysis is based on macroeconomic estimates and short-term forecasts for the two groups of countries, prepared by the IMF for FAO, and on forecasts by the LINK project, prepared in association with FAO, for variables related to agriculture. The time horizon explored is 1993-94.

The broad trends emerging from the analysis confirm the general observations presented in *The State of Food and Agriculture 1992*, i.e. both country groups are forecast to share in the overall improvement of developing countries in general economic and agricultural performances.

However, the improvement for these two groups would be highly uneven and their average GDP growth would continue below that of developing countries as a whole. Beyond those general tendencies, the following salient features emerge from the 1993-94 forecasts:

TABLE 3B

Economies highly dependent on agricultural exports		
Latin America and Caribbean	**Far East and Pacific**	**Sub-Saharan Africa**
Argentina	Sri Lanka	Côte d'Ivoire
Paraguay	Thailand	Malawi
Honduras	Afghanistan	Zimbabwe
Cuba	Viet Nam	Mali
Uruguay	Malaysia	Sudan
Brazil		Madagascar
Guatemala		Burundi
Costa Rica		Cameroon
Colombia		Ghana
Saint Vincent and		Liberia
the Grenadines		Uganda
Ecuador		Kenya
Guyana		Ethiopia
Belize		Rwanda
Dominica		Swaziland
Nicaragua		Mauritius
El Salvador		Central African Rep.
Dominican Rep.		Tanzania, United Rep.
Sao Tome and Principe		Chad
		Burkina Faso
		Somalia
		Benin
		Guinea-Bissau
		Gambia

Note: The criteria for the definition of these groups are explained in *The State of Food and Agriculture 1992*, p. 11-12.

LIFDCs with the lowest capacity to finance food imports.
- GDP growth would accelerate to about 4 percent in both years, with agricultural value added increasing at a slower pace.
- Merchandise imports would expand strongly from the deeply depressed levels of 1991-92. Agricultural imports would also expand significantly, outpacing other merchandise imports in the African countries of this group.
- Agricultural export growth would lag behind that of food imports, so the agricultural trade deficit would more than double from the level of 1991-92.[6]

---

[6] Despite their high dependence on food imports, LIFDCs rely heavily on agricultural exports, which account for about 28 percent of their total export earnings.

- Despite a strong expansion in export earnings (8 to 9 percent, about twice the rate of the previous two years), the value of imports would still be more than twice that of exports. Nevertheless, unrequited transfers (largely official project and technical assistance, benefiting African countries in particular) would help to bring the current account deficit to less than half the level of 1989-90.
- The terms of trade and, more significantly, the purchasing power of exports would show some improvement, thus reversing a negative trend. Gains in purchasing power would arise from a significant expansion in export volumes, since export unit values would rise only moderately.

Economies heavily dependent on agricultural exports.
- GDP growth is expected to accelerate slightly, reaching almost 3 percent in both 1993 and 1994, with agriculture expanding faster than other sectors.
- Economic activity would be boosted by a significant expansion in total and agricultural exports. For the latter, this would mark a recovery from depressed performances in 1992.
- Along with the strong growth in exports would be a slight improvement in barter terms of trade in both 1993 and 1994,

Figure 4

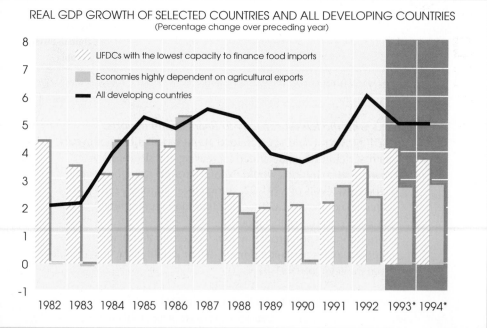

REAL GDP GROWTH OF SELECTED COUNTRIES AND ALL DEVELOPING COUNTRIES
(Percentage change over preceding year)

LIFDCs with the lowest capacity to finance food imports
Economies highly dependent on agricultural exports
All developing countries

Source: IMF and FAO

* Projections

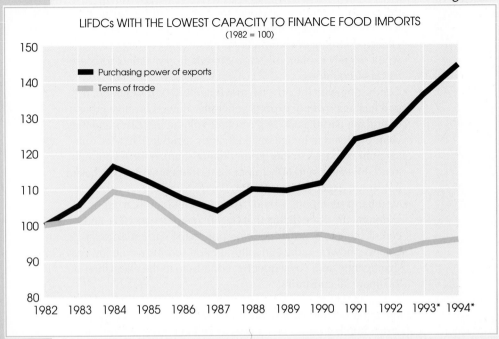

Figure 5A

LIFDCs WITH THE LOWEST CAPACITY TO FINANCE FOOD IMPORTS
(1982 = 100)

■ Purchasing power of exports
▬ Terms of trade

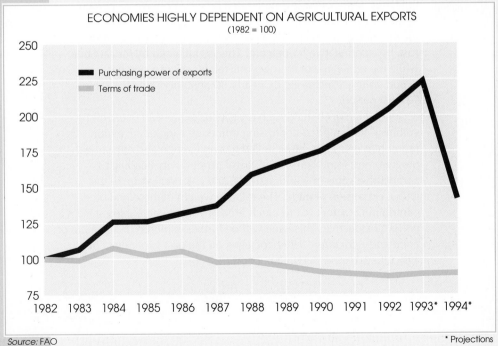

Figure 5B

ECONOMIES HIGHLY DEPENDENT ON AGRICULTURAL EXPORTS
(1982 = 100)

■ Purchasing power of exports
▬ Terms of trade

Source: FAO

* Projections

thereby interrupting a long declining trend. From 1981 to 1992, terms of trade have deteriorated virtually every year. The expected firming of commodity prices in the coming years would largely explain the terms of trade improvement forecast for these countries.

• Contrasting with the adverse movements in terms of trade, the purchasing power of exports generally showed positive growth during the past decade as a result of volume increases and they were expected to increase significantly again in 1993-94. Sub-Saharan countries in this group did not share in the favourable trend, however, and only minor gains in their export purchasing power are expected in 1993-94.

• Merchandise imports would expand even faster than exports, widening the trade deficit that began to emerge in 1991 and contributing to a further deterioration in the current account balance; however, the agricultural trade surplus would increase significantly and, consequently, contribute to the alleviation of the financial constraint.

One of the salient features emerging from the above review is the capacity of both groups of countries to counter adverse terms of trade movements through expanded volumes of exports. In the case of EDAEs, terms of trade deteriorated by a cumulative 27 percent between 1981 and 1992, but the purchasing power of their exports (of which agricultural products typically account for two-thirds) rose by a cumulative 53 percent. This is explained by the fact that, while the unit value of their exports fell by about 5 percent, export volumes increased by nearly 80 percent during the same 12-year period.

General factors behind such a vigorous expansion in export volume – itself a price-depressing influence – included: export promotion measures, often linked to stabilization and adjustment programmes; improvements in factor productivity, leading to competitive gains in world markets; and a general share in the global expansion of trade. The relative weight of these and other contributing factors is a research area of considerable interest from a policy perspective. This issue will be further explored in *The State of Food and Agriculture 1994*, focusing on the past experience of agricultural export-dependent countries.

BOX 2
SPECIALIZATION AND COMPETITIVENESS

Economies highly dependent on agricultural exports (EDAEs) specialize in the production and export of agricultural raw materials. To that extent, they could be expected to be in a better position to strengthen their competitiveness in world agricultural markets than those countries for which agricultural exports matter less.

Historical evidence refutes this simplistic assumption. Not only have EDAEs lost agricultural market share globally but, in the cases of African and Latin American countries in this group, they have lost in relation to other developing countries with a more diversified export base.

While identifying the determinants behind these trends is a matter for further research at the specific country and commodity market levels, one general observation can be made: specializing in agricultural exports – for many countries a fate-determined rather than a chosen course – does not *per se* guarantee competitiveness. The issue is more related to the overall economic situation of the countries concerned. EDAEs are, with few exceptions, relatively poor countries with a limited capacity for introducing technological improvements, investing and providing financial and technical support.

This is likely to reduce their international competitive position even in those trading activities for which they are better suited – all the more so, considering the spurious competitive losses they suffer from farm protectionism practised in many richer countries.

Share of EDAEs in agricultural exports

	1969-71	1979-81	1989-91
	(............................. % ....)		
Share of EDAEs in:			
- *Agricultural exports of all developing countries*	49	56	51
- *World agricultural exports*	18	17	14
Share of EDAEs, by region, in agricultural exports of all developing countries			
- *Africa*	14	12	9
- *Asia and Pacific*	10	13	15
- *Latin America and Caribbean*	31	36	28

SELECTED ISSUES

This section reviews selected issues of current or emerging importance for agriculture. The themes discussed this year concern challenges and achievements in food access and nutrition as a follow-up to the International Conference on Nutrition (ICN); the decline in commodity prices and the current status of the Uruguay Round; forest and forest industries, their status in economies in transition and issues related to forestry trade; high sea fishing and coastal zone fisheries; and opportunities and concerns arising from the development and application of biotechnology in agriculture.

MEETING THE GOALS OF THE INTERNATIONAL CONFERENCE ON NUTRITION

The World Declaration on Nutrition and the Plan of Action for Nutrition were unanimously adopted at the ICN, held in Rome in December 1992. Their adoption was the culmination of more than two years of preparation and collaboration at national, regional and international levels. It also marked the beginning of renewed and vigorous efforts at all levels to reduce global hunger and malnutrition and to improve the nutritional well-being of all populations.

With the adoption of the World Declaration on Nutrition, governments and other concerned parties pledged to make all possible efforts to eliminate before the end of the 1990s: famine and famine-related deaths; starvation and nutritional deficiency diseases in communities affected by natural and human-caused disasters; and major health problems related to iodine and vitamin A deficiencies. They also pledged to reduce substantially starvation and widespread chronic hunger; undernutrition, especially among children, women and the aged; other important micronutrient deficiencies, including iron; diet-related communicable and non-communicable diseases; social and other impediments to optimal breastfeeding; and inadequate sanitation and poor hygiene, including unsafe drinking-water.

The ICN recognized that poverty, social inequality and lack of education are the primary causes of hunger and malnutrition and stressed that improvements in human welfare, including nutritional well-being, must be at the centre of social and economic development efforts. It called for concerted action to direct resources to those most in need in order to raise their productive capacities and social opportunities. It also emphasized the need to protect the nutritional well-being of vulnerable groups through specific short-term actions, when needed, while working for longer-term solutions.

Past achievements and current challenges

An estimated 20 percent of the people in the developing world are chronically undernourished, consuming too little food to meet even minimal energy needs.[7] Approximately 192 million children under five years of age suffer from acute or chronic protein-energy malnutrition; during seasonal food shortages and in times of famine and social unrest, this average number increases. According to some estimates, every year nearly 13 million children under the age of five die from infections or as a direct or indirect result of hunger and malnutrition. Moreover, more than two billion people, mostly women and children, are deficient in one or more micronutrients: babies continue to be born mentally retarded as a result of iodine deficiency; children go blind and die from vitamin A deficiency; and enormous numbers of women and children are adversely affected by iron deficiency. Hundreds of millions of people also suffer from diseases caused by contaminated food and water.

At the same time, a number of impressive achievements have been made in food availability, health and social services throughout the world over the last few decades. The estimated number of people in developing regions suffering from chronic malnutrition has declined consistently (from 941 million people to 786 million between 1969-71 and 1988-90), as has the proportion of malnourished people (from 36 percent to 20 percent), even though the world population has increased. In addition, life expectancy in most developing countries is improving steadily, mainly as a result of reduced early deaths from infectious diseases, while mortality rates among children are also declining.

Average per caput food supplies in developing countries increased in the 1970s and 1980s, although the rate is slowing. By the late 1980s, roughly 60 percent of the world's population lived in countries that had more than 2 600 kcal available per caput per day. Global food supplies (if distributed according to individual requirements) were sufficient to provide well over what would have been required to meet energy needs.

Progress in a number of countries indicates that the goals of the ICN, although ambitious, are attainable. In *Thailand*, for instance, during the past decade the prevalence of protein-energy malnutrition (PEM) among preschoolers was reduced dramatically from 50.8 percent to 17.1 percent, with the almost total elimination of moderate and severe forms. In *Indonesia* food availability increased from 2 072 to 2 605 kcal per caput between 1971-73

[7] Defined as those people whose estimated daily energy intake over a year falls below that required to maintain body weight and support light activity.

and 1988-90 and the prevalence of malnutrition is decreasing steadily.

Chile has made remarkable achievements in improving the health and nutritional status of infants and preschoolers over the last three decades. Both infant and child mortality rates have declined from one of the highest to one of the lowest in the region; the prevalence of child malnutrition has declined from 37 to 8.5 percent.

India has completely eliminated famines over the last two decades. In *Brazil*, national averages of the prevalence of underweight children fell from 18.4 to 7.1 percent between 1975 and 1989. Substantial improvements have been made in the nutritional status of preschoolers in *Zimbabwe* and infant mortality rates have declined sharply. *Botswana*, despite current and persistent drought, has eliminated deaths from famine and starvation.

These country examples illustrate that nutritional status can be markedly improved by the commitment of political will and the formulation of well-conceived policies and concerted action at national and international levels. The immediate challenge to the international community is to build on the progress made and accelerate the pace of improvement in the nutritional well-being of all people.

Nutrition at the centre of development

Malnutrition primarily affects the poor and disadvantaged who cannot produce or procure adequate food, who generally live in marginal or unsanitary environments without access to clean water and basic services and who lack access to education and information for improving their nutritional status.

Moreover, poor health related to malnutrition reduces the resources and earning capacities of households that are already poor, thus increasing their social and economic problems. This, in turn, contributes to further declines in future human, economic and social development.

In the poorest countries, nutrition problems cannot be solved through nutrition programmes alone; efforts are needed to improve the overall social and economic conditions in those countries. In all countries, it is imperative to ensure that the benefits of social and economic development are directed to the poor and malnourished. In many instances, the most effective government strategies to reduce malnutrition on a national scale have been those focusing on national income growth with equity.

However, many national planners and policy-makers have often failed to give adequate attention to the nutritional implications of development policies. Consequently, such policies have not achieved the maximum nutritional benefits possible and, in some cases, they have had a negative impact on nutritional well-being. For example, the pursuit of industrialization policies that are biased against the agricultural sector has contributed to nutrition problems in some instances.

Macroeconomic policies that attempt to correct imbalances between aggregate supply and demand but fail to pay adequate attention to the social and nutritional implications can lead to serious nutrition problems, particularly for poor and vulnerable households. While improvements in nutrition may not be among the prime objectives of sector or subsector development policies, the identification of their potential impacts on nutrition should be given particular attention.

One key strategy emerging from the ICN is to promote better nutrition explicitly through a range of agricultural and development policies and programmes by incorporating nutrition objectives into the planning process. Significant improvements in nutrition can result from the incorporation of nutrition considerations into the broader policies of economic growth and development, structural adjustment, food and agricultural production, processing, storage and marketing of food, health care, education and social development.

Properly implemented development policies can improve nutritional status by providing an economic environment conducive to growth (employment and income creation) or by influencing the prices of and access to goods and services, especially food. Sectoral policies can also maintain or enhance the productivity of resources directly through agricultural and environmental policies or indirectly through health policies that enhance labour productivity. Moreover, public sector policies that develop and expand services such as agricultural extension, health clinics, crèches, schools, farm input centres, roads, bridges, wells and potable water supplies can all have beneficial impacts on nutrition.

The agricultural sector presents the greatest opportunity for socio-economic development and consequently offers the greatest potential for achieving sustained improvements in the nutritional status of the rural poor. In many rural areas, the overriding nutrition problems are more closely associated with a shortage of jobs than with a shortage of food. Often, the most pressing need is for employment creation, both on the farm and off, through activities related to agriculture. Agricultural policies can positively affect nutrition through improved food production, availability, processing and marketing as well as through increased employment opportunities.

Agricultural policies also affect time, labour and energy

utilization, environmental and living conditions and the nutrient content of food. By taking a more comprehensive approach to development, planners may be able to encourage a more equitable distribution and consumption of food, while increasing the purchasing power of the nutritionally deprived, poor and disadvantaged groups of the population.

To safeguard the nutritional well-being of the poor, it is essential that macroeconomic policies do not discriminate against the food and agricultural sector and rural areas, where the poor often live. Public investment in health care services and public sanitation, including both piped water and sewerage, can significantly improve health and nutrition. Investment in infrastructure to promote effective market functioning, especially roads and transportation, and the communication of market information are also likely to promote equitable access to economic incentives.

A growth-promoting external economic environment also has an essential role to play in improving the nutritional status of the poor. Policies in this domain encompass improving the international trade environment, alleviating the external debt problem and increasing the flow of external resources. At the national level, rapid population growth is a serious barrier to achieving a sustainable improvement in living standards. Consequently, the implications of population policies on nutrition are significant, particularly in food-deficit countries where rapid population growth continues and where urbanization is increasing.

Education provides better opportunities and better living conditions which can result in improved health and nutrition. Maternal education and literacy, in particular, have a significant impact on children's survival, health and nutritional well-being. Education and literacy affect development and income which, in turn, contribute to improved nutrition. Education and the training of people to address food and nutrition concerns at the community and regional level may have a great impact in areas where such skills are lacking.

Environmental policies also have a major role in influencing the nutritional status of the poor. Policies should aim at creating an economic environment in which it is more profitable to manage and conserve natural resources than to destroy them.

Intersectoral dialogue, based on a strong government commitment and political will, is indispensable for encouraging realistic and complementary actions to improve nutrition. At local and regional levels, some structure is needed to identify actions that the various sectors should take to improve nutrition and formulate better operational objectives for such actions; for example, targeting the benefits of development preferentially to those most in need.

Action to improve nutrition

Most countries have already made good progress in identifying priority problems, reviewing or preparing plans and establishing intersectoral mechanisms for action. Many countries, including some of the poorest, have taken measures to strengthen food, nutrition, agriculture, education and health and family welfare programmes that have dramatically reduced hunger and malnutrition.

Many have also been successful in improving the nutritional status of their populations through intersectoral committees on food and nutrition and through integrated food, nutrition and health policies. The following country examples are representative of these successes.

Thailand's success is largely attributed to its five-year social, health and food and nutrition plans and, especially, to its Poverty Alleviation Plan (PAP). The PAP, initiated in 1982, is a rural investment programme aimed at improving the quality of life of 7.5 million poor people in the northern, northeastern and southern regions of the country. The plan concentrated on raising the population's living standards from the subsistence level and providing minimum basic services in rural areas with a high concentration of poverty.

The PAP emphasized maximum community participation and low-cost technology that would enable people to do more to take care of themselves. Four key programmes were employed: rural employment creation; village development projects or activities; provision of basic services; and an agricultural production programme. The very strong political support received by the PAP throughout its implementation as well as the emphasis on community participation are considered to have been essential to its success.

Indonesia's long-term development plans focus on food and nutrition policy and programmes as a priority in human development and poverty alleviation. At the national level, policy and planning of food and nutrition programmes are coordinated and approved by the National Development Planning Agency. Rapid and equitable economic growth and increased food availability are responsible for the improvements achieved in nutrition. Indonesia has been self-sufficient in rice since the mid-1980s, for instance.

Chile's remarkable achievements in improving nutritional status have been accomplished through the development of an integrated national food, nutrition and health policy that directly involves specific ministries in different sectors as well as through well-targeted policies and programmes in health, sanitation, education and food production.

Some of the activities implemented include: targeted food interventions for families in extreme poverty; treatment centres for severely malnourished children; nutrition education through the schools and health services; emphasis on elementary education, especially for girls; and a nationwide sanitation programme for the urban population.

Agricultural policies initiated in the mid-1970s have resulted in a complete turnaround in this sector, and food production has increased rapidly. The success of the agricultural sector has led not only to a sharp decline in food imports but also to a substantial increase in rural employment and income and, consequently, to a marked improvement in health and nutrition.

The *Botswana* Government has shown a clear commitment to improving national and household food security and nutrition and has made impressive achievements in improving the economic, social and nutritional status of its population. The country has established an intersectoral framework for improving food security and nutrition as well as for the overall development programmes.

Botswana copes with the ever-present problem of drought through an effective early warning system and comprehensive relief measures to alleviate the effect of drought conditions on the nutritional status of the population. Relief measures combine direct food supplements with income-earning opportunities for vulnerable households. The goals of the Early Warning Technical Committee are to improve drought monitoring activities, maintain the country in a state of readiness to confront drought and facilitate the response to drought situations.

The complete elimination of famine in *India* is a major achievement made possible by government policies on food security over the last two decades. The overall growth in food availability, resulting from the green revolution technologies and a substantial reduction in poverty, has eliminated the threat of famine for India's entire population. India's food security interventions, in particular the Public Distribution System and the National Rural Employment Programme, also provide good examples of both the benefit of government interventions to improve nutrition and the need to target such programmes better.

Many other countries have made important achievements that provide useful examples of effective ways to alleviate hunger and malnutrition. However, the resources, needs and problems vary between and within countries and regions of the world. The situation in each country and region needs to be assessed in order to set priorities for formulating specific national and regional plans of action, giving tangible expression to policy-level commitments to improve the nutritional well-being of the population. This should entail considering the nutritional impacts of overall development plans and relevant sectoral development policies.

National plans of action for nutrition need to be initiated or reformulated in accordance with the goals and objectives of the World Declaration on Nutrition and the Plan of Action for Nutrition. These national plans of action should: establish appropriate goals, targets and time frames; identify priority areas for actions and programmes; indicate the technical and financial resources available, as well as those still needed, for programme development and implementation; and foster continued intersectoral cooperation.

DECLINE IN AGRICULTURAL COMMODITY REAL PRICES AND EXPORTERS' EARNINGS

For at least a decade, the prices of agricultural commodities have tended to fall on international markets while those of manufactures have tended to rise. These contrary movements have resulted in a decline in the net barter terms of trade between agricultural commodity exports and the imports of manufactures and crude petroleum. In 1992 the decline was 2 percent. A comparison of the three years 1990-92 with the years 1979-81 shows a decline of 30 percent, that is an average annual rate of 3 percent. The decline was close to 40 percent for the agricultural commodity exports of the developing countries and 20 percent for those of the developed countries.[8] Some countries have achieved gains in productivity sufficient to outweigh the decline in real prices (the barter terms of trade) but, for many, the decline has reduced earnings per hectare of land cultivated (the single factor terms of trade). Furthermore, the global decline in prices has been so large that it has generally offset the expansion of production, thus actually reducing overall earnings (the income terms of trade).

Examples of the degree to which increases in crop yields and production have been outweighed by declines in the barter terms of trade are provided in Table 4. Coffee exporters have generally been big losers, as the small increases in yields and production have been far outweighed by a 66 percent decline in the barter terms of trade on the international market. Other commodities showing large losses have been cocoa, natural rubber, sugar, rice and maize.

The rise in production despite major declines in these terms of trade may be partly explained by the survival of plantings and other investments made in earlier and more favourable years. In fact, just prior to the start of the 1980s – by 1977-78 – the barter terms of

---

[8] These data are derived from UN world export price indices of primary commodities.

TABLE 4

Changes in yield, production and terms of trade for selected commodities, 1979-81 to 1990-92

Commodity	Change in yield	Change in production	Change in terms of trade		
			Barter	Single factor	Income
		(.. % ....)			
ALL COUNTRIES					
Coffee	3	14	-66	-65	-61
Cocoa	18	42	-66	-60	-52
Tea	27	36	-28	-8	-2
Cotton lint	36	34	-33	-9	-10
Natural rubber	12	34	-44	-37	-25
Sugar	10	27	-55	-50	-43
Soybean	16	26	-36	-26	-19
Rice	29	32	-48	-33	-31
Wheat	36	29	-35	-12	-16
Maize	15	18	-35	-25	-23
DEVELOPING COUNTRIES					
Cotton lint	53	52	-33	2	2
Sugar	9	43	-55	-51	-36
Soybean	21	66	-36	-23	7
Rice	30	34	-48	-32	-30
Wheat	44	53	-35	-6	-1
Maize	28	41	-35	-17	-8

Note: Barter terms of trade = export prices (of agricultural products) deflated by import prices (of manufactured goods and crude petroleum); income terms of trade = export earnings deflated by import prices; single factor terms of trade = net barter terms of trade adjusted by changes in productivity (yields per hectare).
Source: FAO.

trade for coffee and cocoa had been more than twice as high as in 1979-81.[9] The real price of rubber had peaked in the early 1950s but the plantings spurred by this and the succeeding years of favourable prices caused its production to continue. The level of production incentives in earlier years would also explain growth in the production of oil-palm, which rose substantially in the 1980s.

For some commodities there has also been an expansion of

_____

[9] FAO. 1987. *Instability in the terms of trade of primary commodities 1900-1982.* FAO Economic and Social Development Paper No. 64, p. 172. Rome, FAO.

production in areas that have the advantage of low-cost production, often achieved by above-average increases in productivity. Explanations of the persistence and expansion of the area under some crops would also include changes in the relationship between international trade prices and producer prices. In many developing countries, for instance, before the mid-1980s growers' receipts from exported crops were often diminished by the overvaluation of their national currencies, taxation and costly marketing arrangements. These restraints on incentives, and thus on output, applied to a sizeable part of the production of coffee and cocoa and to some production of other crops exported by the developing countries. In the 1980s, these restraints on production incentives were greatly reduced in some major exporting countries, thereby raising prices paid to growers relative to those on international markets.

By contrast, as a result of governmental support and protection of the sector, incentives for agricultural production in the developed countries in many instances exceeded those available from the international market. This protection increased in most developed countries during the 1980s. The producer subsidy equivalent (PSE) measure of this protection increased from an overall average of 30 percent in 1979-81 to 44 percent in 1990-92 for 22 member countries of the OECD. The resulting increase in output was added to supplies on the world market, often with the use of public funds to facilitate exports. The implicit or explicit subsidization of these exports also meant that international market prices of the commodities concerned would often be below domestic producer prices of the exporter country and would also be below domestic costs of production of some importers.

A further explanation of the decline in the real export prices of some commodities in the 1980s was the weakening and removal of economic provisions in international commodity agreements. The suspension of these clauses in the International Coffee Agreement in July 1989 was followed by a steep decline in coffee prices. Earlier, the economic provisions of the cocoa and sugar agreements had been made inoperative.

Slow growth in demand and consumption in the developed countries exacerbated the situation. The population growth in these countries was only 0.7 percent a year. Further, per caput consumption, already generally high, gained little from an income growth of less than 3 percent a year. Coffee was especially affected by slow growth in its markets, as the developed countries accounted for 70 percent of the global market. Similarly, the developed countries accounted for over 60 percent of the global market for cocoa and natural rubber. Changes in technology in the processing industries also reduced demand for a number of commodities,

Figure 6

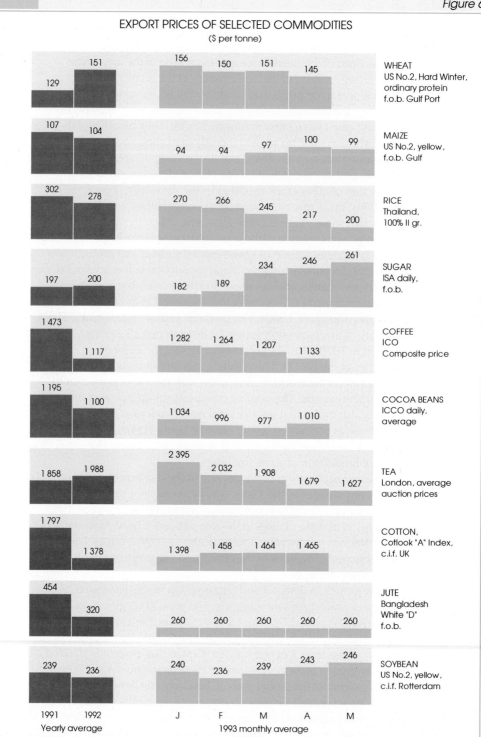

EXPORT PRICES OF SELECTED COMMODITIES
($ per tonne)

WHEAT
US No.2, Hard Winter,
ordinary protein
f.o.b. Gulf Port

MAIZE
US No.2, yellow,
f.o.b. Gulf

RICE
Thailand,
100% II gr.

SUGAR
ISA daily,
f.o.b.

COFFEE
ICO
Composite price

COCOA BEANS
ICCO daily,
average

TEA
London, average
auction prices

COTTON,
Cotlook "A" Index,
c.i.f. UK

JUTE
Bangladesh
White "D"
f.o.b.

SOYBEAN
US No.2, yellow,
c.i.f. Rotterdam

1991   1992   J   F   M   A   M
Yearly average   1993 monthly average

Source: FAO

especially natural rubber and sugar. There was, however, considerable growth in the market for animal feeds, which was of importance to oilcakes and oilmeals, non-cereal feeds and, in some cases, grains. This growth has been reduced of late by a squeeze on animal production in both Eastern and Western Europe and in the former USSR.

Increases in per caput consumption through price reductions also tend to be relatively small in the developed countries. Thus, for many commodities the volume consumed was persistently below that produced, despite decreases in international commodity prices of up to 66 percent from the beginning of the 1980s. Smaller price decreases in the face of high rates of production increase were recorded for commodities where consumption was more responsive to international prices, for example animal feeds in the developed countries and commodities with major markets in the developing countries, such as tea.

URUGUAY ROUND OF MULTILATERAL TRADE NEGOTIATIONS

Since early 1992, the GATT multilateral trade negotiations (MTNs) have proceeded on four tracks.[10] Under track one, negotiations on market access have taken place bilaterally, plurilaterally and multilaterally. Similarly, on track two, negotiations have been conducted on initial commitments in services. Under the third track, work has taken place on the legal conformity and internal consistency of the draft agreement in the Draft Final Act. Finally, the Trade Negotiations Committee (TNC) has held a number of meetings, thus forming the fourth track.

Of particular importance to these trade negotiations were the bilateral discussions between the Commission of the European Communities (CEC) and the United States that concluded in the so-called Blair House Accord of November 1992.[11] The parties reported achieving progress necessary to assure agreement on the major elements blocking progress in Geneva, notably in agriculture, services and market access. Regarding agriculture, the parties resolved their differences over the main elements of domestic support, export subsidies and market access. They also agreed how to resolve their dispute on oilseeds.

The main differences between the Draft Final Act and the Blair House Accord concern the possibility that subsidized export

---

[10] Developments up to early 1992 were covered in *The State of Food and Agriculture 1992*.

[11] GATT document MTN.TNC/W/103 of 20 November 1992.

volumes may be reduced by 21 percent instead of 24 percent and that the 20 percent reduction in the aggregate measure of support would apply not to individual commodities, as envisaged under the Draft Final Act, but to agriculture as a sector. Furthermore, all subsidies decoupled from production would be exempt from reduction. That is, they would be included in the "Green Box" category.

Subsequently, there have been several calls at international meetings, including the FAO Council, for a successful and comprehensive outcome of the Uruguay Round. Further impetus was given by the agreement at the July 1993 meeting of the G-7 leaders of industrialized countries to reduce or eliminate tariffs on a wide range of manufactured goods.

CURRENT ISSUES IN FISHERIES MANAGEMENT
Coastal zone fisheries and local involvement in management
For many years FAO has been promoting local-level involvement in fisheries management. Although Chapter 17 of UNCED's Agenda 21 takes a broader outlook on the issues, particularly those relating to environmental and habitat protection, the basic principles of community involvement still apply and the following observations and guidelines for fisheries management are quite valid in this broader context.

The devolvement of management responsibility to the local level is often a gradual process, linked to the capacity of the community to manage its own affairs effectively. In this connection, careful attention needs to be given to traditional or customary management systems which may already exist with respect to the management of different resources. The recognition and possible legalization of such systems may provide a solid basis for local-level management.

Clearly defined local property and ownership rights to the resource can facilitate the monitoring and enforcement of regulations, including self-policing, and therefore make management more effective. They can also improve the planning and implementation of specific management measures because of the traditional and indigenous knowledge of the resources, their seasonalities and other characteristics that are available to the resource users.

Many of the most vulnerable resources of coastal areas are characterized by the open access condition. Open access implies that the use of the resources is unpriced, as anybody who wishes can exploit the resources without paying a price for them. This did not create problems in the past when resources were abundant relative to the available exploitation technologies and the demand for the resources. However, population growth and technological progress have changed this situation dramatically, with the result that there is widespread misuse and degradation of open access resources in coastal areas.

The open access condition is often particularly badly felt by local communities whose livelihood may depend on such resources. In the absence of local control, people from outside the communities take advantage of the open access condition and, with superior financial and technical means, are often able to appropriate large parts of the resources to the detriment of local users. This has frequently led to conflict, for example between local artisanal fisheries and national and international industrial fleets. Some countries have taken steps to establish local rights to local resources. An example is in the Philippines, where municipalities have been given exclusive rights over coastal waters up to 15 km from the shore.

High sea fishing

Increasing international concern about the sustainable use of the world's fishery resources has focused attention on the manner in which high sea fishing operations are conducted. This matter has been considered in a number of international fora, including the International Conference on Responsible Fishing, UNCED and the FAO Technical Consultation on High Seas Fishing, all of which were held in 1992.

One of the recommendations of UNCED, and in particular of Chapter 17 in Agenda 21, was to convene an intergovernmental conference under the auspices of the UN to consider measures and mechanisms that could be adopted internationally to manage straddling fish stocks and highly migratory fish stocks better. The first session of this conference was held in 1993.

The 1982 United Nations Convention on the Law of the Sea (the 1982 Convention) lacks detailed provisions with respect to high sea fishing. As a consequence, the management of high sea living resources has often been ineffective. Unlike the management of resources falling under coastal state jurisdictions, there is no comprehensive internationally agreed regime for the management of the high seas.

When extended jurisdiction was introduced by most countries in the 1970s, it was anticipated that there would be a significant retrenchment of fleet capacity. This retrenchment did not occur and the capacity of fleets continued to expand. Vessels that could not gain access to the exclusive economic zones (EEZs) of coastal states that had surplus fish stocks were forced to shift their operations to the high seas. Consequently, FAO estimated that, in the 1970s, 5 percent of world fish catches came from areas beyond the

200-mile zones while, in 1990, this share was estimated to have increased to 8 to 10 percent.

As a result of government subsidization policies, many fishing nation fleets targeting high sea resources have expanded since the introduction of extended jurisdiction. These subsidies, estimated to be $54 000 million per year, have enabled fleets to continue operating when, under normal circumstances, such operations would not have been financially viable. Indeed, it is estimated that, to return to the 1970 catch rate per vessel, the removal of at least 30 percent of the existing tonnage in the world's fishing fleet would be required.

The need to secure internationally agreed management mechanisms for the rational exploitation of high sea resources is recognized both by coastal states and distant-water fishing nations. FAO is contributing to the formulation of the Code of Conduct for Responsible Fishing and the Draft Agreement on the Flagging of Vessels Fishing on the High Seas. Such management agreements must necessarily involve consensus on the overall exploitation limits of stocks and resource allocations. For management mechanisms to be effective in securing sustainable resource use, adherence to measures agreed by contracting parties will be critical. There is a risk, furthermore, that the effectiveness of management mechanisms will be eroded by non-contracting parties to conventions.

CURRENT ISSUES IN FORESTRY
Recycling in forest industries
The recovery and recycling of residues has played a major role in the development of forest industries in the last 50 years. Forms of recycling include the utilization of the residue of logs processed in the sawmill to produce chips for pulp and paper and particleboard; the use of small wood previously left in the forest; the use of bark and other residues for energy production; and the recovery of waste paper for use in paper manufacturing.

More than 95 percent of the industrial wood harvested in developed countries is used in primary or secondary production. About 70 percent enters into the actual fibre composition of the final product and 20 percent is recovered or recycled from final residue into energy generation within the industry. The recovery of wood residues is at a much less advanced stage in developing countries, where only 65 percent of industrial wood harvested is effectively used and 58 percent of wood harvested enters into the actual composition of the product. Thus, there remains a potential equivalent of some 30 percent of industrial wood residues which could be recovered.

As environmental concerns have gained importance, the issue

of recycled fibres has increasingly attracted the attention of environmentalist groups and mass media. The paper industry, which has expanded strongly in the last decade, has considerably increased the amount of recycled fibre products utilized. It has also substantially improved the control of effluent and emissions as well as energy efficiency.

Between 1980 and 1991, world consumption of paper and paperboard rose from 170 million to 245 million tonnes, while per caput world consumption rose from 38 to 45 kg per year. To meet the increasing demand for paper, the industry has relied on three major fibre sources: wood pulp, other fibre pulp and waste paper. In the period 1980-1991, wood pulp consumption rose from 126 million tonnes to 155 million tonnes, at a rate close to 2 percent per annum. The consumption of waste paper rose much faster, from 50 million to 88 million tonnes, i.e. at a rate of 5.3 percent per annum. World consumption of other fibre pulp, 16 million tonnes, is concentrated in developing countries, predominantly in China.

Recovered waste paper is today an important raw material for paper manufacturing. Accounting for 40 percent of the fibre input both in developed and developing countries, it totalled 88 million tonnes in 1992. Twelve million tonnes enter international trade, with the United States providing some 50 percent of total exports, mainly directed towards developing countries in Asia.

However, the world disposes of a further 150 million tonnes of used paper, which is a major component of the total 500 million tonnes of solid waste generated each year. Disposal of this massive amount of waste has become a major physical problem for local municipal authorities. Various policy instruments have been considered for reducing the volumes of waste paper to be disposed of, including increase in recycling and the use of incineration for energy production.

The recovery of waste paper for reuse is, under certain conditions, an economically feasible option. When free from contaminants, waste paper may be reused as pulp, thus saving the raw material inputs and the cost of manufacturing paper pulp. Contaminated waste paper requires cleaning, however. In particular, inks, glues, coatings, fillers and additives have to be removed. This process is costly, as it requires special equipment and often produces noxious residues and effluents. This recycling process also results in some deterioration and loss of fibre.

Recycling waste paper is all the more economically viable when the transport distance is limited or the recovered paper is reused in mills in the locality where it is collected. This tends to be the case in densely populated countries with a high per caput paper consumption, such as Germany, Japan, the Netherlands and some other European countries where recovery rates of more than 50 percent have been achieved.

Local and national authorities in some countries are introducing measures to encourage or improve increased recycling. However, policy measures that require paper to have recycled content may lead to the transportation of waste paper to distant mills, making recycling less economical. In addition, mandatory measures may lead to the market being swamped by an oversupply of recovered paper. There is also a risk of forcing the use of excessively costly recycling processes in order to recover low-grade or badly contaminated waste paper. In circumstances of high recycling costs, the incineration of waste paper as well as other urban waste for energy production may be more economical and beneficial to the environment.

In general, recycling is a component of a more efficient utilization of basic raw materials and it contributes to the reduction of urban waste. Its future growth will lead to a change in the demand for wood raw materials from forests and induce adjustments in forest management. In fact, a lower demand for small logs, mainly used by the pulp industry, poses a particular problem because it reduces the market for products of intermediate cutting (thinning), which is necessary to improve the quality of the final harvest.

Forests and forest industries in countries in economic transition
Market-oriented reforms in Eastern Europe and the former USSR have initially led to considerable reductions in their production, trade and consumption of forest products. The output of forest products fell from the peak years of the mid-1980s to 1991 by percentages of about 30 to 40 percent for mechanical wood products and more than 45 percent in the case of paper production.

The collapse of the former marketing and distribution system and the replacement of its predetermined production and price levels with market-determined prices resulted in a very sharp increase in real prices of wood products and lower levels of domestic demand. In Poland, real prices of wood products rose by 50 percent between 1987 and 1991, while the per caput consumption of sawnwood, already well below West European levels, fell by 60 percent. Similar declines in per caput consumption of forest products took place in Bulgaria and Romania.

Trade in forest products among these countries was also hampered by the collapse of the Council for Mutual Economic Assistance (CMEA) trading arrangements and the introduction of pricing in convertible currencies. Exports to other areas suffered as well, reflecting the problems of quality and competitiveness faced on Western markets as well as uncertainties resulting from changes in long-established trading arrangements. Thus, total exports of sawnwood from countries in Eastern Europe and the former USSR dropped from 10.5 million m^3 in 1987 to 6.4 million m^3 in 1991.

The paper industry, which relies heavily on energy and chemicals, suffered severely from the dismantling of intraregional trade in inputs and products as well as from the inadequacy and obsolescence of equipment. In Estonia difficulties with energy imports from the Russian Federation and the need to pay for raw materials in hard currency have practically brought the paper industry to a standstill. The obsolescence of equipment and inadequate pollution controls have forced the virtual closure of the wood pulp industry in the former German Democratic Republic.

By 1993, conditions for the wood industries appeared more favourable in the Czech Republic, Hungary, Poland and Slovakia. In these countries, the first signs of economic recovery have begun to stimulate investments in residential activities using wood. The other countries, less advanced in the process of economic transformation, are seeing a continuation of falling output, trade and consumption of forest products. Production of coniferous sawnwood in the Russian Federation in 1993 is expected to continue to decline because of financial problems experienced by producers and trading organizations and because of uncertainty about forest legislation.

The privatization of property and enterprises is regarded as an important step to speed up the transition process. Given the complexity of the political, legal and administrative problems concerning landownership, the privatization of forest land has tended to be slow and uneven among countries. In Hungary it is expected that 60 percent of forest land will remain in state ownership while some 30 percent will be transformed into private ownership or into joint forest property associations. In the Czech Republic, joint stock companies are expected to be founded to assume ownership of state forests, while in Slovakia publicly owned forest enterprises, financed from the state budget, will be the norm. In Poland the state forests will still provide the basic potential both in economic and ecological terms, but previous owners, whose forest land was nationalized, will be compensated financially. Under the Romanian Land Law of 1992, the state is expected to return to previous owners 300 000 ha of forest land out of a total forest area of 6 million ha. In Estonia only 55 000 ha of forest land have so far been privatized since 1991, but up to half of the total forest land of 1.8 million ha may be privatized in the future.

Some notable progress has been achieved in the important area of forest industry privatization. In Hungary, where the process is most advanced, some 55 percent of the total capital of the pulp and paper industry had been privatized by the end of 1991, with 23 percent of participation being foreign capital. The decentralization of the forest industry in the Czech Republic and Slovakia is expected to be followed by the privatization of the most efficient wood enterprises and the formation of small private companies. In Poland some of the smaller sawmills have been privatized, but this process is complicated by claims from previous owners; the Polish wood-based panel industry, the largest in Eastern Europe, has seen the privatization of eight mills out of a total of 30 while, in the pulp and paper sector, private joint ventures with foreign capital have included seven large enterprises. Important developments have also taken place in some of the Baltic republics. In 1993, Estonia launched a massive privatization programme of state property, open to foreign capital, which included the offer for sale of 11 forest industry complexes comprising three pulp and paper mills. In some countries, such as Romania, the privatization of the sector is still proceeding very slowly; in 1992, for example, only 100 000 m^3 of wood, out of a total of 2 million m^3 harvested, were purchased by private operators. In the future, however, harvesting operations in Romania may be taken over by contractors and wood enterprises may be transformed into commercial societies with state, mixed and private capital.

Trade and sustainable forest management

It is generally agreed that every effort should be made to ensure that forests are sustainably managed so as to permit their survival, but there is less agreement on how to achieve this objective.

It is clear, however, that trade is not a major cause of deforestation and, as such, trade policies alone cannot ensure sustainable management of the forests. Only a minor proportion of the wood harvested actually enters world trade and the linkages between trade policies and forest management are very indirect. In the case of tropical forests, only about 6 percent of the wood harvested enters international trade in any product form and only one-third of the tropical timber produced (logs, sawnwood and solid wood panels) is sold on international markets.

Consequently, trade actions can only play a secondary role in addressing the problem of deforestation. At best, they can reinforce more direct actions; at worst, they may speed up rather than slow down deforestation. Improvements in forest policies and actual forest management practices within the developing countries are the most direct and effective means of ensuring sustainable forests, and it is here that the developing producer countries are placing emphasis, with assistance from many bodies, including FAO.

Nevertheless, a number of actions involving trade have been proposed by the developed countries, which represent important markets for the developing countries. Despite wide disagreement on the most appropriate actions to be taken and especially on what impact trade measures can actually have on encouraging sustainable forest management, interest in trade issues is growing. The main emphasis has focused on tropical forests and trade in tropical timber but, recently, attention has widened to include temperate timber as well.

Many of the trade proposals attempt to link trade in timber to the sustainable management of the forest resource. This may be achieved by encouraging users to purchase only products that are made from timber harvested in sustainably managed forests, or by trying to force producers to manage their forests sustainably under the threat of losing markets.

Groups supporting such trade schemes consider an essential element to be a clear means by which buyers can accurately distinguish sustainably produced timber from other timber. Proposals for achieving this include the certification of producer countries or individual forest concessions that practise sustainable management and the use of product labels to indicate this fact to buyers and users.

Consumer groups, non-governmental conservation groups, governments, timber trade groups and a limited number of producers all have activities in this area, but even those supporting the general idea disagree on what shape and form the schemes should take. Following are examples of current action: German timber trade groups are working on regulations which would identify tropical timber coming from sources that carry out forest management in accordance with the International Tropical Timber Organization (ITTO) sustainable management guidelines; the Dutch Government proposes encouraging importers and traders to deal only in sustainably managed tropical timber from 1995 and is testing the feasibility of timber labels; a United Kingdom environmental NGO's labelling proposal, which relates to all timber, includes the establishment of a body that would accredit labelling agencies; Ghana is providing certificates which indicate that the timber comes from a country which is following sound forest practices; and the African Timber Organization has proposed an African timber label indicating that the timber comes from "controlled origins".

The only formal government action taken to date was introduced by the Government of Austria, which passed legislation requiring all tropical timber and products sold on the Austrian market to be labelled as tropical. In the future, this legislation is also to include the identification of products from sustainably managed resources. This unilateral action, which was considered by many to be discriminatory against tropical timber, was subsequently modified by removing all references to tropical timber.

Despite all this activity, many questions concerning such policies, several of them interrelated, remain to be resolved. For example:

- whether such actions, which are being promoted predominantly by developed importing countries, work against the interests of the producer countries and their right to determine their own trade actions within open market systems;
- whether labelling or certification schemes can, in fact, effectively promote sustainable forest management, since any moves that close markets may in fact reduce the value of the forests and hasten their conversion to other land uses;
- whether such schemes are discriminatory and actually work against current international trading rules, such as those of GATT, which are based on the concept of free trade as an effective instrument for promoting economic and social well-being;
- whether they can only be effective if all, or most, major markets follow similar policies, and whether they will in fact be taken up in many markets;
- whether a reliable and believable labelling or certification scheme, accepted by all, is possible, given the practical difficulties involved, particularly those concerning how and by whom the level of management should be assessed.

These issues need serious consideration before trade policies such as those indicated are implemented.

BIOTECHNOLOGY: CHALLENGES AND OPPORTUNITIES FOR THE 1990s

During the past 40 years, the global output of agriculture, forestry and fisheries has overtaken population growth; however, this result has been achieved in many situations to the detriment of the natural resource base.

The productivity gains resulting from increases in crop and livestock yields have been obtained by means of technologies that rely heavily on high-input use and that have stretched the land absorption capacity to the limit. Biotechnology, a set of powerful tools based on biological knowledge, could play a significant role in reversing this trend. At the same time, it offers novel approaches to conquering diseases, improving food security and reducing environmental pollution.

Broadly defined, biotechnology includes any technique that uses living organisms to make or modify products, to improve plants or animals, or to develop micro-organisms for specific uses. Traditional biotechnologies have been practised in agriculture since the beginning of civilization through plant and animal breeding and food processing. Modern biotechnology has thus far had its greatest impact in the area of human health through the development of new pharmaceuticals, diagnostics and other medical products and it has further potential in the development of drugs, diagnostics and vaccines as well as vaccine therapy.

The application of biotechnology will benefit agriculture with: new and improved agricultural products, resulting in higher-quality food and fibre; improved crop yields; animals with a greater tolerance of stress; and new uses for agricultural commodities. Moreover, biotechnology should make it possible to manage agrosystems better, including the maintenance of soil productivity and water management; to improve diagnostics to help ensure food safety; and to control microbial pest agents.

Many industrialized countries consider that modern biotechnology holds the key to competitiveness and comparative advantages in many fields, including food and agriculture. In these countries, primarily because of economic considerations, the bulk of the research is funded, carried out and controlled by the private sector.

Research institutions in the public sector are now generally required to raise a substantial part of their budget from non-governmental sources, for example via contractual research, licensing agreements and royalties. This is tending to increase secrecy over research findings and to hinder free scientific communication. University professors, researchers and government institution scientists are becoming increasingly entrepreneurial and are entering private industry.

Another important trend is that large multinational corporations are purchasing smaller seed and biotechnology companies and diversifying their holdings. This allows them to develop a package sale of chemicals, seeds and equipment.

The heavy involvement of the private sector as well as market considerations greatly influence the topics and commodities chosen for research. Major crops, commodities and farming systems of great socio-economic importance to the developing world, but of little international market importance, do not figure in the biotechnology research agenda of industrialized countries. Further, these countries are keen to reduce their production costs and increase the productivity, quality and value of their products, thus improving their overall competitiveness in the world market.

On the other hand, despite the fact that biotechnology facilities are being established in most developing countries, the level of research, development and use of biotechnology for agriculture, forestry and fisheries is generally far below the level in the developed countries. Among developing countries, the status of biotechnology varies considerably. A few, such as Brazil, China, India, Mexico and the Republic of Korea have sought to gain full scientific and technological capacity, especially in agricultural biotechnology. Many developing countries face problems of poorly focused research; a shortage of highly qualified personnel; limited access to information; a lack of appropriate policies and priorities; insufficient funding for operational activities; and inadequate linkages between research, development and extension activities. Further, there is a negligible involvement of the private sector, which accentuates the problem of insufficient attention to biotechnology.

Application and potential

Among agricultural and allied fields, *animal production and health* has benefited the most from biotechnology, although practical use of transgenic livestock remains a possibility of the future (transgenics refers to those organisms – both plant and animal – whose hereditary DNA has been augmented by the addition of DNA from a source other than parental germplasm). The wide use of monoclonal antibodies for efficient diagnostics, leading to safe and specific treatments of animal diseases, is a major breakthrough. Through genetic engineering, vaccines for the prevention of viral, bacterial and parasitic animal diseases are rendered safer and more effective. Tailored vaccines exist for pig scours, chicken bursal disease and cattle tick-borne diseases. Pathogen-specific vaccines are attractive goals. Other interesting possibilities are endocrine-directed vaccines to stimulate twinning in beef cattle, immunocastration, livestock growth rate stimulants and vaccines that compensate for various stress-induced production losses.

Advances in genetic engineering will also facilitate the production of male-only populations of screwworms, tsetse flies, ticks and various other ectoparasites for use in the sterile release technique of control and eradication. Further, mammalian tissue culture may replace whole animals in the 1990s for toxicity testing of certain chemicals. The culture technique can also be exploited for studying and analysing pesticide metabolism and for herbicide prescreening. *In vitro* fertilization and embryo sexing techniques have considerably increased the use of embryo transfer techniques for cattle breeding and trade. The value of the approach will be further enhanced if embryo cloning techniques can be reliably employed. Microbial and enzymatic treatment of roughage and genetic engineering of rumen bacteria both have great potential to improve animal nutrition. To accelerate and increase milk and lean meat production, growth hormones can be produced by genetically engineered micro-organisms both in quantities and at the low cost necessary for widespread use. Biotechnological tools (embryo culture, gene cloning, etc.) may also be used for the conservation of genetic resources.

Crops are the other group of agricultural commodities that are benefiting highly and would further benefit from the application of modern biotechnologies, which render greater precision and speed to crop improvement processes. Transgenics have already been reported in 40 crop plants, including maize, rice, soybean, cotton, rapeseed, potato, sugar beet, tomato, potato and alfalfa, but the new varieties are yet to be used commercially. Opportunities for commercial exploitation in the near future include vegetables and fruits (potato, tomato, cucumber, cantaloupe and squash), followed by legumes (alfalfa) and oilseed crops (oilseed rape). A good number of the transgenics are herbicide-resistant plants whose widespread use is somewhat controversial.

Wide use is currently made of tissue culture techniques for the micropropagation of élite clones and for freeing planting materials of pathogens. Monoclonal antibodies are also in use as diagnostic aids in the detection and identification of viruses and viroids. Anther culture and microspore culture, giving rise to haploids,[12] are being used in variety improvement to facilitate and accelerate breeding. Molecular maps and markers are being widely used to identify genes of interest to accelerate conventional breeding programmes. Efficient biological nitrogen-fixation systems and strains for the efficient utilization of soil nutrients are being genetically engineered. Other long-term objectives are the genetic manipulation of photosynthesis patterns and the production of hybrid seed through apomixis (asexual reproduction through seed). A very distant possibility is providing nitrogen-fixation capacity to cereals.

The application of biotechniques in the *forestry* subsector is also of enormous interest. It offers useful solutions for forest tree improvement, even if the benefits are to be felt in the longer term. Cryopreservation, the technique which preserves biologicals at extremely low temperatures, is an important adjunct to germplasm conservation approaches for long-life cycle, woody and recalcitrant seed species.

It allows for successful slow-growth storage for many years of tissues and organs cultured at cool and warm temperatures. There are three areas in which the application of culture storage will have

---

[12] Haploids are organisms or cell lines that have only half of the full chromosome complement of a normally occurring organism.

particular value: storage of germplasm, maintenance of juvenility and germplasm transport.

Another technology that shows huge potential is micropropagation. One of the success stories of the use of tissue culture is that of oil-palm micropropagation for large-scale commercial plantations in Malaysia and Indonesia. Although some of the plantations based on vitroplants in those countries had shown varying degrees of sterility ranging up to 30 percent, concerted research efforts are likely to alleviate this snag. These two countries account for about three-fourths of the world's palm oil production, and oil-palm is one of their major economic resources. Therefore, any improvement in the productivity and production of oil-palm in these countries is of great significance for the overall world economy of edible oils. Other countries, such as India and Thailand, are also embarking on oil-palm micropropagation technology. Rapid growth with vegetative propagation has also been achieved with eucalyptus species in Brazil, the Congo and Zimbabwe.

As regards the application of genetic engineering, plants, including poplars, transformed with genes for insect and virus resistance and tolerance of various types of herbicides are either at or near the stage of commercial application. Another biotechnology application of practical value to forestry, but not yet widely supported by experimental success, is somaclonal variation, which allows variation during cell or callus cultures for many species. For some crops, variants have been produced that show economically useful characteristics, for example as resistance to disease and increased levels of salt. Molecular marker technology permits the screening of species where patterns of genetical variation are not well defined, as in the case of lesser-known tropical hardwoods and non-industrial species. *In vitro* control of the maturation state and *in vitro* embryo rescue technologies are areas where potential for further research exists.

In the *fisheries* sector, the major applications of biotechnology are in the fields of marine species and aquaculture. Marine biotechnology broadly refers to the research and developmental activities in the biological, chemical and environmental sciences that occur in or are related to the sea.

Capitalizing on the biotechnological potential of marine organisms requires the ability to manipulate these organisms genetically. This calls for the study of regulation at the genetic, biochemical and physiological levels, research which should yield not only powerful tools for exploiting organisms, but also diagnostic techniques for studying marine organisms in their natural environments, thus helping to interpret the complex interactions among physical, chemical and biological ocean processes. Marine organisms are the source of a wide range of proteins and other polymeric materials that are useful or potentially useful as commercial products.

Marine organisms have evolved elaborate sensory organelles and some of these seem to be useful for biosensor development. For example, the antennules of the blue crab have been used as a source of chemoreceptive nerve fibres which have been incorporated into biosensors for measuring amino acids. Studies have been conducted on the primary and secondary metabolism of plants, animals and micro-organisms in order to provide the basis for new pharmaceutical compounds, medical research materials, enzymes and other chemical products.

Marine biotechnology also provides rational approaches that have wide industrial applications in the control and prevention of destructive processes.

The marine environment is a potential source of novel biological pathways for processing and degrading a wide variety of natural and human-made substances. Research into bioprocessing and bioremediation is providing new methods for treating hazardous wastes, e.g. estuarine bacteria have been adapted for use in bioreactors to detoxify brines from industrial processing.

As regards aquaculture, raising aquatic organisms in a controlled environment enables the production of environmentally important items such as pharmaceutical agents, food and feed additives, isotopically enriched chemicals, polymers, lipids with potential for substituting petroleum and foodstuffs. Genetically engineered microbes can be used to produce fish growth hormones, which may then be used to improve feed conversion and growth rates. Synthetic reproductive hormones are produced commercially and used to regulate fecundity, breeding cycles, growth rates and sex determination in certain cultured species. In attempts to increase desirable culture qualities such as growth rate, disease resistance, temperature tolerance and marketability, transgenic fish containing genes introduced from other species have been produced on an experimental scale.

Challenges and issues

Modern biotechnology holds considerable promise for increasing the yield, quality, efficient processing and utilization of products; decreasing reliance on agrochemicals and other external inputs; and improving the conservation and use of genetic and other natural resources. However, the development and application of modern biotechnologies has raised the question of whether it is a potential source of imbalance in the global socio-economic, institutional and environmental domains.

The issues at stake are mainly the intellectual property protection systems, biological safety and other environmental concerns, substitution of developing countries' exports, social equity and the widening gap between developed and developing countries in exploitation of the new technologies.

The adjustment of intellectual property rights (IPR) legislation to international standards is progressively considered to be a prerequisite for participation in the global economy, not the least because, in this way, developed countries force the developing countries to re-examine their IPR systems. Most developed countries have extended IPR legislation to cover biotechnology processes and products in order to stimulate and protect research.

However, this trend will make it increasingly difficult for the less developed countries to absorb and diffuse the new technologies for their development. Moreover, they may face high costs and barriers to development brought about by strictly enforced IPR systems.

In addition to the legislative framework, concern has been stressed about the possible environmental and health hazards resulting from biotechnology, especially from field testing and the release of genetically engineered organisms and plants. While data for evaluating such risks are insufficient and valid risk assessment procedures are still under study, countries with inadequate regulatory policies become attractive as test sites for organisms and plants to be genetically modified in ways forbidden in other countries.

Biotechnologies may support the agricultural sector; the direct use of biotechniques for plant breeding could dramatically raise crop productivity and overall food production in developing countries.

The reverse side, however, is that these technologies may also widen the gap between resource-poor and large-scale farmers as well as between developing and industrialized countries.

Biotechnology may jeopardize developing countries' exports. For a country that depends on agricultural products for most of its exports, the development of biotechnologically manufactured substitutes in its main export markets is a threat. Laboratory-produced vanilla may soon threaten the livelihood of 700 000 vanilla bean farmers in Madagascar, while it is conceivable that consumers will soon have a choice between Kenya AA and biocoffee beans made in the United States. Biotechnology could block export markets for many African countries. Exports of sugar, coffee, vanilla, cocoa and cotton are already threatened by the development of fermented maize starch, coffee produced by clonal propagation, test-tube vanillin, cocoa butter produced from artificial emulsions and quality traits introduced via biotechnology into cotton fibre.

Côte d'Ivoire relies on agricultural products for about 80 percent of its exports. Large-scale substitution of coffee and cocoa production – the major sources of foreign exchange of the country – and also of palm oil and rubber would have severe consequences for the Ivorian economy. Therefore, it is imperative for a country to anticipate the possible adverse impacts of biotechnology on the national economy. If substitution hampers exportation to the developed countries, it is necessary for countries depending on raw material exports to encourage national processing activities, the local use of finished products and the diversification of its export markets. Regional markets may be important in this respect but the issue has not yet been explored enough.

One of the greatest challenges of plant biotechnology for developing countries is that it may reduce their dependence on a limited number of export crops and permit agricultural diversification. For example, Côte d'Ivoire is one of the few countries in Africa to export ornamental plants. *In vitro* micropropagation techniques and the diversification of germplasm through somatic hybridization and somaclonal variation will help expand the production and commercialization of these plants. This approach is becoming increasingly popular in Thailand and other South and Southeast Asian countries.

FAO has played an active role in helping to translate developmental concerns relating to biotechnology into policy action. Many of its activities have provided quantitative and policy analyses at global, regional and country levels with a view to identifying issues and constraints to development in biotechnology, exploring prospects for the years to come and defining appropriate policy action.

Since 1983, the FAO Commission on Plant Genetic Resources has been the primary intergovernmental forum for discussions on plant genetic resources and related biotechnologies. Agreements achieved under its guidance include the Agreed Interpretation of the International Undertaking on Plant Genetic Resources, the Resolution on Farmers' Rights and the International Code of Conduct for Plant Germplasam Collection and Transfer. A Code of Conduct for Biotechnology as it relates to Plant Genetic Resources is under discussion with the Commission. Recently, in collaboration with UNIDO, WHO and UNEP, FAO developed a voluntary code of conduct for the release of genetically engineered organisms into the environment.

FAO's initiatives in this area cover both basic and applied research. The Organization has assigned high priority to biotechnology in its programme of work and it perceives that modern biotechnologies should be used as adjuncts and not substitutes for conventional technologies, and that their application should be driven by need rather than by technology. In collaboration with other concerned UN agencies and CGIAR institutes, FAO is committed to enhancing the capabilities of the developing countries to enable them to harness biotechnologies in a balanced and equitable fashion, including support to orphan commodities, i.e. those commodities used by the poor whose research and development needs are generally not catered to by national or international programmes. The challenge for FAO and all humankind lies in maximizing the positive effects while minimizing the negative effects of biotechnology.

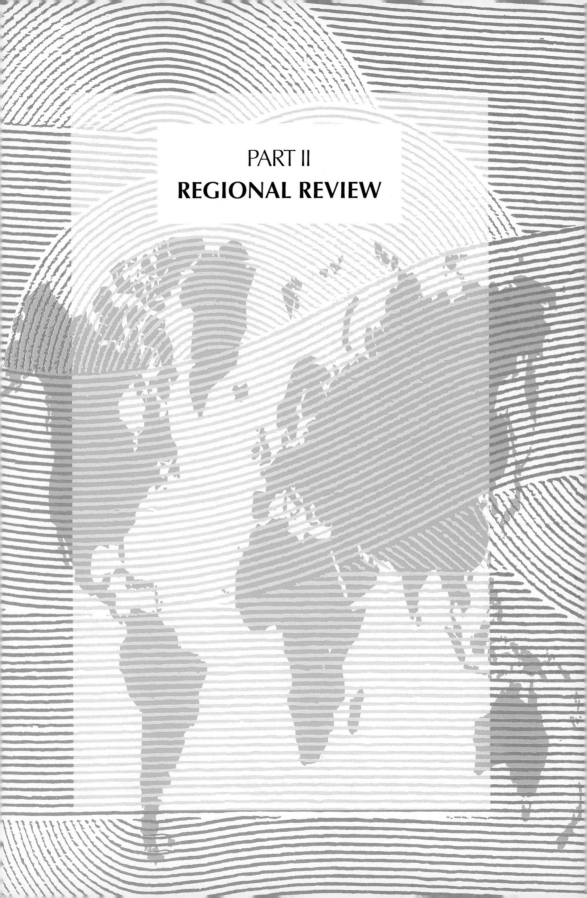

PART II
REGIONAL REVIEW

REGIONAL REVIEW
I. Developing country regions

The following review examines recent economic and agricultural performances in the four developing country regions and highlights the main policy developments affecting their agricultural sectors during 1992 and 1993. Following the customary approach, the review then focuses more specifically on the experience of selected countries in each region: Ethiopia in Africa; Bangladesh and Sri Lanka in Asia; Mexico in Latin America and the Caribbean; and Egypt and the Syrian Arab Republic in the Near East.

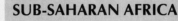

SUB-SAHARAN AFRICA

REGIONAL OVERVIEW
The *economic performance* of sub-Saharan Africa was dismal yet again in 1992. The average growth rate of the region (excluding Nigeria) was 0.9 percent, a slight recovery from the meagre 0.2 percent achieved in 1991.[1] However, these averages mask a great diversity among individual countries. According to the African Development Bank (AfDB),[2] more countries (16) experienced negative growth rates in 1992 than in the previous year (13) and fewer countries (19) experienced growth rates of more than 2.5 percent than in 1991 (23). Moreover, economic growth fell far short of population growth. Consequently, in per caput terms, output shrank by 1.1 percent in 1992, meaning the sixth successive year of decline. Overall, the picture is that of worsening economic and social conditions.

The UN Economic Commission for Africa (ECA) estimates output growth to be about 3 percent in 1993 (for Africa as a whole).[3] That growth rate, if achieved, would merely keep abreast with the projected population growth rates.

The causes of the gloomy performance of sub-Saharan African countries include: *i)* the negative effects of the

[1] UN. 1993. *Economic Recovery*, 6(4).
[2] AfDB. *African Development Report 1993*.
[3] ECA. *Economic Report for Africa 1993*. UN.

Figure 7

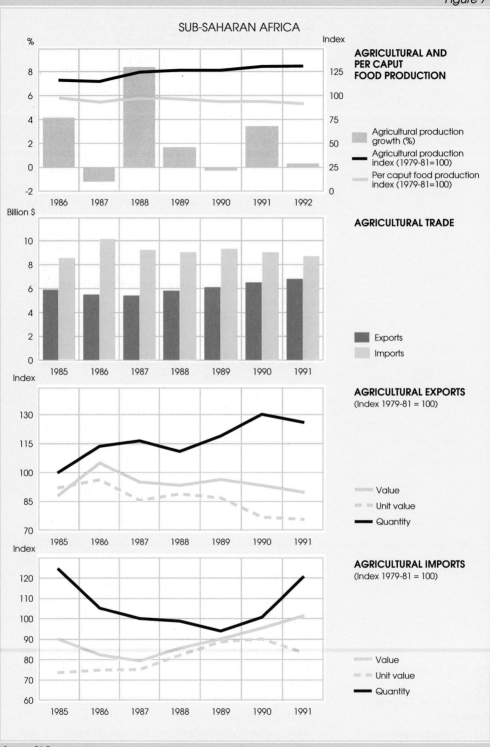

SUB-SAHARAN AFRICA

AGRICULTURAL AND PER CAPUT FOOD PRODUCTION

- Agricultural production growth (%)
- Agricultural production index (1979-81=100)
- Per caput food production index (1979-81=100)

AGRICULTURAL TRADE

- Exports
- Imports

AGRICULTURAL EXPORTS
(Index 1979-81 = 100)

- Value
- Unit value
- Quantity

AGRICULTURAL IMPORTS
(Index 1979-81 = 100)

- Value
- Unit value
- Quantity

Source: FAO

SUB-SAHARAN AFRICA

depressed global environment on trade and capital flows; *ii)* the continuing decline in terms of trade for primary exports which represent the bulk of foreign exchange earnings for most countries in the region; *iii)* the undiminishing debt burden that continued to frustrate the process of recovery and structural adjustment in many countries (see Box 3); *iv)* the declining inflow of external resources from both official and private sources; *v)* civil strife in parts of the region; and *vi)* low agricultural production as a result of drought.

The slow growth (1.7 percent) in the combined output of industrialized countries constrained demand for developing country imports and capital flows to the developing world. Moreover, the demand for primary commodities remained weak and their prices declined in spite of a small recovery in world trade during the year.

Terms of trade for sub-Saharan exports deteriorated further in 1992. Despite lower inflation in the industrialized countries, the main trading partners of sub-Saharan Africa, import prices rose by 3.2 percent during 1992. Meanwhile, prices of exports fell, albeit less pronouncedly than in 1991. Among the main agricultural commodities exported by the region, only logs, tea and sugar registered higher export prices in 1992 than in 1991. Cocoa and coffee recorded their eighth and sixth consecutive years, respectively, of falling prices. Prices of almost all metal and mineral exports from sub-Saharan Africa fell during the year. Moreover, in 1993, improvements are expected only in aluminium and diamond prices.

With continuing poor prospects for export earnings relative to the value of imports, sub-Saharan Africa requires an increasingly large volume of external *resource flows.* However, foreign direct private investment in the region has traditionally been small ($1.7 billion in 1991) and can be expected to remain so, particularly as private resource flows to countries labelled as bad debtors are rare. The hope that structural adjustment programmes would accelerate the flow of foreign private finance seems to have been misplaced.

Unfortunately for sub-Saharan Africa, which has traditionally depended on official resource flows, the flows of Official Development Assistance (ODA) to the region have actually declined of late. ODA net disbursements, which amounted to $11.5 billion in

BOX 3
THE DEBT PROBLEM IN SUB-SAHARAN AFRICA

Total debt for sub-Saharan Africa was more than $183 billion in 1992, up from about $178 billion in the previous year. At that level, the debt stock exceeded the 1992 annual regional GDP by 6 percent. Interest arrears on long-term external debt alone were a staggering $14 billion. Nearly one-fifth of hard-earned export revenue was used to service debt in 1992. Although that figure signifies a third consecutive year of decline, the debt-service ratio remains stubbornly high.

A significant share (some 10 percent on average between 1985 and 1991) of total debt originates from loans for projects in the agricultural sector. In 1991, the latest year for which data are available, outstanding agricultural long-term external debt was just over $13 billion, up from about $12.5 billion in the previous year. For 1991 alone, net long-term flows on debt (or net lending) to agriculture, at $727 million, were the lowest since 1985; nevertheless, they represented 23 percent of total net flows on debt.

Despite years of efforts to reduce the sub-Saharan African debt burden through rescheduling and debt forgiveness, only a small amount of debt has so far been affected. In 1991, only $3.8 billion of Africa's debt (mostly in sub-Saharan Africa) was cancelled. During 1992, only nine countries secured the "enhanced Toronto terms", which allow for a cancellation of or reduction in the interest charges offered by some creditor countries. The amount of debt involved is significantly less than it would have been with the cancellation of two-thirds of the entire stock of eligible debt, as envisaged under the "Trinidad terms". Furthermore, only two countries had recourse in 1992 to the IDA Debt Reduction Facility, which is oriented towards reducing commercial debt, because of the creditors' reluctance and debtor countries' domestic constraints as well as debtors' failure at times to comply with structural adjustment conditionality.

Multilateral debt, rather than commercial or official bilateral debt, is fast becoming the major problem in sub-Saharan Africa. During the 1980s, most countries were lured away from contracting commercial market debt by the prestructural adjustment experience, commercial banks' reluctance to lend to debt-burdened countries and donor persuasion, and they consequently resorted to heavier borrowing from multilateral financial institutions. Almost 40 percent of total sub-Saharan Africa's official long-term debt in 1992 was owed to multilateral institutions from which the debtors can not expect debt rescheduling or cancellation.

SUB-SAHARAN AFRICA

1990, were down by about $1 billion (in real terms) in 1991. Meanwhile, at $6 billion, total multilateral net disbursements remained the same in 1991 as in the previous year.

The growing disparity between resource inflows and debt service payments resulted in reduced net transfers to the region in 1991 relative to 1990. For example, for the agricultural sector alone, the net transfers of $377 million in 1991 (the latest year for which data are available) represented less than one-half of net transfers in 1990.

Wars and civil strife, notably in Angola, Liberia, Mozambique, Somalia and the Sudan, contributed significantly to the overall economic decline in 1992, as did the sometimes chaotic political situations in such countries as Togo and Zaire where looting and rioting destroyed the infrastructure required for economic development.

The level of agricultural production in 1992 remained virtually unchanged over that of 1991, the major cause being the drought that affected East and southern Africa. As a whole, the latter experienced a decline of 7.7 percent over the previous year and accounted for 16 million of the 40 million people estimated by FAO to be facing food shortages in sub-Saharan Africa. Elsewhere in Africa, growth was slow; in central Africa, agricultural output grew by 1.4 percent and, in West Africa, the growth rate was 2.9 percent. Civil strife exacerbated the already disastrous food supply and access problems in Mozambique and Somalia.

Cereal production fell by more than 5 percent for the region as a whole. In southern Africa, where cereals are the main staple, output fell to less than one-half of the 1991 level. Thanks to less dramatic changes in cereal and non-cereal food items elsewhere in the region, notably in Ethiopia, the Sudan and in West and central African countries, the aggregate food production sector increased slightly – by nearly 1 percent – over the previous year. The output of non-food agricultural commodities, on the other hand, fell by about 5.7 percent.

Over a longer period, sub-Saharan Africa has, contrary to popular belief, maintained trend growth rates in agricultural production comparable to other regions of the world.[4] In fact, from 1981 to 1992, aggregate production increased at a rate of 3 percent per year, with

---

[4] UN. 1992. *Economic Recovery*, 6(3).

slight declines in 1982, 1986 and 1990. The problem in the region has always been the population growth rate which has outstripped growth in production, thus resulting in a declining per caput output. For instance, although agricultural output increased marginally (0.3 percent) in 1992, per caput production declined by nearly 2.8 percent. The prospects of a reversal of this trend depend on both the region's ability to slow population growth as well as its capacity, assuming more benevolent weather conditions and fewer wars and civil disruption, to increase production through sustainable and intensive agriculture.

With the return of favourable weather conditions for the 1992/93 growing season, a rebound of agricultural output in countries affected by drought in 1992 is expected in 1993.

With respect to policy developments, structural adjustment programmes with emphasis on short-term objectives continued to guide policy reforms in most countries in the region. The pursuit of adjustment with transformation and the harmonization of short-term policy goals with medium- and long-term development objectives were hardly in evidence. The latter were the objectives of the African Alternative Framework to Structural Adjustment Programmes for Socio-Economic Transformation (AAF-SAP) adopted recently by the Organization of African Unity (OAU).

Fiscal reform played a central role in efforts to strengthen domestic economic management. The success rate in reducing budget imbalances varied considerably, however. Benin and the Gambia, for instance, were able to reduce their budget deficits as a proportion of GDP, but many other countries failed to do so.

Monetary policy emphasized a tight control of money supply as well as adjustments of interest rates. Going against the grain, however, Zaire embarked on a course of monetary expansion, and its inflation rate reached huge proportions. Interest rate adjustments were an important plank of monetary policy and real interest rates were raised by several countries, including Cape Verde, Comoros, Côte d'Ivoire, Djibouti, the Gambia, Guinea-Bissau, Kenya, Malawi, Mali, Mauritania, Tunisia, the United Republic of Tanzania, Zambia and Zimbabwe. Ghana and Mauritius adjusted their nominal bank rates downwards but they remained positive in real terms.

SUB-SAHARAN AFRICA

The move towards market-determined exchange rates continued in many sub-Saharan countries in 1992 either through outright devaluation of national currencies (e.g. Ethiopia, Malawi, Mauritania and Rwanda) or by flotation (Nigeria) and foreign exchange liberalization (e.g. Algeria, Uganda, the United Republic of Tanzania and Zambia).

Public sector reforms, which have included trimming the size of the civil service and curtailing government consumption, were a continuing feature of the reform programme. Privatization also played a major role in public sector reforms of such countries as Chad, Côte d'Ivoire, Ghana, Mozambique, Nigeria, the Sudan, Uganda and Zambia.

Policy reforms in agriculture continued in most countries, often within the overall framework of structural adjustment programmes negotiated with the World Bank and the IMF. Market liberalization remained an important component of agricultural policy reforms, with agricultural parastatals being dismantled, privatized or restructured in countries such as Burundi, Côte d'Ivoire and Mozambique. In some other countries (e.g. Ethiopia, Kenya, Malawi, Mali, Uganda, the United Republic of Tanzania, Zambia and Zimbabwe), some or total decontrol of agricultural marketing has been effected. Agricultural market liberalization has also been planned for implementation in other countries, including Lesotho and the Central African Republic.

Some countries have embarked on a policy of diversifying the agricultural export base, moving away from a reliance on one or few export crops, as international prices for traditional exports continue to crumble. For example, Benin is promoting the production of palm oil, coconut and groundnuts as well as pineapple and exotic fruits and vegetables, along with the traditional export, cotton. Uganda is planning to diversify into sesame, tobacco, hides and skins, spices and fish after regaining a market share in its traditional exports: cotton, tea and coffee. Typically, the fisheries sector has featured prominently in the drive towards diversification. Mozambique, Namibia, Nigeria and Sierra Leone are just four of the countries that have embarked on aggressive fish farming campaigns.

The drought in southern Africa has led to the region's agricultural development policies being focused mainly on drought relief, increased food production and

SUB-SAHARAN AFRICA

diversification within the food sector. In Malawi, in addition to supporting maize production (the main staple for most of the population), the government is promoting the production of cassava – a drought-resistant crop – as a security crop, as well as promoting local production of vegetable seeds. Zambia is encouraging the production of sorghum, millet and cassava in its food crop diversification strategy to reduce dependence on maize. In Zimbabwe, price and non-price incentives have been provided to farmers to ensure an increase in grain production. Other countries in the region have followed similar trends.

Food security has also been a major preoccupation elsewhere in the region. Nigeria's five-year ban on wheat imports (lifted temporarily at the end of 1992) was designed to promote domestic production and was a partial success. Senegal has launched a programme intended to achieve an 80 percent self-sufficiency in food. In Burkina Faso, a project to prevent seasonal hunger and malnutrition has been launched; and in Djibouti, efforts are under way within the broad arena of food security to encourage greater consumption of local products, including food.

The drought in the southern part of the region has been a catalyst in the reorientation of agricultural policies towards a more efficient exploitation of irrigation potential in the region; Malawi is one of the countries that are actively addressing this issue.

Environmental protection has also received some attention within the context of agricultural policies. The Global Coalition for Africa, in its first annual report, contends that four-fifths of the cropland and pasture land in sub-Saharan Africa is at least partly degraded; and that deforestation might have been a cause of the significant decline in rainfall in the Sahel, in coastal areas along the Gulf of Guinea, in Cameroon, northern Nigeria and East Africa.[5] Environmental concerns have led, for example, to a government ban on the felling of some tree species in Zaire and to a ban on the exportation of 18 log species in Ghana. Several other countries have outlined strategies to develop forests and rationalize the exploitation of fisheries resources.

In addition to desertification, which was Africa's primary concern at the United Nations Conference on Environment and Development (UNCED) in 1992, the countries in the region have given priority to the issues

_____

[5] The Global Coalition for Africa. 1992. *African Social and Development Trends.* Annual Report, p. 11.

SUB-SAHARAN AFRICA

of increased finance and technology transfers during the UNCED follow-up discussions. In doing so, they are echoing the thoughts of part of the donor community. The World Bank, for example, has made it clear that environmental issues are at the top of the priority list of the Bank's concessional lending arm – the International Development Association (IDA).

Although policy emphasis was heavily weighted towards national concerns in 1992, intra-African trade, in particular, but also economic and political integration, generally, received a boost through a number of important decisions.

The Preferential Trade Area for Eastern and Southern African States (PTA) amended the PTA Rules of Origin: all goods originating from member states, regardless of the nationality of the producers, are now subject to preferential tariffs.

In August 1992, the Southern African Development Coordination Conference (SADCC) was renamed the Southern African Development Community (SADC) in anticipation of the potential accession of post-apartheid South Africa.[6]

The year also witnessed ratification by a few more countries of the 1991 Abuja Treaty establishing the Pan-African Economic Community (PAEC).

The apparently renewed commitment to economic integration results from the recognition that the region's future may lie in collective self-reliance as the international economic environment becomes increasingly hostile, thereby threatening accelerated growth in the small, often fragmented, individual economies of sub-Saharan Africa. Self-reliance was one of the themes of the international conference, held in Dakar from 16 to 18 November 1992, entitled "Trampling the Grass: Is Africa's Growing Marginalization in the Newly Emerging International Order Reversible?" The conference was hosted by the African Centre for Development and Strategic Studies (ACDESS), a major new African think-tank.

---

[6] The prospects of a settlement of the political quagmire in South Africa have been enhanced by the announcement of a tentative date (April 1994) when the country will hold multiracial elections.

ETHIOPIA
The country: general characteristics

Situated in northeastern Africa, Ethiopia constitutes the largest part of the Horn of Africa.[7] It spans an area of 1 223 600 km² (one of the largest countries in Africa) and has an altitude ranging from 100 m below sea level to more than 4 000 m above sea level. The second most populous African country after Nigeria, Ethiopia has a population of 55.1 million.[8]

The main characteristic of the climate is its erratic rainfall patterns. The southwest highlands receive the highest average rainfall, while precipitation decreases towards the northeast and the east. Even in areas with a high mean annual rainfall, the variations can be extreme. Chronically drought-prone areas cover almost 50 percent of the country's total area and affect about 20 million people.[9]

Drought was at the root of at least ten famine episodes in the last 40 years which have affected large areas and significant portions of the population. In the last 20 years, the most serious droughts in terms of human suffering were those of 1972-73 and 1984-85.[10]

The economy

Ethiopia is one of the poorest countries in the world, with a per caput GDP of $120 and 60 percent of its population living below the poverty line.

Agriculture accounts for 50 percent of the country's GDP and 90 percent of exports. In terms of area under cultivation, cereals (teff, maize, barley, wheat) are the major crop category, followed by pulses (horse beans, chickpeas, haricot beans) and oilseeds (mainly *neug* and linseed). Coffee is the main export (accounting for 57.3 percent of total agricultural exports), followed by hides and skins (28 percent), live animals (3.3 percent) and vegetables.[11] About 78 percent of the total value of production from manufacturing industries is based on the processing of agricultural products (food processing, beverages and textiles).

The smallholder sector accounts for 90 percent of the country's agricultural output. The average farm size is estimated to be between 1 and 1.5 ha.

The overall growth of GDP during the 1970s and 1980s (1.9 and 1.6 percent, respectively) closely follows the trends in the growth of agricultural production (0.7 and 0.3 percent, respectively) and both magnitudes

---

[7] Eritrea, officially independent since May 1993, is included in most of the reported data because of insufficient information to permit systematic reporting on Ethiopia only.

[8] 1992 estimates.

[9] T. Desta. *Disaster management in Ethiopia: past efforts and future directions.* Presented to the United Nations Sudano-Sahelian Office (UNSO) Workshop on Drought Preparedness and Mitigation. Early Warning and Planning Services Relief and Rehabilitation Commission, Addis Ababa, May 1993.

[10] For more information, see T. Desta, op. cit., footnote 9.

[11] AGROSTAT data for 1990.

SUB-SAHARAN AFRICA

are well below the population growth rate (estimated to be 3 percent).

Economic policies affecting agriculture

The search for proximate causes of both agricultural and general economic stagnation in Ethiopia since the mid-1970s leads to a set of interrelated structural constraints and policy factors. In addition to the harsh agroclimatic conditions, inadequate and poorly maintained infrastructure, environmental degradation and inadequate technology have contributed to the decline of agriculture.

At the policy level, macroeconomic and sector-specific policies have contributed to the creation of a negative environment for agricultural growth. The rise to power of the revolutionary government in 1974 marked the beginning of an era of tight direct government controls on the production and distribution systems. A brief description of the policies implemented as well as their effects help explain the nature and magnitude of the problems facing Ethiopia today.

Macroeconomic policy: a deceptive internal balance. In Ethiopia, macroeconomic policies have traditionally been characterized by prudent fiscal management. The fiscal deficit was kept at an average of 7 percent of GDP for most years between 1975 and 1989, with the exception of drought years.

Relatively low deficits were achieved despite increasing public expenditure (from about 17 percent of GDP in fiscal 1974/75 to 47 percent in 1988/89). An aggressive policy of fiscal receipts prevented the deficits from ballooning. The budgetary effects of external shocks were mitigated by foreign disaster-relief flows. In general, foreign flows of grants and loans left about half the deficit to be financed internally. As the government avoided recourse to inflationary financing, average inflation was kept close to 9 percent during the 17 years ending in 1991.[12]

While a macroeconomic balance and price stability are necessary for growth, Ethiopia is an example of how these two factors may not be sufficient. Public fixed investment expenditure grew by almost 16 percent annually after 1975, while recurrent expenditure grew by 5 percent. It was chiefly channelled towards directly productive activities (mainly in manufacturing and

---

[12] **For details, see World Bank. 1990.** *Ethiopia's economy in the 1980s and framework for accelerated growth.* **Washington, DC.**

public utilities), which often had questionable efficiency performances. During the 1980s, 30 percent of real capital outlays were devoted to agriculture (including state farms and land settlement) and only 15 percent to infrastructure (transport and communications).[13] Of the recurrent expenditures, approximately 2.2 percent were devoted to agriculture and settlements while close to 55 percent were spent on security and defence.

An aggressive revenue policy brought total fiscal revenues from 20 to 29 percent of GDP in the 1980s. Tax collection was divided evenly among domestic indirect taxes, business profit taxes and taxes on foreign trade. Taxes on coffee exports amounted to 30 to 40 percent of the f.o.b. coffee export values. Profits made by the lucrative state enterprises (mainly airways, mining and shipping) constituted an increasing share of total revenues. Occasionally, emergency levies and surcharges were imposed.

Institutional constraints on private business activity, for example a ceiling of 0.5 million birr (br) of fixed assets per manufacturing enterprise and a lack of investment opportunities and consumer items increased the amount of deposits (demand and savings) made by households and private businesses. High levels of deposits could be attracted at low interest rates (forced savings) and they were, in turn, mobilized for financing the domestic deficit. As a result, 85 to 90 percent of domestic financing came from the banking system.[14]

On the expenditure side, the relative neglect of infrastructure and less than optimum public investment allocation in agriculture weakened the overall productivity of the economy. Likewise, the emphasis on security in the recurrent budget and the maintenance of uneconomical projects further aggravated the situation. Furthermore, non-inflationary financing of the budget deficit was achieved at the expense of private investment opportunities. Thus, overall domestic balance was achieved but basic sources of productivity and growth were neglected or suppressed.

Agricultural sector policies
Between 1974 and 1993, the agricultural policy environment as well as that of the economy as a whole can be divided in three periods:
- 1974 to 1988, when "command economy" measures were implemented and consolidated;

[13] For detailed Ministry of Finance data, see A. Teferra. 1993. *Ethiopia: the agricultural sector – an overview, Vol. II – statistical annex.* Paper prepared for the Policy Analysis Division, FAO.

[14] See footnote 12, p. 85.

• 1988 to 1991, when a number of previous measures were abandoned and reforms were made towards a more liberal economy;
• the post-1991 period (the revolutionary regime collapsed in 1991), during which several of the 1988-1990 reforms were consolidated and additional measures were taken to liberalize the economy.

Given the country's variable agroclimatic conditions, three sets of interdependent factors shaped the environment for agricultural growth: the institutional framework; pricing and marketing policies; and the distribution of budgetary allocations.

The pre-1988 situation. In March 1975, the government announced sweeping changes in the structure of land tenure and labour relations in rural areas. The major elements of the law (Proclamation 31 of 1975) were: *i)* the nationalization of land and the abolition of private landownership; *ii)* a ban on tenancy contracts; *iii)* the prohibition of hired rural labour in private farming; *iv)* guaranteed access to cultivable land for all households.

Individual farm units were organized in peasant associations (PAs) which allocated and reallocated land among households, collected taxes and production quotas and organized voluntary labour for public works. The PAs, in turn, formed service cooperatives (SCs) which carried out supply, marketing and extension functions. Producers' cooperatives (PCs) were composed of individual households which *commonly* managed their consolidated farms. A number of large state farms were also established. By 1989, there were 17 000 PAs and 3 700 SCs, while the socialized sector (PCs and state farms) comprised 3 300 PCs with a total of 290 000 members.

Despite efforts directed towards the "socialization" of agriculture, the structure of production basically remained private because peasants strongly resisted integration in PCs. By 1988, the share of individual peasant holdings in total cultivated land was around 94 percent, with the remainder divided between PCs (2.5 percent) and state farms (3.5 percent). The allocation of public resources between the socialized and the non-socialized sectors was not proportionate to their importance, with the bulk of financial resources, modern

inputs and extension personnel allocated to the socialized sector whose productivity performance often did not justify this disproportionate allocation.

"Villagization" (the grouping of the population in designated villages) became national policy in 1985. By 1989, one-third of the rural population had been transferred to villages. In 1985, in the wake of the drought, the campaign to resettle peasants from drought-stricken areas to uncultivated lands was intensified. Poor organization and settler selection transformed the scheme into an extremely costly project which required continuous subsidies in order to survive.

Pricing and marketing policies also reflected the tendency towards heavy state control. The Agricultural Marketing Corporation (AMC) was responsible for wholesale domestic procurement of grains, oilseeds and pulses and for cereal imports. The AMC was responsible for collecting all the marketable produce from PCs and state farms and required individual farms to deliver a quota based on their assessed capacity to produce a marketable surplus. From 1980, a pan-territorial pricing system was in effect for the quotas, with procurement prices remaining fixed until 1988 when they were increased by 7.7 percent.

Even after their increase in 1988, procurement prices for teff, wheat and barley were, respectively, 37, 61 and 45 percent of free market prices. There were intermittent bans on private trading in major producing regions until 1988. In addition, private traders were obliged to sell the AMC a share of their purchases (ranging between 50 to 100 percent) at br 4 to br 5 more than the price paid to farmers. AMC procurement was not particularly successful and its share of grain purchases reached a peak of 11 percent of the total grain crop in 1986/87, as both individual farmers and traders had strong reason to evade controls.

The functioning of the public procurement system created a market "dualism". On one side, there was the public distribution system which delivered to mills, hospitals, urban associations (*kebeles*), educational institutions and the army. On the other, there were (poorly integrated) free markets where grains and pulses were sold at substantially higher prices.

Exports of pulses and oilseeds, coffee and livestock were also handled by parastatals. Livestock products for export were procured at market prices while domestic

trade was free. Coffee farmgate prices have been kept low (at 35 to 45 percent of their f.o.b. value) even under the overvalued official exchange rate.

The reforms of 1988. Faced with economic stagnation and mounting social problems, in 1988 the government initiated a programme of economic reforms aimed at liberalizing the economic system. The government pointed to the following causes for the economic stagnation:[15] *i)* the negative effects of suppressing private economic activity; *ii)* the unbalanced allocations of investment in peasant agriculture in favour of the low-performance socialized sector; and *iii)* neglect of market forces and the private sector in favour of central planning that led to resource underutilization and inefficient investment.

In response to the diagnosis above, the government endorsed and started implementing a series of measures, including increases in price incentives as well as institutional reforms. Official procurement prices were increased and crop quotas for delivery to the AMC were reduced. Price incentives for coffee were improved substantially. The number of licensed traders was increased, interregional restrictions on the movement of agricultural produce was abolished. Participation in PCs became voluntary and, by the end of 1989, 95 percent of these cooperatives had disintegrated. Several PAs also disappeared.

Another set of reforms was introduced in 1990, liberalizing the foreign investment code, while plans existed to allow the hiring of rural labour. As the country plunged increasingly into civil strife, political instability and institutional disintegration, those policies were not put into effect.

The post-1991 economic environment. In May 1991, the Transitional Government of Ethiopia (TGE) assumed power. It faced an economy that was devastated by the long period of civil strife, with low living standards and deteriorating infrastructure and social conditions. In addition to the deep-rooted problems of poverty in the country, there was the challenge of providing a livelihood for 350 000 demobilized soldiers and their families as well as for a large number of war refugees and displaced civilians.

Along with measures to establish peace and security

---

[15] Presidential Address to the Ninth Plenary Session of the Central Committee of the Workers's Party of Ethiopia, November 1988.

SUB-SAHARAN AFRICA

in the country, a wide-ranging programme of economic and social reforms was introduced by the government with support from the donor community.

On the macroeconomic side, the government devalued the birr from br 2.07 to br 5 per US dollar and, in May 1993, a limited exchange rate auction system was established for essential items.

In agriculture, the government guaranteed use, lease and inheritance rights to land. In the transition period, land redistribution has stopped and the hiring of rural labour is now allowed. The TGE has announced that an elected government should handle the land tenure issue by referendum. The AMC lost its monopoly power so most grain is now marketed by private traders and the quota system has been abolished. Since January 1993, all export taxes have been abolished, with the exception of the coffee export tax. A 15 percent subsidy on fertilizer has been instituted as partial compensation for the effects of the devaluation. In the transport sector, trucking has been liberalized and there are plans to parcel and sell the government trucking company.

The impact of policies on agriculture

The effects of the policies (both macroeconomic and sector-specific) followed from 1974 to 1991, especially those applied before 1988, created an overall negative environment for agricultural growth, thereby contributing to the virtual stagnation of agricultural output.

Institutional changes with respect to land caused a drastic reduction in the size of farms which often were not sufficient to support a household. Tenure uncertainty had serious environmental implications while the small size of the holdings and the lack of timely distribution of fertilizers and seeds (exclusively distributed by the public sector) have contributed to the stagnation of yields.[16]

There has been insufficient research on appropriate technologies and inputs (seeds and fertilizers) adapted to the agroclimatic conditions of the country. The Ethiopian Seed Corporation distributed about half of the 40 000 tonnes of seeds that were estimated to be needed by the traditional farm sector. The erratic distribution of seeds and a lack of extension services caused many farmers to rely on traditional seeds and refuse new varieties.

Although the land actually controlled by PCs and state

---

[16] **Average cereal yields are about 1.2 tonnes per hectare for the smallholder sector, two-thirds as high as those in Kenya for comparable soil fertility and climatic conditions. For pulses and oilseeds (at 0.65 tonnes and 0.5 tonnes per hectare, respectively), yields are among the lowest in the world.**

farms was only a small percentage of the total land area cultivated, according to the Ten-Year Perspective Plan 1982/83-1993/94, most individual farmers were to be organized into PCs. The final objective was for 44 percent of the cultivated land to be allocated to individual farms, 49 percent to PCs and 7 percent to state farms. Although the plan was never implemented, its provisions – along with the uncertain land tenure system and the frequent land reallocations within PAs – created great uncertainty among individual farm households and acted as a disincentive to long-term investments by farmers as well as to sustainable farm practices.

Furthermore, the marketing system was not conducive to the production of a marketing surplus, as low prices were paid for quota deliveries. Restrictions on interregional movements prevented the integration of deficit and surplus areas, a situation that was exacerbated by the poor condition of rural roads, tight controls on the transport and hauling system and the long distance of the majority of small peasant holdings from all-weather roads. The relative neglect of rural infrastructure greatly reduced overall investment efficiency.

It is difficult to single out the impact of the liberalization measures taken between 1988 and 1990, as their effects are clouded by the severe disruption of markets caused by the war. There is evidence of a reduction of spatial price dispersion and increased market integration for cereals following liberalization, despite the worsening security situation.

Thus far, the response of the economy and agriculture to the post-1991 reforms is encouraging, although it is difficult to establish with precision a correspondence between policies and performance. Exogenous factors (favourable weather) and non-economic factors (increased peace and security) have played a positive role in expanding economic activity.

On the macroeconomic side, after a reduction of 5.2 percent in 1991/92, real GDP is expected to grow by 7.5 percent in 1992/93, one percentage point above the government target. Inflation fell from 45 percent in the period June 1990/June 1991 to 14 percent in the corresponding period 1991/92. It is believed that the country had already absorbed the effects of the devaluation, as a large number of foreign exchange

transactions were taking place on the parallel market at br 7 per US dollar.

The projected strong performance of real GDP is linked to the agricultural sector's continuous strong performance during the last three years. Cereal production showed a strong recovery, with a total production of 7.3 million tonnes in 1990/91 (a record crop), followed by a near-record crop in 1991/92 of 7.1 million tonnes and a projected 7.7 million tonnes in 1992/93.[17]

The variations reflect changes in weather patterns and localized droughts. The peasant sector accounted for most of the increase in output, while state farm production was static. Fertilizer consumption was 30 percent higher in 1992 and cropped land area expanded in response to strong cereal prices. Increased deliveries of coffee have been observed in the Addis Ababa market during the first months of 1993.

Current issues in agricultural development

Recent policy reforms constitute the beginning of deep structural changes needed to set the Ethiopian economy on a sustainable development path. Ethiopia is, and will stay for some time, an economy in transition between two different economic development models. Among the numerous issues currently facing Ethiopian policy-makers, two are analysed more extensively in this report: *i)* food security and poverty alleviation; and *ii)* natural resource degradation.

Poverty and food insecurity. The extent of the problem and its root causes. Food insecurity (defined in its most basic form as a situation where the food needed for a healthy life is not accessible to all people at all times) is both a chronic and a transitory phenomenon in Ethiopia. It is estimated that 50 percent of the country's total population (between 23 million and 26 million people) are subject to food insecurity. More than 20 million of these people live in rural areas. In cases of consecutive periods of natural and human-caused calamities, poor households sell their assets, deplete their food stocks and become highly vulnerable or destitute and in need of continuous flows of food assistance to survive. Over the last two decades, transitory food insecurity has manifested itself in the famines following the droughts of 1972-73 and 1984-85.[18] In Ethiopia, refugees and people

[17] *Sources:* For 1990/91, Central Statistical Authority data; for 1991/92, Ethiopian Ministry of Agriculture estimates; for 1992/93, FAO. 1993. *Food supply situation and crop prospects in sub-Saharan Africa.* Rome. *Note:* Data include non-food uses.
[18] Similar consequences were averted in the 1987 drought because of early warning and adequate preparation.

SUB-SAHARAN AFRICA

[19] For instance, the period 1979-1984.

[20] For more information, see IFAD. 1989. IFAD: Special Programming Mission to Ethiopia. Working Papers Nos 1 (*Macroeconomic performance and trends*) and 7 (*The dynamics of rural poverty*). Rome.

[21] Ethiopian National Institute data. See I. Loerbroks. *Statement on the occasion of World Food Day 1992*, 16 October, Addis Ababa, Ethiopia.

[22] In addition to the level of per caput income, access to social services is another dimension of poverty. Such access, if it exists, can compensate for some of the consequences of low income. In this report, only the elements of poverty *directly* affecting access to food are examined. For a detailed analysis of the different dimensions of poverty in Ethiopia, see *The social dimensions of adjustment in Ethiopia: a study on poverty alleviation*. Addis Ababa, Ministry of Planning and Economic Development. May 1992.

[23] Using 1982/83 survey data, IFAD estimated that only 5 percent of rural income was saved.

displaced by the civil war are highly vulnerable groups requiring assistance.

With respect to chronic food insecurity, data show that even in normal periods (i.e. not characterized by abnormal climatic or socio-economic conditions)[19] the average national level of food intake was 14 percent below the minimum daily requirement of 500 g of cereal equivalent per caput. "Average" data may be misleading because they mask differences in the ability of people to gain access to available food supplies. Data from the Ministry of Agriculture show that, in 1982/83, average incomes per household in the low-income areas were less than one-third of those in higher-income regions. Poor regions were also food-deficit areas and, given the lack of market integration, grain prices were much higher in those areas, thus further exacerbating the access problem.[20] It is estimated that, although food aid has prevented the average food availability from falling dramatically, acute malnutrition during periods of drought and civil disturbances has affected 8 percent of the population.[21] FAO has estimated that the current level of food production (including grains, pulses, vegetables, fruits and livestock products) could provide a total of 1 600 to 1 700 kcal per caput per day. Food aid and imports increase total per caput caloric intake to 1 800 to 1 900 per day which is below the minimum recommended 2 100 kcal per day.

Poverty is at the root of the problem of access to food supplies.[22] In the rural sector, the poor have limited productive assets, mostly of low quality (small farm size, poor soil quality, variable rainfall, a small number of livestock); limited opportunities for alternative employment; poor access to social services; and they use traditional production techniques. The poor also spend a large part of their incomes on food and energy, while a minimal amount is saved.[23] Thus, they are highly vulnerable when emergencies occur. Urban poverty is the result of high unemployment and wages fixed at low levels. The problem has been aggravated recently by the influx of demobilized soldiers and displaced people and by increases in food prices on the free market.

Policies for alleviating poverty and food insecurity. Broad-based economic development is essential for a long-term sustainable improvement in the lives of the poor. For Ethiopia, the role of agriculture is critical in this respect. Agricultural growth will address the supply

side of the food security issue (i.e. increasing food production and foreign exchange for food imports) as well as the access side, through employment creation and income opportunities. On the other hand, policies that promote growth are often slow to work and it may take several years of growth to absorb productively the unemployed and underemployed labour force and raise the living standards of the most needy groups.[24] As a major restructuring of the economic system is taking place, some of the short-term adjustments (especially food price increases) will negatively affect the most vulnerable parts of the population.

Thus, in addition to policy reforms aimed at growth, urgent targeted measures must be taken to deal with poverty in the short and medium term. Issues related to emergency (drought) preparedness and relief as well as to the most appropriate use of the (substantial) food aid flowing into the country need to be examined in the light of the changing economic conditions. Following are some of the issues and actions being taken by the government.

Safety net measures. Past policies for poverty alleviation emphasized untargeted commodity subsidies administered mainly through the public distribution system. Beneficiaries of the subsidies were members of the *kebeles*, PCs and cooperatives who were issued rations of subsidized food and other commodities (soap, salt and kerosene). Families had access to the same rations irrespective of income, the intention being (especially in the urban areas) the creation of a self-targeted system where the more privileged households would not be willing to queue in the *kebele* shops to obtain lower-quality items. The problems with the system of generalized commodity programmes were: *i)* it had a strong urban bias, i.e. urban consumers, representing 15 percent of the population, were receiving about 60 percent of the subsidies; *ii)* although it provided significant relief to poor households, it benefited disproportionately the middle- and higher-income ones, as very poor households could not afford to buy their ratio at subsidized prices; and *iii)* the economic costs of those programmes (i.e. using border prices at equilibrium exchange rates) were extremely high. As prices were liberalized and the exchange rate was devalued, the programmes became unworkable.[25]

In the wake of the complete liberalization of

[24] According to the World Bank, assuming 5 percent real GDP growth and 3 percent population growth, it will take 35 years for the per caput GDP of Ethiopia (of $120) to double.

[25] World Bank calculations show that, at the shadow exchange rate of br 5 per US dollar (which, after 1991, became the actual exchange rate), the benefits to the poorest 30 percent of the urban population amounted to about 16 percent of the *total cost of the urban commodity subsidies.* For the rural sector the share was 5 percent (after adding the cost of the fertilizer subsidy). The total weighted share (urban plus rural) was about 12 percent.

SUB-SAHARAN AFRICA

commodity markets in 1991, the TGE instituted a programme to mitigate the effects of food price increases on the poor. The programme contained a number of safety net features, including a limited public sector wage adjustment to cover food price increases; severance pay and retraining for employees of abolished public enterprises; and a food/kerosene voucher scheme to assist the poorest groups in the urban areas. The scheme uses the *kebele* administrative infrastructure to target the poorest households which, depending on their income, receive a voucher either free or in exchange for community service or public works. This targeted income transfer scheme is more efficient than the previous system of untargeted commodity subsidies. In the rural areas, a programme to provide fertilizer and other input vouchers for poor farmers is under consideration, as is a rural public works programme to help generate income for unemployed rural workers.

Food aid for development. Food aid increased from about 3.5 percent of total food availability in the first half of the 1980s (up to 1984) to 17.2 percent during the second half, reflecting the effects of the 1984-85 drought.[26] The TGE has taken a clear position against free food distribution in its programming of food aid resources. This position is based on the belief that free food distribution is ineffective in arresting or reversing the trend towards impoverishment and that it could destroy the survival mechanisms of the poor. Thus, a number of proposals exist for the use of food aid as a development tool through employment-generating public works programmes. The basic elements of these proposals are: *i)* selection of labour-intensive projects, mainly in the rural areas, based on food-for-work or cash-for-work compensation – the latter being funded with proceeds from monetized food aid; *ii)* a self-targeting mechanism by which the cash or food-equivalent wage is set below the market wage, thus attracting only the truly poor and vulnerable.

The extent to which such a programme can be implemented will depend on the capacities of the line ministries, the Early Warning and Planning Services Relief and Rehabilitation Commission, NGOs and the regional governments to resolve a number of issues, including the following:

• a system for setting the appropriate wage level has to be established;

---

[26] See footnote 20, p. 93.

• the main orientation of the projects must be decided, i.e. whether projects will be selected strictly in terms of economic cost-benefit criteria or whether such economic efficiency will be compromised in favour of projects that make a significant difference in the level of employment (putting more emphasis on the project's social safety net features).

Natural resource degradation.[27] Degradation of natural resources constitutes one of the major constraints to increasing agricultural production in Ethiopia. According to FAO, about half of the highlands (270 000 km²) are already significantly eroded; of this, 140 000 km² are seriously eroded and have been left with relatively shallow soils. Close to 20 000 km² of agricultural lands are so badly eroded that they are unlikely to sustain cropping in the future. About 1 900 million tonnes of soil are being eroded annually, of which about 10 percent is carried away by rivers and cannot be retrieved, while the rest is redeposited as sediment within the highlands but mostly in places that cannot be of much agricultural use. If the trend continues, land covered by soil with a depth of less than 10 cm will constitute 18 percent of the highland area by the year 2010. This implies a dramatic fall in yields, frequent crop failures and a high probability of famines, especially in the low-potential cropping areas (LPCs) of the highlands. In addition to on-site agricultural production losses, erosion reduces the effective lives of dams and reservoirs through siltation as well as increasing the extent and intensity of droughts and flooding.

Soil erosion is not a necessary consequence of cropping but rather a result of inappropriate cropping practices. Factors contributing to high erosion rates are the removal of natural vegetation for cropping, fuel, grazing and building; short, intense storms in the rainy season; high erodibility resulting from deforestation; and highly sloped topography. In the Ethiopian highlands, population pressures forced the cultivation of increasingly steeper slopes and progressively shortened the fallow between periods of annual cropping. It is estimated that four-fifths of the erosion in the highlands occurs from the overexploitation of croplands, while most of the remainder is caused by the overgrazing of grasslands and deforested areas.

[27] This section is derived for the most part from FAO. 1985. *Ethiopian Highlands Reclamation Study.* Project report. Rome.

SUB-SAHARAN AFRICA

Deforestation constitutes another serious environmental problem. In less than a century, the country's forest and woodland cover has been reduced from 40 percent of the total area to 16 percent in the 1950s and an estimated 4 percent at present.

Past policies concerning the agricultural sector amplified the adverse resource degradation and depletion effects of agroclimatic parameters. Villagization schemes placed an excessive demand on forest resources for building material. No effort was made to explore and introduce new energy sources in the rural sector, so wood and dung remained the only sources of energy. As the demand for such resources grew with population, deforestation and the deprivation of land from valuable nutrients increased. Uncertainty about land tenure acted as a disincentive to investments in soil conservation. Inadequate funding for agriculture and its disproportionate distribution in favour of state farms and cooperatives resulted in a shortage of funds for research on appropriate peasant technologies. In general, the policy environment discouraged the integration of conservation activities into the farming practices of peasants. The situation was exacerbated by a lack of appropriate land-use and forest policies. While the resettlement of rural populations may be, in principle, an efficient method of addressing imbalances between patterns of human settlement and available resources, the way it was implemented in the past in Ethiopia made it ineffective.

In its 1985 Ethiopian Highlands Reclamation Study, FAO recognized that isolated conservation measures are bound to be both highly costly and ineffective. The study suggested a broad-based development strategy (conservation-based development strategy or CDS) so that conservation measures are integrated into mainstream agricultural development activities at all levels (farm, agricultural, national).[28]

Within the agricultural sector, the strategy identified proper farming and livestock management systems and practices to be promoted in each agro-ecological zone in the highlands. Emphasis was given to the provision of proper incentives for conservation and to proper relocation practices. The strategy recognized that agriculture cannot by itself solve all factors associated with degradation (such as low growth and poverty). It suggested that the links of agriculture with other sectors

[28] "The term Conservation-based Development implies not only the allocation of more resources for conservation but, even more importantly, ... the integration into agricultural and rural development objectives and criteria of improved land-using systems. This could result in a significant reduction, if not the removal, of absolute poverty." Executive Summary, p. 12, in FAO. 1985. *Ethiopian Highlands Reclamation Study*. Rome.

and complementary activities (small-scale industry, agroforestry, energy generation) be exploited to generate alternative income sources, especially in low-potential areas. At the national level, increased overall spending for agriculture was recommended in favour of the peasant sector; the need for an increased capacity of the ministries to carry out conservation programmes; and the full utilization of the capacities and skills of the private sector.

A number of policies included in the recommendations of the Ethiopian Highlands Reclamation Study have already been implemented (more secure tenure, more freedom for the private sector, voluntary resettlement and better incentives to farmers) but much more needs to be done. Land-use and forest resource policies are necessary prerequisites for a successful environmental resource conservation strategy. Accordingly, a forestry action plan is an important component of the national conservation strategy that the Ethiopian Government plans to complete by April 1994. Within a well-established set of rules for forest management and conservation, a greater role will be allowed for private sector participation in wood harvesting and processing. Incentives will be given to farmers and rural communities for reforestation and tree planting.

ASIA AND THE PACIFIC

REGIONAL OVERVIEW

Asian and Pacific countries continued to show strong and steady economic growth in 1992. The Asian Development Bank (AsDB) estimates the average annual GDP growth rate for the region to be 7 percent in 1992, up from 6.3 percent in 1991. Despite the prolonged global recession, the AsDB expects regional GDP to increase by 7.2 percent in 1993. Three significant factors contributing to the region's ability to maintain this solid growth performance are: *i)* a continuing increase in disposable incomes, which is sustaining domestic demand; *ii)* the continuing expansion of intraregional trade; and *iii)* positive results from earlier policy reforms in many Asian economies.

Following are some individual country experiences in 1992:

- The output of China's industrial output increased by 20 percent in 1992, contributing to the country's impressive 12.8 percent increase in GDP. Even though drought affected many parts of the country, total grain production increased by 1.7 percent to an estimated 443 million tonnes. Tea, sugar, tobacco, fruit and vegetable production also increased compared with 1991 levels.
- All of India's economic sectors improved in 1992 – the country's GDP increased by 4.2 percent. Agriculture, which was aided by a good monsoon, grew by 3.5 percent. Foodgrain production increased to a record 177 million tonnes compared with 167 million tonnes in 1991. However, heavy monsoon rains and floods in July 1993 are likely to have serious implications for this year's grain production.
- In Pakistan, a 30 percent increase in cotton production spurred agricultural GDP to a 6.4 percent increase in 1992. The large cotton crop is attributed to higher farmgate prices, a wider use of improved seeds and favourable weather. In contrast, Nepal experienced unfavourable weather in 1992. Its agricultural GDP increased by only 0.5 percent and foodgrain production declined by 6.5 percent.
- Southeast Asia reported mixed agricultural performances. Agricultural GDP increased by 3.5 percent in Thailand and 1.2 percent in Malaysia, but

Figure 8

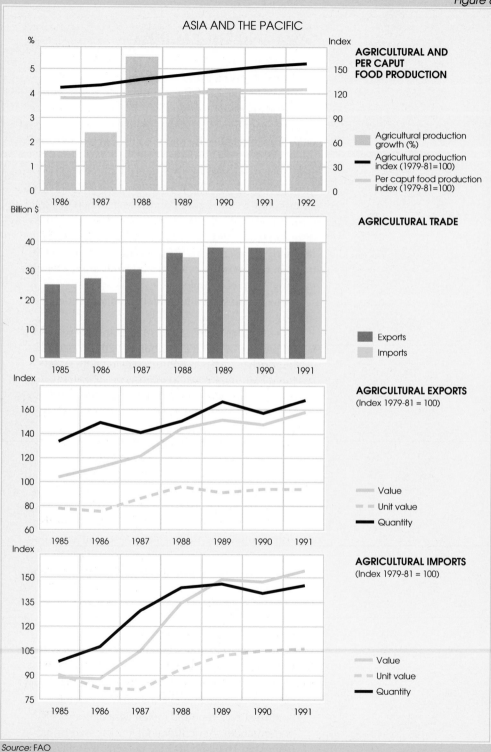

ASIA AND THE PACIFIC

AGRICULTURAL AND PER CAPUT FOOD PRODUCTION

- Agricultural production growth (%)
- Agricultural production index (1979-81=100)
- Per caput food production index (1979-81=100)

AGRICULTURAL TRADE

- Exports
- Imports

AGRICULTURAL EXPORTS
(Index 1979-81 = 100)

- Value
- Unit value
- Quantity

AGRICULTURAL IMPORTS
(Index 1979-81 = 100)

- Value
- Unit value
- Quantity

Source: FAO

fell by 1 percent in the Philippines. In Malaysia, the production of palm oil, sawlogs, livestock and fish increased, while rubber and cocoa declined. In the Philippines, a severe drought reduced corn and rice production while the logging ban and related conservation measures curtailed forestry production in 1992.

- Viet Nam produced a record rice crop of 21.1 million tonnes, 1.2 million tonnes more than 1991. Total food production increased by 9 percent and agricultural GDP increased by 6.3 percent in 1992. Wide access to inputs and agricultural policy reforms are credited with improving yields and expanding area under cultivation. Laos' agricultural sector also recorded an outstanding year in 1992. Its agricultural GDP increased by 8.3 percent, with rice production growing by more than 20 percent.

Growing intraregional trade and investment flows
Despite a slow-down in the world economy in 1992, the international trade performance of the developing countries of the Asia and Pacific Region continued to be buoyant. Exports rose by 13 percent as a result of improvement in production efficiency, low inflation rates and favourable impacts of the policy reforms initiated in recent years.

One key factor sheltering the Asian economies from the global recession was the significant growth in intraregional trade and investment. In 1991, intraregional trade expanded by 23 percent compared with a 15 percent increase in exports to the rest of the world. This development is strongly supported by the ongoing regional division of labour, specialization and the relocation of production within the region in response to the opportunities offered by the various countries' relative factor endowments, macroeconomic policy environments and resulting comparative advantages.

In addition to large inflows of direct foreign investment, substantial flows of investment capital from Japan and newly industrialized Asian economies to the developing countries within the region continued. In particular, vast investment opportunities and the spectacular rate of growth in China attracted millions of dollars of investment by overseas Chinese.

The outcome of the ongoing Uruguay Round of

multilateral trade negotiations (MTNs) is keenly awaited in view of its influence in shaping the application of the principles of non-discrimination and market access for exports from the region. The emergence of the North American Free Trade Association (NAFTA) is, however, viewed with some wariness because of the likely diversion of direct foreign investments from Asian countries.

Against the backdrop of these changes in the external environment, Asian countries have moved ahead with the creation and promotion of subregional trade arrangements. The member states of the Association of Southeast Asian Nations have launched the ASEAN Free Trade Area (AFTA) with a goal to remove tariffs on most commodities traded within the region in the course of the next 15 years. Likewise, the South Asian Association for Regional Cooperation (SAARC) summit in Dhaka earlier this year adopted a resolution to create a South Asian Free Trade Area (SAFTA). However, because of differences in size and the state of economic development between member nations, many difficult issues need to be resolved before these regional arrangements can emerge as an effective means for coordinated action.

The challenges of economic transition
During the past two years, the number of Asian countries undergoing transition from a centrally planned to a market-oriented economy more than doubled when six former Soviet Asian republics (Azerbaijan, Kazakhstan, Kyrgyzstan, Tajikistan, Turkmenistan and Uzbekistan) joined China, Laos, Mongolia and Viet Nam in this process. There is considerable variation among these countries in terms of the problems of transition, approaches followed and the degree of success achieved. Most of them require structural transformation which can only be achieved over a number of years through persistent and consistent efforts. There are also problems of short-term stabilization and macroeconomic management as well as the need to create and strengthen institutions necessary for a market economy. Both problems seem to be more acute in the case of former Soviet Asian republics than others.

While, initially, all countries undergoing transition faced high inflation, unemployment and underemployment, China, Viet Nam and to some extent

Laos have been able to reduce these by stimulating agricultural production, private investment and foreign direct investment. Mongolia and the former Soviet Asian republics, on the other hand, are facing severe shocks of transition.

For example, in 1992, in contrast to the economic growth of 12.8 percent and an inflation rate of 6.4 percent in China, Mongolia's real GDP fell by 7.6 percent and the inflation rate spiralled to 320 percent. In China and Viet Nam, the rural communities – whose production systems are based on the household unit and are equipped with labour-intensive technologies – responded well to market signals. In contrast, farming communities in Mongolia and the former Soviet Asian republics, which have a longer tradition of communal farming using heavy equipment and depending on input supplies from state enterprises, face more difficulties in adapting to the new situation. It also appears that, in the latter group of countries, price liberalization did not bring about the expected supply response because of a monopolistic control over inputs and the tendency of the monopolistic enterprises to curtail production and raise prices.

Judging by the experience of some countries in transition (China and Viet Nam), which suffered initially from short-term macroeconomic instability and inflation, it appears that an appropriate institutional structure is equally as crucial as macroeconomic stability for a successful transition. The transition process requires the public sector and foreign donors to have an active supporting role in creating and consolidating a favourable policy framework and institutional environment that will enable the efficient functioning of a market economy.

In addition, improvements are essential in the government's capacity to deliver public goods (research, extension, transport and communications infrastructure, health, education and other social services), which remain in the domain of the public sector even in a highly developed market system.

The environment and sustainable agriculture
Rapidly increasing population pressure, urbanization, the excessive use of chemicals in production processes and the unsustainable use of natural resources are contributing to serious water and air pollution,

deforestation, soil erosion, desertification and flooding throughout the region.

While the improved seed and fertilizer technology, complemented with a vast expansion in irrigation facilities, removed the spectre of hunger from many populous Asian countries, in some cases it also added to environmental degradation. Moreover, maintaining or raising the present yield levels demands a more intensive use of natural resources, which has adverse environmental consequences. For the Pacific countries, global warming and the resulting rise in sea level are the most serious, although uncertain, environmental threats. The externalities involved with these types of environmental issues require concerted group actions by the international community.

Developing Asian countries have realized the close connection between rural poverty and environmental degradation. Increasing population pressure on agriculture, the result of inadequate growth in off-farm employment opportunities and a lack of access to yield-improving technologies, is forcing many Asian farmers to cultivate marginal lands and overuse other natural resources for their immediate survival. In many Asian countries that are striving for equitable and sustainable development, poverty alleviation is a core element of the national development plan.

Many countries are grappling with the complex task of achieving poverty alleviation and environmental protection goals within a somewhat conflicting framework, containing socio-political commitments to achieving equity as well as market liberalization policies aimed at resolving macroeconomic imbalances. It is argued that market-based policy instruments emphasizing the removal of input subsidies, output support prices and protective tariffs may act as a two-edged sword. While tending to discourage uneconomical and unsustainable input use, with positive effects on the environment and the evolution of sustainable farming practices, these policies tend to increase food prices, consequently having negative income effects on the poor, who often are net buyers of food, and thus mitigating the achievement of poverty alleviation goals in the short term. Policy formulation in such situations may call for a compromise between economic efficiency and a pragmatic understanding of the short-term socio-economic political situation.

Finally, the cost of reversing environmental degradation is very high. For most developing Asian countries, investing in such activities would entail drawing resources away from other important development projects. It has also been realized that preventing environmental damage costs less than restoring the loss. Thus, there is an increasing emphasis on the incorporation of environmental considerations in policy formulation as well as in development project selection and the evolution of appropriate production systems.

Sectoral policies following macroeconomic and structural reforms

Having established a growth-oriented macroeconomic policy framework in the course of implementing stabilization and structural adjustment programmes, a number of market-oriented Asian countries, such as Bangladesh, Indonesia and the Philippines, have moved on to sectoral reforms. It is realized that the macroeconomic policy reforms cannot be fully effective in improving efficiency and unleashing the farmers' production potential unless sectoral constraints on growth are tackled.

A comprehensive package of agricultural sectoral policy reforms generally consists of the withdrawal of input subsidies, the dismantling of expensive public food distribution systems and the removal of subsidized credit and protective tariffs as well as other barriers. It also entails freeing import restrictions, encouraging private sector participation and investing in infrastructure to promote the efficient operation of market mechanisms.

The task of designing efficiency-oriented equitable agriculture sector policies is not easy, however. Among other things, policy-makers have to take into account the differential impacts of sector policy changes on various sections of society as well as dealing with diverse coalitions and interest groups who react differently to policy changes. These reforms are therefore being carried out selectively and in sequence, with due consideration given to the socio-political realities of the countries concerned. For example, in some cases fertilizer subsidies have been gradually reduced (in India and Indonesia) while an active public sector role in foodgrain procurement, distribution and buffer stock management has been maintained.

ASIA AND THE PACIFIC

In some Asian countries, the reluctance to carry out agricultural sectoral policy reforms seems to have been reinforced by the delayed finalization of the Uruguay Round of GATT negotiations as well as by protective trade policies and trade blocks outside the region.

BANGLADESH

With an estimated per caput GNP of $225 in 1992, Bangladesh is among the poorest countries in the world. Moreover, with approximately 115 million inhabitants and 149 000 km², the country is three times more densely populated than India and seven times more than China. This intense population pressure on a relatively narrow resource base, together with the frequent natural disasters suffered, present formidable challenges to poverty alleviation efforts in Bangladesh.

Over the years, floods, droughts and cyclones have undermined progress and hampered the country's efforts to stimulate growth and reduce poverty. Cyclones and resulting storm surges are particularly destructive. The Bay of Bengal is the most cyclone-prone area in the world, having been hit by 15 cyclones during the past 25 years. These natural disasters cause immeasurable human suffering, devastate large crop areas and destroy property and infrastructure. The government estimates that the cyclone of April 1991 killed approximately 140 000 people. Such disasters impede economic and social progress by diverting attention and resources away from development programmes and towards crisis management.

Despite all these obstacles, Bangladesh has made significant economic progress over the past decade. The country has reduced external and internal deficits, stabilized the inflation rate, promoted non-traditional exports and achieved a modest growth rate. Stabilization policies have helped lower the budget deficit from about 8 percent in 1990 to 5 percent in 1992. The inflation rate fell to around 5 percent in 1992, the lowest rate in more than ten years. Real GDP growth during the period 1990-92 has been in the range of 3.5 to 6.5 percent and is forecast to be 5 percent in 1993.

Bangladesh has also initiated a number of structural reforms in the industrial and financial sectors, public enterprises and trade and exchange rate policy. Financial sector reforms include abolishing credit ceilings and increasing reliance on cash and liquid asset reserve requirements to regulate liquidity. Public enterprises are being given more administrative and managerial autonomy. Trade policy is shifting from import substitution to export promotion; a tariff system is replacing prohibitions and quantitative restrictions on imports.

Perhaps even more important to the overall economy are the agricultural policies, programmes and projects that have expanded the use of high-yielding variety (HYV) rice seeds, fertilizers and shallow tube wells for irrigation. As a result, rice production has increased by more than 40 percent in the past ten years. Today, Bangladesh is close to self-sufficiency in rice and, for the first time in the country's history, the government is discussing the possibility of exporting rice.

In addition to the stabilization programme and economic policy reforms, human resource development and poverty alleviation remain top priorities. Public spending on health care, primary education and family planning increased in real terms in 1992. Food distribution programmes aimed at vulnerable groups and the poor are being overhauled to reduce costs, increase efficiency and improve coverage.

Many human development programmes have proved successful in Bangladesh. For example, family planning efforts have resulted in a lower population growth rate which is currently down to 2.1 percent. At the same time, the country still has a low literacy rate (around 35 percent), a low primary school enrolment rate (72 percent) and a low life expectancy (56 years). Moreover, half of total mortality is due to child death below the age of five years, of which more than half is due directly or indirectly to malnutrition. Household food security is another persistent problem; half the households in Bangladesh cannot afford an adequate diet and an estimated 22 to 30 percent of the population lives in dire poverty (less than 1 805 kcal per caput per day).

The agricultural sector

The agricultural sector is Bangladesh's largest source of income, employment, savings and investment. Agriculture accounts for about 40 percent of GDP and more than 60 percent of employment. Rice not only dominates all other agricultural products, it also dominates all other economic activities. Production, trade, processing and transportation of rice amount to more than 25 percent of the country's GDP. Rice represents 75 percent of the cropped area, 95 percent of foodgrain production, about 80 percent of caloric intake, 60 percent of protein intake and about 30 percent of total household expenditures – the weight of rice in the consumer price index (CPI) is about 60 percent. For

these reasons, policies that affect rice production, trade and consumption have a profound impact on Bangladesh's entire population.

Over the past two decades, rice production and distribution policies have adjusted with changing economic circumstances and pressures. The growth in rice production is attributed primarily to policies that encouraged wider use of new irrigation technology, HYVs and mineral fertilizers. The introduction of tube well irrigation, particularly low-cost shallow tube wells, is the main reason for the rapid expansion of total irrigated area and the shift away from traditional irrigation methods.

Rice and foodgrain policies

Rice production. During the 1980s, the area under shallow tube well irrigation expanded annually by nearly 30 percent, increasing from 227 000 ha in 1981 to 1.8 million ha in 1991. Today, tube wells account for 55 percent of the 3.3 million ha under irrigation, compared with 14 percent in 1980. Moreover, tube well irrigation has encouraged more rice production in the dry season and less in the early monsoon season. In 1992, irrigated dry season rice accounted for 37 percent of the record harvest (18.25 million tonnes) compared with 20 percent in the early 1980s. In contrast, the total area planted to rice during the early monsoon season declined from 3.2 million ha in 1982 to 1.9 million ha in 1992.

Initially, government policies encouraged rice production through the direct provision of irrigation equipment. During the 1970s and 1980s, the Bangladesh Agricultural Development Corporation (BADC) monopolized imports and domestic distribution (sales and rentals) of all irrigation equipment. An increasing number of procedural difficulties, however, led to a series of policy changes in 1989. These changes included: restructuring the BADC's tube well sales practices; allowing the private sector to import and market tube wells; and eliminating licensing requirements for shallow tube wells (many restrictions still apply to deep tube wells).

The resulting increase in access to and availability of irrigation equipment, combined with lower prices, contributed to a rapid expansion in tube well irrigation. Half of the 40 000 units sold in 1989 came from the

private sector. In the three-year period from 1989 to 1991, the irrigated area expanded by almost 700 000 ha, which is more than the total irrigated area added during the previous eight years.

Other production policies provided a guaranteed floor price as well as subsidized inputs, including HYV seeds, credit, pesticides and fertilizers. In recent years, the government has removed subsidies on fertilizers and allowed private sector imports and sales of mineral fertilizers, even though it remains the sole domestic producer of most types of fertilizers.

Rice and foodgrain distribution. To ensure an affordable food supply for poor consumers, the government manages a variety of food distribution programmes and open market sales operations to help stabilize foodgrain prices. Public food distribution programmes provide approximately 13 percent of all foodgrains consumed in the country.

Past policy measures aimed at foodgrain distribution and prices include: a ban on exports; a monopoly on imports; restrictions on the movement and storage of rice; prohibitions against extending bank credit for rice storage; open market sales of wheat and rice at predetermined ceilings during times of price peaks; and public sector procurement at predetermined floor prices in the postharvest season. The objectives of price stabilization policies are to protect poor consumers from sharp price increases, protect poor farmers from a postharvest price collapse and achieve foodgrain self-sufficiency.

The public food distribution programmes include disaster and famine relief, seasonal food-for-work development projects and year-round rationing. Many food distribution programmes and food policies have recently been restructured, reformed or eliminated. For example, in August 1992, the government allowed private sector imports of foodgrains for the first time. Private traders responded by importing more than 300 000 tonnes of wheat by the end of the year.

The government also abolished the rural rationing programme in May 1992 because of the high costs of maintaining it (an estimated $60 million per year) and large leakages (between 70 and 100 percent).[29] The rural rationing programme had provided an outlet for half of all government rice stocks. Its elimination resulted in a

[29] IFPRI's series, *Food Policy in Bangladesh*, Working Paper Nos 1-6, contains well-documented analyses of food distribution issues in Bangladesh.

large buildup of government stocks and prompted several additional reforms in procurement policies. In November 1992, the government cancelled "millgate contracting" (millgate contracting involves government contracts with the rice mills to support farm prices), introduced tendering operations, lowered procurement prices and raised procurement grades.

Procurement by tender was substituted for millgate procurement because of the high costs of millgate contracting, which involved above-market purchase prices. The higher-quality standards were established to increase storage life and obtain export-quality rice.

These various policy changes and reforms are under way for a number of reasons. First, the structure of rice markets has evolved substantially over the past two decades. Twenty years ago, farmers marketed only 15 percent of their production; today, they market more than 50 percent. Second, the proportion of privately held rice stocks has been increasing over the years, now accounting for 75 percent of total stocks. Moreover, the share of privately held stocks located on farms has increased while the share held by traders and millers has fallen.

The increasing importance of an irrigated winter rice crop is an additional factor influencing foodgrain policies. By decreasing both the frequency and severity of seasonal price changes, this third annual rice crop reduces the need for price stabilization measures. Finally, today's rice markets are much less fragmented and much more competitive than in the past: more than 20 000 rice mills and 30 000 husking mills now provide services throughout the country.

Rice policies and agriculture: short-term issues. As rice production and productivity continue to increase and as the market structure evolves further, additional policy adjustments and reforms are likely in the future. Achieving rice self-sufficiency has already raised a number of important policy questions. For example, can Bangladesh compete with its Asian neighbours, especially Thailand and Viet Nam, in world rice markets? What kind of trade and exchange rate policy reforms are necessary to enhance the country's ability to export rice? What is the role of the private sector relative to that of the public sector in this new era of rice self-sufficiency and exports?

BOX 4
THE FISHERIES SECTOR IN BANGLADESH

Although Bangladesh's fisheries sector is relatively small (around 3 percent of GDP), it contributes to the national economy in a number of significant ways. First, marine and inland fisheries provide full-time jobs for some 1.7 million people and part-time work for more than 11 million. Second, fish consumption represents 80 percent of animal protein intake and 7 percent of total protein supplies. Finally, frozen shrimp and other fish products are among the country's fastest growing exports. Exports of frozen shrimp have increased annually by around 15 percent during the past decade and it has become the fourth most important export after ready-made garments, jute products and leather.

Already significant, the sector's current contribution to growth, income, employment and foreign exchange earnings nevertheless remains below its potential. Much of Bangladesh is a vast delta dissected by three major rivers and more than 700 other rivers and streams. The flood plain is rich in fish (as a source of food) and about one-third of the country is under water for six months each year.

These freshwater resources explain why inland fisheries account for nearly three-fourths of the country's total fish production. Yet, despite its importance, this resource base is being displaced or disrupted by flood control, drainage, road embankments, irrigation systems, pesticides and fertilizers. Ironically, the same agricultural policies and projects that allowed rice farmers to increase their productivity and helped some landless to find more work have done so often at the expense of open access capture fisheries. Water control projects, intended to create favourable conditions for rice production, frequently decrease flood duration and area. The resulting decline in inland capture is especially threatening for those Bangladeshis who depend on this open access resource as their only source of animal protein.

Few water-related projects or policies take the needs of fisheries into account or include the physical structures needed to achieve fisheries objectives. These projects can disrupt fisheries in a number of ways. Embankments and regulators prevent fish from successfully carrying out breeding migrations. Structures to stop bank overtopping and lateral flooding lead to sedimentation further downstream, adversely affecting fish production in river channels. The large-scale clearing of flood plain forests to create agricultural land for rice production is degrading the flood plain and wetland habitats. Inundation-tolerant tree species are gradually being reduced, as are their benefits for fisheries and other flood plain and wetland activities.

Fisheries are also harmed by pollution from agricultural activities as well as industrial effluent and raw sewage which are frequently discharged into rivers or enter the aquatic environment during monsoon flooding. At the same time, some fishing practices themselves contaminate water and cause environmental degradation; for instance, the improper disposal of feed, faeces or shrimp shells from intensive aquaculture and the excessive clearing of mangrove forests.

Bangladesh is attempting to address many of these environmental problems by improving public awareness, enforcing pollution regulations, strengthening environmental impact assessments and implementing measures to mitigate environmental damage to fisheries.

These and many other planned improvements can expand Bangladesh's opportunities for both domestic and export production. To meet this potential, however, more public and private sector investment is needed in harvesting, processing, marketing, extension, research, training and community development. In addition, the sector requires improved inputs, technology, credit, public agency coordination and policy analysis.

While there is much to be done, the fisheries sector could contribute much more to the country's social and economic development.

Source: FAO. 1993. *Fishery Sector Programming Mission to Bangladesh.* TSS-1. Rome.

The heavy concentration on rice production and distribution over the past 20 years has often been at the expense of other agricultural products and economic sectors, both financially and environmentally (see Box 4, The fisheries sector in Bangladesh). Policy-makers must now face the challenge of deciding how to reduce rice and foodgrain subsidies while also maintaining secure stocks, stable prices and well-targeted relief programmes.

At the same time, even with the most optimistic benefits from further liberalization, agriculture is unlikely to absorb Bangladesh's rapidly expanding unemployed population. Faster growth in manufacturing, services and commerce, which account for some 60 percent of GDP, is essential to reduce poverty and absorb the one million new entrants into the labour force each year.

ASIA AND THE PACIFIC

SRI LANKA

One of Sri Lanka's most striking features is its enduring commitment to progressive social welfare policies. Even before independence in 1948, Sri Lanka promoted three major social policies: a food subsidy, an entirely free education system and free universal health care. By the 1970s, Sri Lanka had become a unique example of a developing country capable of attaining a high level of social welfare despite a very low average per caput income. Today, the country ranks high among both developed and developing countries in terms of a wide range of human development indicators. Sri Lanka's citizens enjoy a long life expectancy, advanced health standards and one of the highest literacy rates in the world.

These impressive achievements in social and human development were not matched, however, by a similar performance in economic growth. An expanding population and a persistently sluggish economy kept per caput incomes low. In addition, the country's inability to generate budget and trade surpluses limited public and private savings, resulting in a low rate of investment. While enlightened social policies were contributing to human capital development, there was no corresponding growth in capital formation necessary to increase productivity and expand the economy.

Over time, high unemployment, high inflation, balance of payments deficits and economic stagnation made it more and more difficult for successive governments to pay for the country's food, health and education programmes. In an attempt to compensate for deteriorating economic conditions, policy-makers gradually turned the economy inwards, pursuing an industrialization-led development strategy based on import-substitution policies. By the mid-1970s, the government had nationalized the tea estates, established strict controls on foreign exchange and foreign investment and placed tight restrictions on both domestic and international trade.

However, the import-substitution policies failed to generate enough growth in income and employment and, in 1977, a new government introduced fundamental changes to the country's economic policy. Sri Lanka essentially reversed its economic development strategy, shifting from an inward-looking, state-controlled economy to an export- and market-oriented

system. Policy-makers eased controls on foreign exchange transactions and foreign investment; unified the multiple exchange rate into a single, floating rate; replaced trade monopolies and quotas with tariffs; and liberalized producer and consumer prices and interest rates.

The economy responded impressively to this new policy environment for nearly a decade. GDP growth, which averaged less than 3 percent per year between 1970 and 1977, grew to more than 6 percent on average between 1978 and 1986. This growth was also well balanced – agriculture, industry, services and international trade all performed well. Nonetheless, the economy was unable to build on or sustain this momentum, with the result that slow economic growth, high unemployment and poor agricultural sector performance recurred during the late 1980s.

The economy faltered for a number of reasons. First, the country's ongoing civil conflict, which escalated after 1983, diverted public resources and discouraged foreign investment. Second, bad weather, including periodic droughts, hampered agricultural production and exports. Third, the stabilization policies, aimed at containing the fiscal deficit and controlling inflation, suppressed demand and slowed economic growth. Finally, because many policy-makers remained focused on key macroeconomic aggregates, important sectoral reforms were neglected.

Since 1989, the government has focused much more attention on sectoral reforms. A number of high-level commissions, comprising public and private sector representatives, have analysed and recommended policy actions to address specific economic issues. At present, reforms are either planned or already under way for taxation, tariffs, public administration, public sector enterprises, the banking system, private sector management of the tea estates and agricultural diversification. The agricultural sector in particular is undergoing noteworthy changes.

In the last several years, the economy has grown at a relatively strong pace. GDP increased by 4.8 percent in 1991 and 4.6 percent in 1992. The industry and services sectors were the main sources of this growth. Industrial output increased by 6.1 percent in 1992, mostly a result of growth in the manufacturing of textiles and garments for export. Demand for tourism, trade, transport, banking

and financial services has stimulated growth in the services sector, which increased by 6.1 percent in both 1991 and 1992 and now accounts for half of the country's GDP.

In contrast to the strong growth in the industry and services sectors, agricultural growth was completely flat in 1992, rising by only 0.1 percent. Agricultural performance continues to be affected by bad weather and civil unrest. A severe drought in the first half of the year reduced tea production by approximately 25 percent. Rubber and coconut production were less affected by the drought and output remained close to the levels of 1991.

The rice crop was not seriously affected by the drought, which began in March, because it occurred towards the end of the harvesting season. In Sri Lanka, rice is cultivated in two seasons, corresponding to the two monsoons. The major rice crop is produced during the northeast monsoon from October to February, known as the Maha season. The minor crop is produced during the Yala season – the southwest monsoon from May to September. The drought only slightly delayed the planting of the 1992 Yala crop.

The agricultural sector
In many areas, Sri Lanka's agricultural economy and rural life have changed little over the past three decades. For example, agriculture's contribution to GDP has remained relatively stable – it generated 28 percent of GDP in 1965 and 25 percent in 1992. Agriculture continues to be the main source of income and employment for rural Sri Lankans; today, the sector employs approximately 50 percent of the workforce – the same proportion as in the late 1960s.

Sri Lanka's economy still relies on four crops – tea, rubber, coconut and rice – just as it did 30 years ago. Tea remains the dominant agricultural export; it accounted for 67 percent of agricultural exports in the period 1969-71 and 62 percent in 1989-91. Likewise, agriculture still consists of two distinct sectors: the estate sector, which produces the bulk of tea and rubber; and the small farm sector, which produces rice and most of the coconuts and spices for export.

In other areas, the agricultural sector has undergone major structural changes. The 1977 macroeconomic reforms and subsequent sectoral policy reforms affected

the small farm and estate sectors in a number of different ways.

The small farm sector

Sri Lanka's small farm sector produces rice on approximately 40 percent of the agricultural land, while growing fruits, legumes, non-traditional export crops and a few other grains on about 10 percent. Most rice farms are very small and are becoming increasingly fragmented. More than 50 percent of today's rice production comes from parcels of less than 0.5 ha, compared with about 12 percent in the mid-1960s. Crops such as cinnamon, cocoa, coffee, cardamom, chilies, peppers, cloves and citronella are grown on a relatively small scale, but are increasingly important and now account for 4 percent of total exports.

For decades, rice policies have shared the same four objectives: to ensure national food security; to create employment; to enhance farm income and social welfare and to reduce imports. On the other hand, the policy measures used to meet these objectives have varied greatly. Before the 1977 reforms, rice production and distribution were strictly regulated by the government. The Paddy Marketing Board had sole responsibility for domestic procurement and the Food Commissioner's Department controlled distribution at officially fixed prices. Not only were producer and consumer prices controlled, rice could not be freely marketed or transported from one of the island's 25 districts to another.

The 1977 reforms served to: liberalize agricultural prices; replace the rice ration with a discriminatory food stamp programme; transform the guaranteed price scheme for rice producers into a minimum producer price scheme to shelter farmers from large seasonal price fluctuations; and allow private traders to operate throughout the country. The improved markets and increased real producer prices had an impressive impact on rice production, which grew at a rate of well over 10 percent per year between 1977 and 1980.

From 1978 to 1986, rice output rose from 1.7 million to 2.7 million tonnes and yields from 2 500 to 3 500 kg per hectare. This was an important accomplishment for Sri Lanka's economy because the country imported from 40 to 50 percent of its total rice consumption during the 1960s and most of the 1970s. From 1970 to 1977, the

country's rice imports averaged 400 000 tonnes per year, then fell to 150 000 tonnes between 1978 and 1985. By the mid-1980s, the country had attained 90 percent self-sufficiency in rice.

Rice producers responded to the 1977 policy changes by expanding area and increasing yields; about one-third of the increased production is attributed to expanded area and the remaining two-thirds to yield improvements. Successes in rice research and extension, HYV seeds, improved irrigation facilities and better management practices have all contributed to higher yields. Today, more than 80 percent of the rice area is irrigated and most farmers use HYV seeds and fertilizers.

In contrast to the rapid output increase of the early 1980s, production slowed and became highly variable towards the end of the decade. The highest level of paddy production was achieved in 1985 with 2.7 million tonnes while yields peaked in the mid-1980s at 3 500 kg per hectare. By 1989, output had declined to a low of 2.1 million tonnes, as civil conflict and adverse weather conditions led to a reduction in cultivated area. In recent years, reduced fertilizer use has also affected yields. Fertilizer subsidies were removed in 1990, doubling prices paid by farmers and causing fertilizer use to drop by approximately 20 percent.

Present small farm sector policies provide incentives for crops with high export potential. Numerous regulatory systems, such as quarantine procedures on imported seed materials, are being re-examined, streamlined, simplified or eliminated. The agrarian regulations that have restricted certain lands to the cultivation of paddy have been relaxed and wider crop choices permitted. The public sector has divested itself of several commercial enterprises in the agricultural sector and reduced its level of intervention.

The estate sector

The estate sector has also undergone significant structural changes over the past two decades. For instance, tea no longer accounts for 80 percent of total exports as it did in the early 1970s. Textiles have overtaken tea as the island's principal export, accounting for some 40 percent of total export earnings. The primary export crops (tea, rubber and coconut) have dropped to below 30 percent of total export earnings.

Two decades of import-substitution policies indicated

a relatively strong bias against agriculture, especially export-oriented agriculture. During this time, the government increased tax rates on export crops, controlled producer prices, managed input and product distribution and nationalized the estates.

The 1977 reforms attempted to encourage traditional exports by reducing export taxes on tea, rubber and coconuts. Tax rates declined from 40 to 50 percent in 1977 to 10 to 20 percent by 1987. Nonetheless, the tree crop sector did not benefit as much from the reforms as did the small farm sector. The highest average levels of output in tree crop production today are still below the maximum average levels of the 1950s and 1960s. In 1990 and 1991, tea production improved only marginally on the highest output level since the mid-1960s. There has been a substantial and continuing decline in rubber production, with 1990 output 40 percent below the level of the 1960s and 20 percent of the 1984 level.

Despite these declines in production, the estate sector remains important to Sri Lanka's economy in terms of income, employment, land use and exports – especially processed export products of tea, rubber and coconut. Today, about 20 percent of the rural population is employed in the estate sector where permanent crops occupy about half the agricultural land (40 percent of the area is in tea and rubber and 10 percent is in other perennial crops).

A persistent problem for tea and rubber producers has been declining international prices, which discourage replanting and, in turn, lead to falling productivity and a lower economic capacity to adjust to international price cycles. In coconut production, the absentee ownership structure of medium-sized and large estates has limited replanting and intercropping.

Until 1992, two state corporations owned and operated the tea estates, which occupied more than 200 000 ha and employed 425 000 workers. But the declining yields, large state subsidies and lagging investment in replanting and maintenance forced the government to begin the privatization-of-management programme. In January 1992, 449 state-owned estates were regrouped into 22 independent regional enterprises, each comprising between 15 and 25 estates. The government then put out to tender and selected 22 private sector companies to manage these estates on a

profit-sharing basis. Approximately 95 000 ha of tea, 59 000 ha of rubber and 11 000 ha of coconut are now under this private management contract arrangement.

The privatization of plantation management, combined with substantial investment in rehabilitating estates and new planting in recent years, should improve short-term agricultural prospects. Agricultural output is projected to grow by about 3 percent in 1993 and 1994. Nonetheless, Sri Lanka's relatively slow transformation to a more industrialized economy is placing enormous pressure on its agricultural sector and, especially, on its natural resources.

The agricultural sector has a limited capacity to absorb labour and all of the good agricultural land has already been developed. In the long term, Sri Lankan policy-makers face the daunting task of expanding the industrial base and diversifying both export products and markets. Without access to more jobs in agro-industrial and agro-processing enterprises, Sri Lanka's rural population may be forced on to economically marginal and environmentally fragile lands.

LATIN AMERICA AND THE CARIBBEAN

REGIONAL OVERVIEW

Overall economic activity in the Latin America and Caribbean region rose by an estimated 2.3 percent in 1992, down from 3.1 percent in the previous year. The slow-down in growth mainly reflected the depressed economic situation in Brazil, where GDP declined by 1.5 percent in an economic environment dominated by hyperinflation and pronounced fiscal and external account imbalances. Excluding Brazil, the regional GDP growth in 1992 was 4.3 percent (5 percent in 1991), still a robust performance in the context of earlier trends and especially in view of the depressed state of the OECD economies. Several countries consolidated the stabilization process and some appeared to have entered a long-awaited recovery phase. Stabilization efforts in some cases achieved spectacular reductions in inflation rates: from 1 400 percent in 1991 to 20 percent in 1992 in Nicaragua; and from 173 to 23 percent in Argentina.

In the external sector, an outstanding feature was the reversal in the trade balance, which turned negative in 1992 for the first time since the outbreak of the debt crisis in the early 1980s. Indeed, imports rose to $132 billion (19 percent higher than in 1991) while exports reached $126.1 billion (only 4 percent higher than in 1991). Although the negative trade balance to a large extent reflected the huge trade deficit of Mexico, other countries such as Argentina, Bolivia, Paraguay and a number of Central American countries also recorded significant trade deficits. While much of the increase in imports was in consumption goods – a typical phenomenon in the early phases of economic opening – capital goods imports appear to have also expanded significantly in recent years. The negative net trade balance contributed to a widening in the current account deficit, which represented nearly 19 percent of the region's exports of goods and services compared with about 11 percent in 1991.

A parallel and related process was a sharp increase in capital inflows which more than covered the increase in the current account deficit, allowing an expansion in reserve holdings. This reflected to a large extent the climate of renewed confidence in the region's economic outlook.

Figure 9

LATIN AMERICA AND THE CARIBBEAN

AGRICULTURAL AND PER CAPUT FOOD PRODUCTION

- Agricultural production growth (%)
- Agricultural production index (1979-81=100)
- Per caput food production index (1979-81=100)

AGRICULTURAL TRADE

- Exports
- Imports

AGRICULTURAL EXPORTS
(Index 1979-81 = 100)

- Value
- Unit value
- Quantity

AGRICULTURAL IMPORTS
(Index 1979-81 = 100)

- Value
- Unit value
- Quantity

Source: FAO

However welcome, the large and sudden increase in capital inflows also introduced a number of new issues. The extent to which they are really contributing to capital formation, rather than being speculative, is a debated question. Furthermore, as in the case of Mexico and several other countries, large capital inflows are associated with a complex set of problems. First, they have contributed to an overvaluation of currencies, running counter to one of the key objectives of current development strategies, i.e. export expansion. Also, capital inflows have introduced risks of inflation and greater stringency in monetary policies. Higher interest rates are in turn dampening growth prospects and accentuating the public debt burden beyond what would be expected from the size of fiscal imbalances. Finally, capital inflows have created greater interdependence with international capital markets and increased vulnerability to changes in external macroeconomic conditions.

Foremost among those problems in the short term is probably currency overvaluation. Indeed, a major challenge for countries that have so far made significant progress in stabilization will be to overcome the exchange rate dilemma in a way that does not lead to renewed instability and inflation. The other major, longer-term challenge remains that of extending the benefits of stabilization and adjustment to the widest possible segments of population, particularly the poorest.

The agricultural sector

As is by now a well-known characteristic of the region, agricultural performances have been largely determined by factors exogenous to the sector, i.e. domestic macroeconomic policies and international market conditions, with the specific sectoral policy playing a relatively subordinate role. Currency overvaluation has been a major influence behind the weakness of the agricultural export sector. To this must be added the dramatic fall of commodity prices, affecting several of the main export products of the region.[30] Contrasting these generally depressing influences in the external sector, agriculture benefited from the overall favourable turn of events in the domestic economic situation, to the extent that domestic demand and investment in the sector were stimulated.

[30] In 1992 price declines for the main export products of the region were: banana, -10.1 percent; cocoa, -7 percent; coffee, -25 percent; beef meat, -8.8 percent; maize, -3.2 percent; soybean, -0.4 percent; and cotton, -15.8 percent.

Overall, the year 1992 witnessed a relatively lacklustre growth in agricultural value added, estimated to be less than 2 percent. However, there were wide variations among countries. A combination of favourable climatic, price and credit conditions resulted in increases in agricultural value added exceeding 6 percent in Brazil, Ecuador, El Salvador and Uruguay. Chile, Costa Rica, Guatemala and Honduras achieved increases of around 3 percent while Bolivia, Colombia, Mexico, Paraguay and Peru experienced stagnating or falling agricultural output. In some cases, such as that of Paraguay, the most important single factor behind poor agricultural performances was the fall in prices of export commodities (soybean and cotton). In Brazil, the strong increase in agricultural output was mainly associated with agricultural support policies, while Uruguay benefited from improved terms of trade and better trading opportunities within the framework of the Southern Common Market (MERCOSUR) agreement.

In the external sector, several countries succeeded in expanding agricultural export earnings despite the collapse in the prices of some of their main export products. This was the case in Brazil, Chile, Guatemala, Honduras and Uruguay. Other countries experienced declining export earnings from agriculture despite varying degrees of success in expanding their volume of exports. These included the Dominican Republic, Nicaragua and Paraguay. Still others, for example Bolivia, experienced both volume and price declines.

Agricultural policies

The general market-oriented policies now followed throughout the region emphasize a more neutral role of the state as an economic agent. Nevertheless, general tendencies in recent years have been for a broader and more active government involvement in sectoral policies. There are major differences between the current schools of thought and those that determined previous policies, however. The state has abandoned its pervasive presence in agriculture and its top-down approach in transferring subsidized resources. Rather, current policies increasingly emphasize the objectives of helping farmers to help themselves and promoting the agrarian and institutional reforms required for this purpose. Another leitmotif of recent policy statements is integration at two general levels: *i)* within agriculture, in

the context of maximizing interregional and intercrop complementarity while reducing gaps between modern and traditional agriculture; and *ii)* between agriculture and upstream and downstream activities. These are not new ideas but, in many instances, they have recently been translated into more decisive action than in the past.

Within this general framework, specific country examples include Mexico's deep process of reform involving a revision of its agrarian law, supportive and compensatory measures to facilitate the transition to a fully liberal market regime and commitment to NAFTA. This remarkable experience is reviewed in more detail in the section on Mexico.

In Argentina the implementation of the Convertibility Law,[31] introduced in March 1991, helped deepen the process of adjustment and economic opening but also introduced a dollar-peso parity regime that resulted in a strong overvaluation of the peso. In order to compensate the tradables sector for the losses involved, the government introduced a number of measures in late 1992. These included reduced taxes on agricultural exports; a softening of agricultural credit conditions; the application of a 10 percent "statistical" tax (previously 3 percent) on imports; and an increase in import duties of up to 20 percent for some products. Furthermore, an important package of farm support measures was introduced in May 1993, particularly directed at non-pampean producers. This included financial support to cooperatives; preferential interest rates for producers facing emergency situations or working in disaster-prone areas; financing facilities for small producers; regional development support; and early payment of the value of shipments to agricultural exporters on the principle of "credit on trust".

The case of Brazil is illustrative of a more active recourse to the traditional instruments of support while maintaining a commitment to the basic principles of market liberalization. In the context of major macroeconomic instability, which rendered producers' decisions particularly difficult, the government announced guarantee prices for the main food products in 1991-92 as well as special rural credit facilities.

The measures enacted contributed to a significant recovery of the sector, whose performance rose by 5 percent in 1992. Such a positive performance of

[31] The Convertibility Law established free convertibility of the national currency at a fixed exchange rate.

agriculture helped, once again, to offset the negative impact of the industrial recession following the failure of the Collor Plan.

Several countries introduced or strengthened measures to reform agricultural institutions with the general objectives of redefining the state's role in agro-economic activities and promoting decentralization. This was done, for instance, in Peru through a new organic law of the Ministry of Agriculture and Food; in Jamaica through the reorganization of the Rural Agricultural Development Authority; and in Bolivia, where the Ministry of Peasant Affairs initiated an important process of institutional decentralization.

A number of countries in Central America also initiated important measures of institutional and legal reform affecting agrarian structures. In Honduras, the Congress approved in March 1992 the Law for Modernization and Development of the Agricultural Sector. This law forms the normative framework for institutional reorganization and creates a Council of Agricultural Development, a Direction of Agricultural Science and Technology and a Land Bank. The new law also introduces major changes to the previous Agrarian Reform Law of 1975.

Land allocated to farmers became their full property, enabling the renting of such land for productive purposes or its use as collateral for credit. Also, the occupation period required before granting full ownership rights was reduced to three years; and women were recognized as beneficiaries of land allocation under agrarian reform. These measures are generally aimed at achieving greater stability in agrarian structures so as to promote investment and capital formation in the sector.

In El Salvador, the peace agreements concluded in 1992 created a favourable environment for strengthening sectoral policy formulation and implementation. Actions included reform of the public sector institutions and the introduction of a new agrarian code.

In both Honduras and El Salvador, new institutional frameworks seek to develop markets and improve efficiency in the existing market channels from the farmgate to industrial processing and external trade. To this end, parastatals have been privatized, basic foodstuff marketing boards abolished and external trade deregulated. At the same time, the state is promoting

producer organizations, credit through private and cooperative banks and basic extension services.

Subregional integration schemes have gained further momentum and depth, aiming not only at strengthening commercial complementarity but also at productive or financial integration. NAFTA, the first such scheme involving developed and developing countries, is discussed in Box 6 in the context of its likely impact for Mexico. Preliminary discussions are under way for the purpose of building on NAFTA and achieving a hemisphere-wide free trade area. The MERCOSUR members (Argentina, Brazil, Paraguay and Uruguay) agreed to establish a common external tariff of 20 percent for most products as of June 1993. The Central American Integration System (SICA) entered into function in February 1993, replacing the former Organization of Central American States. The Panama Agricultural Agreement, signed within the SICA framework, aims at eliminating the existing systems of permits, licences and quotas affecting agricultural trade within the subregion. At the same time, it was agreed to harmonize tariffs on maize and sorghum applied within the system of common price bands for imports in El Salvador, Guatemala, Honduras and Nicaragua.

Despite the continuing emphasis on regional integration, there is a wide awareness of the importance of improving trade relationships with countries outside the region. It is felt that, while the existing regional free trade schemes are compatible with GATT principles – to the extent that they lower trade barriers and work towards reducing trade diversion – trade policies should ultimately aim at global integration. Countries in the region have strongly pressed for a successful conclusion to the Uruguay Round of GATT negotiations.

BOX 5

DEBT AND EXTERNAL FINANCING IN LATIN AMERICA AND THE CARIBBEAN

In 1992 the region's stock of external debt amounted to $447 billion, about 2 percent above the previous year's level. Only four countries, Argentina, the Dominican Republic, Honduras and Paraguay, experienced a decline in their debt stock.

The total debt service-to-exports ratio was estimated to be 30.5 percent in 1992, a slight increase over the previous year. Total debt service on all debt paid by the region was $54.5 billion in 1992 against $50.2 billion in 1991.

Recent institutional developments affecting debt include the Paris Club agreement to restructure Argentina's and Brazil's debt for a consolidated $13 billion. This agreement provides for a graduated amortization schedule for restructuring debt so as to reduce the need for further rescheduling. The Paris Club also agreed to consolidate the debts of the Dominican Republic and Ecuador under the Houston terms.

Commercial bank debt and debt-service reduction under the Brady Plan continued. In December 1992, Argentina signed an important agreement which should reduce the country's $23 billion commercial debt and $9 billion of interest arrears by an equivalent of $11 billion, i.e. more than one-third of its public debt. Another important agreement, concluded by Brazil, involves $44 billion of eligible bank debt and provides for a parallel agreement to convert 1991 and 1992 interest arrears into bonds.

A development of major significance for the region was the strong increase of net capital inflows, primarily from private sources, which reflected the generally improved economic outlook, interest rate differentials and the catalytic effects of commercial debt-reduction agreements for many countries of the region. Private portfolio flows reached $15.3 billion in 1992, four times the level of 1990. Net foreign direct investment amounted to $13.8 billion, the major recipients being Mexico ($6.2 billion), Argentina ($2.5 billion) and Brazil ($2 billion).

**LATIN AMERICA
AND THE CARIBBEAN**

MEXICO
Overview

The Mexican experience is an important reference in the recent history of development. It was the Mexican moratorium in 1982 that marked the beginning of the debt crisis of the 1980s. Ten years later, Mexico was again attracting worldwide interest, this time as a case-study of bold market-oriented reform and remarkable initial stabilization achievements. It still has a long way to go to full recovery and many uncertainties cloud the mid- and long-term horizon. Nevertheless, the economic improvements achieved over the past three to four years augur well for a consolidation of the stabilization process. The recent decision by the world's major industrial countries to allow Mexico to join the OECD is a manifestation of international confidence in the country's prospects.[32]

At the basis of the recent improvements was a package of policy measures, initiated in the late 1980s, which introduced pervasive and, indeed, revolutionary change. These measures included: a reduction of the public sector's size and a redefinition of its economic role; fiscal reform, involving tight discipline in public expenditure; a shift towards free trade principles, including unilateral trade liberalization and commitment to NAFTA.

Agricultural liberalization, possibly the most radical and far-reaching element of the reform package, included the reduction of subsidies on agricultural product and factor prices; privatization of support services; reform of the juridical status of the "ejidos";[33] and exposure to external competition.

Agricultural performance is expected to improve as a result of the experience, since the opportunities and risks associated with market liberalization should enhance its competitive efficiency. However, as in any revolution, there will be winners and losers. The more competitive sectors, particularly those producing fruit and vegetables, will benefit from enhanced market opportunities, provided competitiveness is not dampened by currency overvaluation. On the other hand, the full enforcement of trade liberalization measures and the country's likely adherence to NAFTA will entail major risks for peasant and medium-sized farmers who are responsible for the bulk of staple food production. Exposure to external competition,

---

[32] The June 1993 OECD Ministerial Council requested that the dialogue with Dynamic Non-Member Economies be deepened and that consideration be given to an extension of membership to include Argentina, Brazil, Chile and Mexico. Mexico has long been involved in OECD activities and the terms of conditions for its early membership are now under examination.

[33] The "ejido" is a form of rural communal association which gained importance after the agrarian reform of 1917 but has pre-Columbian roots.

combined with reduced access to subsidized inputs, will force many in the sector to undergo a difficult process of adjustment.

The government is making a major effort to meet the challenges of transition by offering rural support and social welfare schemes as well as financial and agricultural development services.

Economic setting

The major policy reforms carried out since the late 1980s must be considered in the light of the critical economic situation preceding their introduction. After the crisis of 1982-83, when economic activity fell by a cumulative 5 percent, a therapy of orthodox stabilization measures permitted a period of mild recovery. However, this improvement came to an abrupt halt in the mid-1980s when a period of new shocks began: a disastrous earthquake in late 1985 (with damages estimated to be 2 percent of GDP) and a collapse in oil prices caused the GDP to fall by 4 percent in 1986. With growth remaining weak the following year, the economic and financial situation sharply deteriorated.

By 1987 the fiscal deficit had increased to an equivalent of 13 percent of GDP, inflation had soared to 132 percent and debt-service obligations were absorbing 36 percent of total export earnings. Altogether, the period 1983-1988 saw virtually no growth; during that period public consumption rose by 1.6 percent annually, private consumption stagnated and public investment fell by an annual average of more than 11 percent. Exports did expand faster than imports, thereby allowing a trade surplus which rose as a share of GDP from 4.7 percent in 1982 to 8.7 percent in 1988; however, since much of the surplus was absorbed by debt servicing, current accounts failed to improve commensurately – indeed, the balance fell into the red for several years in the 1980s and has worsened dramatically recently.

The new policy framework and economic performance

Confronted with such a difficult situation, the new administration that took office in late 1988 initiated a bold programme of stabilization and structural reform. The new strategy introduced orthodox fiscal, monetary and exchange measures; unorthodox wage and income measures, combining fiscal restraint and price and wage control; and structural reform through privatization,

deregulation, a redefinition of the state's role and liberalization of the investment regime. The external sector was also extensively liberalized, accelerating the process that had been under way since the mid-1980s.[34] Maximum import duty rates were reduced from 45 percent to 20 percent, their weighted average falling to about 11 percent, while the volume of imports subject to import licensing was reduced to less than 4 percent of the total. Thus, from being heavily restrictive in the early 1980s, Mexico's trade regime became one of the most open in the world. Furthermore, the government actively engaged in NAFTA negotiations which, if ratified, will further enhance liberalization and regional integration (see Box 6).

The normative framework for the new set of economic measures was the National Development Plan 1989-1994, which aimed at a GDP growth rate of 6 percent by the end of the period and inflation rates similar to those of Mexico's main trading partners. As an instrument to check inflation, the Pact for Economic Stabilization and Growth (PECE), a government agreement with the business and labour sectors, was introduced in December 1988 and has been periodically renewed since then. The PECE provided for the adjustment of minimum wages as well as public sector prices and tariffs and for a preannounced depreciation rate of the Mexican peso against the US dollar.

The stabilization/reform package can be credited with several remarkable achievements so far. Economic growth during the first part of the plan period (1989-1991) exceeded the 2.9 to 3.5 target, although it fell to an estimated 2.7 percent in 1992. The inflation rate fell to an estimated 12 percent in 1992 and may fall further in 1993. From a staggering 13 percent of GDP in 1987, the public sector deficit turned into a surplus equivalent to 1 percent of GDP in 1992.

These achievements were largely due to the stabilization and reform measures introduced by the government, but other factors also played a positive role. In particular, debt-relief operations under the Brady Plan and IMF-World Bank resource transfers helped alleviate financial constraints. Financial inflows were also attracted by interest rate differentials, the regaining of investors' confidence – particularly as a result of bank and parastatal privatization – and hopeful expectations regarding NAFTA.

[34] A significant step in this process was Mexico's entry into GATT in 1986.

One area where Mexico did not succeed, however, was in reducing the current account deficit which reached about $20 billion, or more than 6 percent of GDP, in 1992. The difficulty of checking import demand and inflationary concerns prompted a tightening of monetary policies, which had an inhibiting effect on economic growth. Indeed, it now appears unlikely that the 5.3 to 6 percent annual growth rate set for 1992-1994 will be met. Moreover, the steady overvaluation of the peso has helped to accentuate the trade deficit, affecting in particular the agricultural sector which has already been penalized by the removal of most subsidies.

The economic role of agriculture
Agriculture has played an uneven and declining role in Mexico's economy. While the sector contributes 7 percent of GDP, the rural population still accounts for 27.5 percent of the total population while agriculture's economically active population (EAP) represents about 23 percent of the total EAP. Agricultural performances have shown a gradual deterioration since the mid-1960s, except for temporary upsurges (e.g. from the late 1970s to the early 1980s, when a self-sufficiency drive under the Mexican Food System [SAM] helped boost maize production). Overall, agricultural production rose by about 4 percent annually during the 1970s, allowing moderate gains in per caput food production, but by only 2.3 percent annually during the "lost development decade" of the 1980s when per caput food production stagnated altogether. During the latter period, only the most export-oriented crops maintained a strong expansion, helped in particular by the currency devaluation – a process that has reversed in recent years. The 1990s have so far seen a continuation of lacklustre performances. After having shown virtually no growth in 1991, agricultural output expanded only moderately in 1992.

The poor performances of the food sector caused growing food import requirements and a marked deterioration in the agricultural trade balance. From being a net earner of foreign exchange until 1987, agriculture has emerged as a major deficit sector: the agricultural export/import ratio has moved from an average of 130 during the 1970s to barely more than 60 in recent years, while agricultural imports currently

BOX 6
NORTH AMERICAN FREE TRADE AGREEMENT

In June 1990 the Presidents of Mexico and the United States announced their decision to start negotiations for a free trade agreement between the two countries. Soon afterwards, Canada expressed its wish to join the negotiations, which took place from May 1991 to August 1992.

At the outset, an agreement text was issued for an expanded NAFTA, and this was signed by the presidents of the three countries on December 17, 1992. The text was then submitted for parliamentary approval by the three countries. Should it be ratified – the main question mark being the decision of the United States Congress – NAFTA would enter into force on 1 January 1994.

The expanded NAFTA agreement contains separate bilateral undertakings between Mexico and its United States and Canadian trading partners. It also incorporates the Canada-United States Free Trade Agreement, leaving intact those rules on agricultural tariff and non-tariff barriers and transitional safeguards that went into effect in 1989. Certain trilateral provisions deal with domestic support and export subsidies. Mexico and the United States agreed to negotiate "side agreements" dealing with environmental and labour issues in an attempt to allay concerns of the incoming United States Administration and congressional critics.

Under the agreement, both countries would convert all their agricultural non-tariff barriers either to tariff-rate quotas (TRQs) or to ordinary tariffs. During a ten- or 15-year transition period, depending on the commodity, no tariff would be charged for commodities within the TRQs. The longer transition periods apply to certain highly sensitive products, such as maize and dry beans for Mexico and orange juice and sugar for the United States. Duties imposed on commodities exceeding the TRQs – initially set to replace the protection provided by the former non-tariff barriers – would decline progressively to zero by the end of the transition period. Existing tariffs on a broad range of agricultural products would be eliminated immediately. Among the United States' major agricultural exports – which include feedgrains, oilseeds, meat and dairy products – grains and oilseeds were expected to benefit most. For Mexico, whose leading exports to the

United States are tropical products, horticultural exports such as fruit and vegetables would probably be the most favoured.

The agreement also contains special import safeguards for specified products whose trigger levels would be increased progressively over the first ten years of the agreement. The NAFTA countries made only a very general commitment to move towards less trade-distorting domestic agricultural policies, with new policies expected to be in compliance with GATT obligations. As a general principle, the use of agricultural export subsidies within the NAFTA area was considered inappropriate, except as a means to counter subsidized exports from non-NAFTA countries.

absorb about 17 percent of the country's total export earnings.

What determined the long-term stagnation of agriculture? Multiple natural, infrastructural, political, socio-economic and market factors played a role not covered in this review. One influence of major importance, given the large segments of agricultural population involved, was the low productivity of the large smallholder sector, which was marginalized to a large extent from state support as well as access to markets, credit and public services. Associated factors were the rigidities of the ejido legal framework and distortive state interventions. The removal of these constraints is at the core of the current agricultural reform strategy.

Agricultural reform

While the new policy orientation is having a profound impact on all economic sectors, agriculture will be one of the most affected. The liberalization of agricultural markets has meant breaking with deep structural rigidities and legislative norms dating from the early decades of the century.

The broad orientations of the new policies were defined in the National Programme for Rural Modernization 1990-1994, issued in 1990. The programme's general principles are that commercial agriculture (smallholder) must assert itself as the sector showing the most dynamic growth, while the "social" sector (ejidos and farm communities) must modernize through cooperative arrangements allowing economies of scale, a redefinition of the state role in productive and marketing activities and association contracts with commercial agriculture and agro-industry.

The most far-reaching area of policy reform was in land tenure legislation. The importance of changes in this area must be appraised in a historical context. Under the previous agrarian regime, regulated by Article 27 of the Mexican Constitution of 1917, the government was expected to provide land to any group of citizens requesting it. The objectives were to reduce the gross inequities that characterized landownership at the time and to alleviate rural poverty. Those granted land entitlements entered the ejido system, whose membership expanded to include a large majority of Mexico's rural population. By 1988, the "social" sector

(made up of ejidos and communities) was estimated to include about 28 000 units comprising more than three million *ejidatario* (ejido member) and *comunero* (community member) heads of household. The sector accounted for 70 percent of the total number of farmers. About 15 million people (19 percent of the country's population) depended totally or partially on production and employment generated by the social sector.

Designed mainly as a political instrument to meet popular demands rather than to create economically viable productive units, the ejido systems became rigid and inefficient. The progressive decline in land area available for redistribution led to the extreme fragmentation of land, with 61 percent of ejido land units falling to an average size of less than 4 ha. Furthermore, under the former provisions of Article 27, ejido land could not be sold, rented or used as collateral for loans.[35] This hampered farm investment as well as modernization of the sector and ultimately defeated the ejido's poverty-reduction objective (according to the Economic Commission for Latin America and the Caribbean [ECLAC], 24 percent of Mexico's rural population lives in extreme poverty, compared with 8 percent of the urban population). Ejidos were also subject to distortive and cumbersome state intervention and tutelage mechanisms which regulated the economic life of the ejido while also exerting political control over it.

These problems prompted a radical reform of the ejido regime. The new agrarian law, which entered into force in February 1992, modified Article 27 in the following main areas:

- Ejido members possessing proper land titles may, with the approval of 75 percent of the ejido assembly, gain full rights for selling, renting or otherwise disposing of their land. Communal ejido land, usually forest and pasture land, may not be sold or used as collateral, however.
- Inheritance and succession rights need no longer benefit the family of ejido members on a priority basis. In other words, ejido landowners may freely choose their successors, which is a break with the previous family-based concept of rural society.
- Ejido land can be sold or leased to private enterprises or corporate entities which may exploit the land directly. Nevertheless, the size of the holding controlled by such enterprises may not

[35] Despite being forbidden by law, the sale and renting of land was a widespread underground practice. For instance, 25 to 30 percent of all productive land was estimated to be rented prior to the amendments to Article 27.

exceed 25 times the size of a smallholding ("small" meaning up to 100 ha of irrigated land or its equivalent in a non-irrigated area). Ejido holders of special shares (type T) are given preferential rights to recover the land should the enterprise close down. The objective of this regulation is to encourage farmers' association with agricultural entrepreneurs and foster technological and production modernization.

• In line with the general principle of granting the sector autonomy, the legal foundation for government involvement in ejidos was dismantled, thus bringing an end to the much criticized bureaucratic paternalism of the state.

The other major area of agricultural policy reform was the liberalization of agricultural markets. The following measures were introduced in this field:

• *Trade liberalization*, including a reduction in the proportion of agricultural imports subject to import licensing from 57 percent in 1988 to 35 percent in 1991. Products still subject to licensing include maize, beans and wheat. At the same time, average import tariffs for agricultural products fell to a mere 4 percent in 1991.

• *Price liberalization*, particularly the elimination of price guarantees for all basic foodstuffs excluding maize and beans (about $1.3 billion were earmarked for supporting maize and bean prices in 1993). NAFTA envisages the gradual elimination of price support for maize and beans within a 15-year transition period. For other cereals and soybeans, government procurement at guaranteed prices was replaced by "agreement prices" whereby private dealers must purchase the whole crop at an agreed price before imports are allowed. For animal products, consumer prices and marketing margins continue to be fixed, with beef and pork prices generally below, and those of poultry above, international market prices.

• *The reduction or elimination of input subsidies*. Agricultural input subsidies, which accounted for more than one-third of the value of agricultural production in the early 1980s, represented only 17 percent of production value in 1989. One consequence was the alignment of fertilizer prices

with international market levels. Subsidies on water and electricity supply were also greatly reduced while the parastatal that sold concentrated animal feed was privatized. Imports of agricultural inputs and machinery were liberalized, which partially offset the effects of higher input prices and production costs. Credit subsidies were also reduced and interest rate controls eliminated, the result being a sharp increase in real interest rates from -37 percent in 1987 to 19 percent in 1989.

- *The reduction of state intervention* with the elimination or drastic downscaling of parastatal market control on sugar, cocoa, maize, tobacco, henequen and cocoa. Specialized institutions previously in charge of credit, insurance, technical assistance and marketing were privatized or foreclosed or had their functions redefined. The number of parastatals depending on the Secretariat of State for Agriculture and Water Resources (SAHR) were reduced from 94 in 1982 to only 20 in 1992, and another 11 were to be eliminated in 1993.

State support to agriculture. In order to compensate farmers for the double blow dealt by agricultural reform and the opening of borders, important agricultural and rural support programmes – of both a welfare and developmental nature – were introduced or strengthened. The basic criteria for providing support were defined as follows: support should *i)* benefit all producers regardless of their size and geographical location; *ii)* provide compensatory assistance against the effects of subsidized agriculture in other countries; *iii)* promote associations among producers as well as between farmers and entrepreneurs, so as to achieve competitive efficiency.

An important new instrument for rural welfare and modernization is the National Solidarity Programme (PRONASOL). Introduced in December 1988, this programme devotes about 60 percent of its budget to social welfare activities and the rest to regional development and financing of production projects. Its main feature is the high degree of decentralization and grassroots participation in its project and activity formulation and implementation. Through its regional branches, and interacting with indigenous coordinating centres, PRONASOL supports programmes originated by

the local communities themselves. Represented at the programme's consultative council, the main peasant communities participate at the highest managerial and executive levels.

Since its creation, PRONASOL has expanded and diversified its activities considerably. From an initial $621 million in 1989, federal allocations for the programme increased in real terms by 54 percent in 1990, 36 percent in 1991 and 19 percent in 1992. PRONASOL currently supports more than 150 000 activities and projects, implemented by 82 000 solidarity committees. About one million peasants, working on 3 million ha, are benefiting from PRONASOL funds, while more than 1 100 peasant organizations are supported by regional funds for the development of indigenous populations. A large number of farmers also rely on PRONASOL for loans under the *crédito a la palabra* (credit on trust) scheme. In 1992, 2.5 million ha of maize were financed under this scheme, i.e. about 500 000 more than in the previous year. Solidarity Enterprises, a body formed more recently under the programme, also provides credit and risk capital for enterprises managed by producers' organizations.

The main sources of *agricultural financing*, however, remain development and commercial banks. Official credit is provided through three main channels: Fideicomiso Instituido en Relación con la Agricultura (FIRA), Banco Nacional de Crédito Rural (BANRURAL) and Nacional Financiera (NAFINSA). FIRA, now the most important of the three, combines loan operations with programmes of technical assistance, research and technological development. It currently benefits about 50 000 farm units, primarily medium-sized and large farms but also ejido and community farms.

Oriented more specifically towards rural development, BANRURAL was the major source of agricultural and rural financing until the late 1980s. However, large-scale defaulting led to a drastic reduction of its credit disbursements, the transfer to PRONASOL of bad outstanding loans and a revision of lending and management policies. An effort is being made at present to replenish BANRURAL's lending resources (planned to increase by 15 percent in 1993 over the previous year) and to restore viability to rural support operations. The other main source of official credit, NAFINSA, works primarily with agroprocessing and marketing enterprises.

Despite current efforts to strengthen the volume and efficiency of official lending, the basic issue remains access to credit, mainly by the small farm sector, following the decline of subsidies, the sharp increase in interest rates and the reduction of BANRURAL's rural support operations.

Another major constraint to agricultural development is the heavy underinvestment that resulted from former landownership regulations hindering access to credit and private financing. This problem was further accentuated during the years of stabilization from 1982 to 1988, when sharp cuts in public expenditure were effected. While rural reform is expected to create a more favourable environment for private financing, the government is also making a major effort to expand public investment. Between 1988 and 1991, SAHR investment rose by 59 percent in real terms and investment in agricultural development by 61 percent. By comparison, total public investment increased only by 20 percent during the same period. Priority areas for public investment are irrigation, agro-industry and small and medium-sized infrastructure. Another initiative to promote rural investment was the creation of the Fund for Rural Investment and Capitalization (FOCIR). Together with resources from PRONASOL funds, this new investment fund was allocated a total of 400 million pesos for 1993, with an additional 30 million pesos allocated for programmes to strengthen project formulation and implementation capacity.[36]

Outstanding issues and prospects for agriculture

The success of future agricultural reform is crucially linked to the sustainability of overall economic recovery. After a period of euphoria over the initial results of the reform, the slow-down in economic activity and the widening current account deficit have generally led to more sober assessments of Mexico's economic prospects. While the current account deficit is largely the counterpart of capital inflows, there is some uncertainty regarding the extent to which such inflows are speculative in nature or stable, long-term investments (for instance, foreign participation in parastatal privatization). In any case, capital inflows contributed to real exchange rate appreciation, thereby raising another set of problems. The overvalued currency is likely to reduce the competitiveness of domestic

[36] US$1 was equivalent to approximately 3 pesos during the first half of 1993.

industry, including export and import-substitution agriculture. On the other hand, devaluation is a difficult policy option at a time when the country needs investors' confidence in its financial stability.

The long-term environment for investment and, more generally, the overall economic outlook also depend to a large extent on NAFTA. While the agreement is expected to result in major gains from trade expansion for Mexico, the main benefits would be in terms of greater economic and political stability and a more favourable climate for foreign investment. More foreign investment would in turn allow a reduction in interest rates and, possibly, an increase in public expenditure, with both factors combining to boost economic activity. The perceived importance of NAFTA for Mexico is shown by the sensitivity of financial markets to opposition voices in the United States, the close scrutiny of its implications by Congress and, more recently, challenges to its compatibility with the constitution.

In the more specific area of agricultural reform, the outlook for the current transition period is also uncertain. In general, the possibility of selling ejido land, and the consequent concentration of landholdings, are likely to create better opportunities for economies of scale, investment and market dynamism. The process also involves risks, however. Although the new legislation contains precautionary clauses against the emergence of neo-latifundia, there are fears that market forces and capital concentration may overturn such regulations in the long term.[37] Moreover, even limited land concentration is likely to accentuate inequalities. Along with enhanced income and employment opportunities for many farmers, distress selling, migration and proletarianization are potential threats for many others. This risk is also latent in the closer association that is sought between ejido members and private entrepreneurs. Will the former be able to maintain a fair share of influence and control in such a partnership?

Some analysts believe those fears are largely unfounded, pointing out the "organic" nature of the links between farmers and their land. Given their reluctance to lose ownership or control, farmers would be more likely to rent than sell their land.[38] The strong sense of identity and solidarity among farmers would also resist disintegrating influences. It is also pointed out that,

[37] Legislation forbids concentrations of more than 2 500 ha of irrigated land and sets a limit of 5 percent on ejido landownership by any one member.

[38] Although forbidden by law, land renting was quite common before reform. However, because of their clandestine character, rents were very low, accounting for an estimated 10 to 15 percent of production costs. The legalization of renting is likely to increase these rates significantly.

whatever the direction of the process, it is likely to be a lengthy and gradual one. Land transactions will only be possible after ownership titles are regularized, a process that may require another three to five years.

In any case, it will be the government's task to counter undesirable developments by monitoring the process and effectively enforcing legislation and, even more important, by helping farmers adjust to the changing situation. A cornerstone of current strategies to this end is the promotion of better organized and trained farmers' associations, giving them more participatory and negotiating power and enabling lower transaction costs in their access to credit, technology and market information. Thus, along with the primary efficiency objectives underlying liberalization and elimination of state paternalism, equity objectives are being pursued.

The other major area of concern for many farmers regards NAFTA. While a minority of competitive farmers would benefit immediately from NAFTA, the large majority, mainly maize producers, would be bound to suffer to varying degrees.

The immediate effects for subsistence farmers, who are largely isolated from market forces, would be relatively minor, although they may lose temporary off-farm employment opportunities. In any case, their marginalization may tend to worsen, although they could still be assisted in modernizing their productive systems and lowering costs of self-consumption.

At the other end of the scale are the reasonably competitive commercial farmers who account for about 10 percent of maize-producing units and for whom subsidies currently account for only 18 percent of their crop. This subsector would probably survive external competition and also has the greatest potential for diversification at little cost to income.

The real problem is posed by the large majority of maize producers who depend on the part of their output that is sold to the market but who cannot possibly remain competitive in an open market regime. How many will abandon maize production is an open question. Much will depend on the impact of compensatory and safeguard measures contemplated under NAFTA. For those pushed out of agriculture, the challenge will be to mobilize welfare programmes such as PRONASOL and to create off-farm employment as well as the conditions for an orderly process of

migration. These are daunting tasks to be tackled in the ten- to 15-year period before liberalization is fully enacted.

These problems raise fundamental issues for the long term. What will be the sector's future role as a contributor to income, employment and food security? Can the major transformations under way be achieved without creating massive problems of proletarianization and rural migration? Will the resources available for developmental, compensatory and welfare action be sufficient to ensure an orderly process of diversification and modernization while preventing major political and social disruptions? To what extent can reliance on the determinism of the market be made compatible with the consolidation of a popular democracy?

Beyond the specificity of the Mexican situation, the answer to these questions has a broad relevance. For many countries around the world, similarly committed to the free market paradigm, Mexico's ability to meet the challenges of reform will be a point of reference and, hopefully, an encouragement for their own efforts.

NEAR EAST AND NORTH AFRICA

REGIONAL OVERVIEW

In 1992, the Near East's recovery from the Persian Gulf conflict was well established. Petroleum export volume increased, although prices declined during 1992 to pre-conflict levels, benefiting oil-importing countries in the region. Reconstruction activity helped energize the region's economy, creating renewed opportunities for migrant employment and raising remittance income. Trade and tourism revenues also rebounded while declining import demand, debt forgiveness and foreign transfers – including support provided by the Gulf Crisis Financial Coordination Group to Egypt, the Syrian Arab Republic and Turkey – helped to improve current account balances.

These positive developments have been clouded by the continued political tensions in the region, however, which have created disincentives for private investment and slowed market reforms in some countries, consequently harming long-term growth prospects.

Agricultural output increased in most countries in 1992. Good weather was the major determinant of increased farm output in countries that have primarily rain-fed agriculture, including Algeria, Cyprus, the Sudan, the Syrian Arab Republic, Tunisia and Turkey. Drought in Morocco caused a sharp decline in its farm output in 1992, with continued drought expected to reduce the 1993 harvest. In Egypt, changing price signals and a lifting of planting controls have resulted in a substantial shift in crop mix since 1986. Wheat area has increased and, combined with the widespread adoption of HYVs, contributed to Egypt's sixth consecutive record crop of wheat in 1992.

Regional agricultural production rose by 40 percent between 1979-81 and 1992. Growth in output has generally enabled regional food production to keep pace with population growth, except in cases of weather-induced shortfalls. Country performances vary: most of the major agricultural producers have achieved substantial gains in per caput food production since 1979-81, including Algeria, Egypt, the Islamic Republic of Iran, Morocco and the Kingdom of Saudi Arabia.

The regional agricultural import volume rose by 40 percent between 1979-81 and 1991, but declining

Figure 10

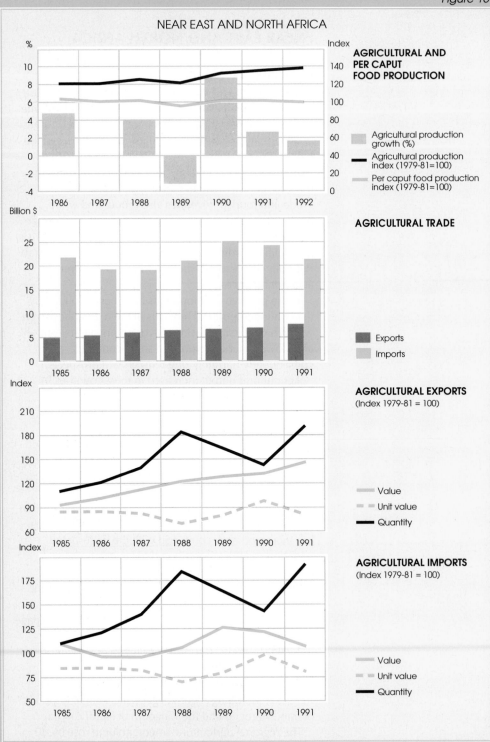

NEAR EAST AND NORTH AFRICA

AGRICULTURAL AND PER CAPUT FOOD PRODUCTION

■ Agricultural production growth (%)
■ Agricultural production index (1979-81=100)
■ Per caput food production index (1979-81=100)

AGRICULTURAL TRADE

■ Exports
■ Imports

AGRICULTURAL EXPORTS
(Index 1979-81 = 100)

■ Value
■ Unit value
■ Quantity

AGRICULTURAL IMPORTS
(Index 1979-81 = 100)

■ Value
■ Unit value
■ Quantity

Source: FAO

import prices kept the value of imports constant. Regional agricultural exports rose in value between 1979-81 and 1991, as a near doubling in export volume offset declining export prices during that period. Overall, the region's agricultural trade balance remained in heavy deficit. In 1991, regional agricultural imports fell by 8 percent to $21.3 billion. Agricultural exports rose by 11 percent to $7.8 billion.

Policy developments

Regional economic and agricultural performance in 1992 has occurred in the context of nearly a decade of profound policy change. Many countries in the region, including Algeria, Egypt, Iran, Jordan, the Libyan Arab Jamahiriya, Morocco, Tunisia, Turkey, the Sudan and Yemen, initiated major policy reform programmes during the 1980s to transform themselves from inward-oriented economies, with extensive government intervention, into more market-oriented economies based on outward-oriented growth. Generally, policy reforms were initiated to deal with the economic crises which unfolded during the 1980s and were reflected in large current and fiscal account deficits, unsustainable foreign debt obligations, inflation and high unemployment. The two prongs of their reform programmes were the short-term stabilization of deficits through austerity policies, and long-term economic restructuring. Long-term strategies included reduced or eliminated price distortions, the liberalization of trade and foreign exchange markets and institutional reforms.

Policy reforms have helped stimulate economic activity in these countries, as trade and domestic markets have become more open, thus leading to greater competitiveness and economic growth. Turkey, for example, was the first in the region to implement a comprehensive structural adjustment programme, which it initiated in 1980. The programme contributed to accelerated growth in GDP, averaging 5.1 percent annually during the period 1980-1990. More recently, Iran has recorded impressive economic growth, averaging 9 percent during 1990-91. Since the end of the Iran-Iraq war, Iran has moved to revitalize and liberalize its economy, removing most of the wartime controls on its economy.

Agricultural and food policies in the region differ widely. Most of the countries that have implemented

major policy reform programmes are at the same time the region's leading agricultural producers and their farm policies have also undergone a transformation. Until the 1980s, they intervened extensively in agriculture with interrelated producer and consumer policies. Generally, the objectives of consumer food policies were to assure an adequate and affordable food supply, improve diets and maintain political stability in urban areas. Consumer policies included fixed retail prices, food subsidies and, in some countries, rationing systems. Producer policies were intended to stimulate domestic agricultural production in a setting of low market prices. Producer policies included subsidized inputs, controls or quotas on planting and procurement, fixed producer prices and government monopolies in marketing and trade. Generally, these consumer and producer policies were set in a macroeconomic context of overvalued exchange rates and low government investment in agriculture, which created disincentives for domestic farm production.

In agriculture, factors that stimulated policy reform were weak agricultural performances, the unsustainable costs of government intervention and the general shift of the policy paradigm in the region towards market-based economies. Common features of agricultural policy reform in Algeria, Egypt, Jordan, Morocco, Tunisia, Turkey and Yemen have been the elimination of guaranteed prices for all or most crops, the reduction or removal of producer and consumer subsidies, the privatization of input supply and the liberalization of agricultural trade.

Agricultural policy reform has been implemented gradually. In 1992, important developments in agricultural trade liberalization included the privatization of wheat imports in Morocco and Turkey, and of wheat flour imports in Egypt. Morocco's drought in 1992 accelerated its import liberalization plans because of the country's tremendous demand for wheat imports. In Egypt, flour import privatization was linked with the liberalization of consumer prices for flour and high-quality breads. Tunisia lowered its staple food subsidies further in 1992, in combination with an increase in its subsidies for low-income households. Algeria removed its food subsidies in 1992, except for those on milk, bread, flour and semolina.

In contrast, agriculture has been excluded from market

liberalization efforts in some countries. Saudi Arabia's Fifth Development Plan (1990-1994) stresses economic diversification and an increased role for the private sector in industry but a continued role for the government in its agricultural sector (see *The State of Food and Agriculture 1992*). Iran has adopted some market liberalization policy reforms but has maintained a food self-sufficiency policy, with controlled and subsidized inputs and producer prices that exceed world prices.

Implications of agricultural policy reforms
Agricultural policy reforms will have important implications for agricultural development and performance in the region. They will also have important environmental implications: in particular, the need to conserve the region's scarce water and land resources has emerged as one of the most critical issues now facing the region. Water problems are most serious in Jordan, the Libyan Arab Jamahiriya and the Persian Gulf countries, including Bahrain, Kuwait, Oman, Qatar, Saudi Arabia and the United Arab Emirates, which face potential water shortages in this decade. In Egypt, increased efficiency in the use of its limited water and land resources forms the core of the country's agricultural strategy for the 1990s.

An excessive consumption of water and the degradation of water quality has partly been a response to agricultural policies in the region. Free irrigation water has led to the overexploitation of groundwater and created salinity and waterlogging problems that have lowered crop yields in Bahrain, Egypt and the Syrian Arab Republic. Subsidized fertilizer and pesticide inputs have contributed to the pollution of available water supplies. Rapid population growth and developing industrial needs have also raised the regional water demand, while the inadequate handling of human and industrial waste has accounted for a significant portion of the region's water pollution.

Many countries in the region are adopting policies that rely on market signals to improve the efficiency of water use and encourage its conservation. These policies include the pricing of irrigation water, the elimination of fertilizer and pesticide subsidies and the provision of incentives for farmers to adopt more efficient irrigation technologies. Egypt, for example, is eliminating pesticide

and fertilizer subsidies, except for cotton, and is studying possibilities for the introduction of fees for irrigation water. Jordan has made major technological advances in its use of drip irrigation and sewage treatment. Tunisia has developed a long-term strategy for soil and water conservation, including the construction of more than 1 000 small dams. Saudi Arabia has increased government control over well drilling and instituted stricter regulations on water use.

Many countries of the region are dependent on the same water supply. Assuring adequate water supplies will raise difficult allocation issues while the conservation of such supplies will require regional cooperation. Among the countries that rely on shared water sources are Israel, Jordan and the Syrian Arab Republic, which share the Yarmuk River. Jordan, Saudi Arabia and the Syrian Arab Republic draw jointly from underground aquifers while Egypt and the Sudan are both dependent on the Nile.

Only 4 percent of the land in the Near East and North Africa is arable. Desertification, deforestation and urban encroachment are the region's major challenges in managing and conserving its limited land base. Two elements of agricultural policy reform have implications for improved land management practices. The first is price policy reform. Artificially low agricultural prices in many countries of the region had depressed land prices. In turn, this had removed incentives to invest in sustainable land management practices and made non-agricultural land uses relatively profitable. Higher farm prices, which raise farmland values, should provide farmers with a structure of incentives to improve their management and conservation of land. Second, measures affecting landownership legislation can contribute to improved land management by clarifying proprietary rights to the long-term returns from conservation investments and by providing access to credit to finance the adoption of conservation technologies.

Efforts in the area of landownership have been part of agricultural policy reforms in Algeria, Egypt, the Sudan and Tunisia. In Algeria and Tunisia, state farms have been dismantled and privatized. Egypt has implemented land rental reform. Land rents, formerly fixed at seven times the land tax, will be market-determined by 1997. Egypt's low land rents created disincentives for the

efficient use of land and water. The Sudan has moved to delineate grazing rights in an effort to prevent overgrazing on common land.

Policy reform in the region has had major institutional implications. It is transforming the role of government from participation and regulation to one of creating a stable environment in which the private sector can function efficiently and be unhindered. This institutional change is perhaps the most difficult aspect of policy reform to implement. On one hand, the privatization of many government functions is expected to achieve efficiency gains and generate fiscal savings for governments. Yet, privatization also entails a degree of dislocation as public sector employment falls and the profitability of economic activity that was based on government intervention is changed. In agriculture in particular, policy interventions had created a pervasive role for governments in input supply, the procurement and distribution of crops, trade and food manufacturing and retail.

The privatization of agricultural input supply, marketing and trade has been at least partially implemented in many Near East and North African countries, including Algeria, Egypt, Morocco, the Sudan, Tunisia, Turkey and Yemen. Privatization plans are probably most extensive in Egypt. All public enterprises have been consolidated into diversified holding companies as a prelude to selling most of these public assets. However, this component of Egypt's policy reform has moved more slowly than any other.

Agricultural policy reform in the region has increasingly taken on a long-term perspective. For example, Egypt's farm policy reform has been formulated in the context of a strategy for the 1990s. Tunisia's resource conservation plan extends to the year 2000, the Sudan has adopted a ten-year agricultural sector strategy, while the development of a long-term agricultural development strategy for Yemen is in progress. A longer-term perspective in agricultural planning reflects the increased awareness of intersectoral linkages within economies as well as the sectoral implications of macroeconomic policy. Most of the countries that have made major reforms in farm policy have implemented these sectoral policy changes in conjunction with economy-wide policy reforms under structural adjustment programmes. Longer-term planning

has also been influenced by the increased urgency of the environmental issues facing the region. These are issues that call for immediate changes in the utilization of natural resources as well as investment in their conservation, which has long-term intergenerational benefits.

EGYPT
Agriculture's role in the economy

Egypt has targeted agriculture, along with tourism and industry, as a sector with strong potential for supporting economy-wide growth under the economic reform and structural adjustment programme (ERSAP) adopted in March of 1990. This is a comprehensive policy reform effort designed to correct structural weaknesses of the economy and achieve macroeconomic stability. Under the ERSAP, Egypt's objective is to restructure economic activity to achieve a decentralized, market-based and outward-oriented economy. This marks a complete break with the centrally planned, inward-oriented economic policies that the country has pursued for more than four decades.

Several factors account for the expectation that agriculture can help support economy-wide reform and stabilization. First, the share of agriculture in the Egyptian economy, while declining, continues to be important. In 1990, agriculture accounted for 17 percent of Egypt's GDP, 41 percent of employment and 20 percent of its export earnings.

Second, the farm sector has potential for additional gains in productivity. Egyptian farmers are already among the most productive in the world, aided by good soils and a mild climate that permits three crops per year. Further productivity gains are expected to come from increased yields in some crops, efficiency gains from crop substitution as remaining price distortions are removed and better management of limited water resources.

Third, the agricultural sector has already achieved considerable progress in implementing market liberalization. Major policy initiatives undertaken since 1986 have removed most sectoral price distortions in agriculture, exposed Egyptian farmers to decision-making in a competitive market and achieved a role for the private sector.

Economic policy reform

The economic difficulties confronting Egypt in the late 1980s necessitated major economic policy reforms. In the 1970s and early 1980s, the country had achieved impressive GDP growth rates, based on high petroleum prices, worker remittances and foreign assistance and borrowing. Economic growth slowed in the second half

of the 1980s when oil prices and export earnings fell but Egyptian policies did not adjust to the decline in resources. Continued large government expenditures on food and energy subsidies as well as on support of public sector enterprises helped generate massive fiscal deficits which exceeded 20 percent of GNP annually. Egypt financed its fiscal and current account deficits partly through foreign borrowing, but capital inflows slowed as Egypt's creditworthiness deteriorated and foreign arrears began to accumulate. By 1990, Egypt's total foreign debt had reached $51 billion, equivalent to 144 percent of GDP, with repayment obligations equal to one-half of its export earnings. An expansionary monetary policy was also used to help fund the fiscal deficits and consequently contributed to high inflation.

In response to the deterioration in the Egyptian economy, the government initiated the ERSAP in March of 1990. The three broad principles of an ERSAP are:

- the rapid achievement of a sustainable macroeconomic environment;
- economic restructuring to lay the foundation for medium- and long-term growth;
- improvements in social policies to minimize the negative effects of economic reforms on the poor.

The measures implemented during the first stage of Egypt's ERSAP included: a reduction in the current account and fiscal deficits; the liberalization of foreign exchange markets and interest rates; the privatization and restructuring of public enterprises; and a reduction in trade barriers. In addition, a social fund was created to cushion the effects of market reforms on vulnerable populations.

The ERSAP is being implemented with support from the international community. The IMF is supporting the macroeconomic stabilization component of the programme. The World Bank is supporting structural adjustment to improve efficiency as the country shifts towards an export-led growth strategy based on the private sector. The IDA and other donors are supporting a review of social policies to minimize the effects of economic reforms on the poor.

In addition, Egypt received substantial foreign assistance following the Persian Gulf conflict. The Gulf Crisis Financial Coordination Group and United States and Arab donors cancelled nearly $13 billion of

Egyptian debt. The Paris Club of lenders also granted debt relief. Combined, these measures reduced Egypt's foreign debt to $38.3 billion at the end of FY 1992. Additional debt relief by the Paris Club in 1994 is contingent on Egypt's performance under its structural adjustment programme.

Egypt made significant progress during the first three years of the ERSAP and, in some areas, moved ahead of schedule in implementing policy reform. It reduced its fiscal deficit to 7 percent of GDP by 1992 while growth in money supply slowed, causing inflation to decline from 27 percent in 1989 to 14 percent in 1992. Exchange rate restrictions were removed and the exchange rate system unified ahead of schedule in November 1991. Egypt's balance of payments improved and a current account surplus was achieved in 1991 and 1992. The surplus partly reflected the effects of foreign debt reduction. It was also due to a recovery in earnings from tourism, worker remittances and Suez Canal revenues, combined with declining imports. Prices were liberalized in the energy, industrial and agricultural sectors.

Only the restructuring and privatization of public sector enterprises have moved behind schedule. Public enterprises were consolidated into a small number of diversified holding companies in preparation for the sale of their assets to the public. The slow pace of privatization illustrates some of the challenges Egypt faces in its economic reform efforts. Privatization has been slowed by both bureaucratic inertia and Egypt's need to maintain economic stability. Slow implementation of privatization places a potential drag on long-term economic growth in Egypt by discouraging foreign investment flows. A revival of foreign investment is particularly important given the external economic conditions facing Egypt, including weak oil prices and stagnating growth in the industrial economies.

Agricultural strategy in the 1990s
Until the mid-1980s, Egyptian agricultural policy was characterized by extensive government intervention and an inward orientation. Egypt's objectives were to attain self-sufficiency in basic food products; provide food to consumers at low prices; generate sufficient rural employment to absorb a rapidly growing labour force; and tax agriculture to support industrial growth and

generate government revenue. Its policy tools were: controlled producer prices; area and marketing quotas; controlled agricultural trade; and government monopolies in trade and marketing.

Under this policy regime, agricultural GDP growth slowed, increasing by an average 2.5 percent annually in the 1980s. The main reasons for slow growth in agriculture were the disincentives that price distortions created for farmers and declining government investment in the sector.

As agricultural production failed to keep pace with population growth, dependence on food imports increased. Cereal self-sufficiency declined from an average of 65 percent in 1978-80, to 52 percent in 1986, when agricultural policy reforms were initiated. Food imports increased by more than 10 percent annually during that period, reaching $2.6 billion in 1986. Slow growth in agriculture also helped induce urban migration. During the period 1980-1990, Egypt's urban population grew by an average of 3.1 percent annually, compared with a 2.4 percent average annual growth in the national population. By 1990, 47 percent of a population of 52 million lived in Egypt's cities, where population densities are among the highest in the world.

In response to these trends, in 1986 Egypt introduced agricultural policy reforms which were pursued gradually up to 1992. They included:

- the removal of crop area allotments with delivery quotas at fixed procurement prices, except cotton and sugar cane;
- the liberalization of producer prices for all crops except cotton and sugar, with the cotton price raised to 66 percent of the border price equivalent in 1992;
- a reduction of subsidies on fertilizers and pesticides;
- encouragement of the privatization of processing and marketing of agricultural products and inputs;
- the implementation of a programme for divesting land held by public enterprises; and
- lower trade barriers and a shift of agricultural trade to a free foreign exchange market.

Egypt's agricultural strategy for the 1990s builds on the policy reforms initiated in 1986. Its objectives are to complete those reforms and to increase agricultural productivity and incomes. The strategy targets increased agricultural productivity per unit of land and water – the

key constraints in Egyptian agriculture – with a reliance on free market price signals to achieve more efficient resource allocations. The strategy for the 1990s differs from the 1986 plan in that its drive for better agricultural performance incorporates programmes designed to alleviate hardships felt by the poor, particularly women and the landless, during the policy transition period.

The targeted growth rate for agriculture under the plan is 3 to 4 percent annually, which would signify a per caput increase in agricultural output.

Land availability is a key constraint in Egyptian agriculture. Only 3 percent of Egypt's total land mass is cultivable. Farms are small and mostly privately owned and 50 percent of them are less than 1 feddan (0.416 ha). Egypt's water resources are also limited: Egyptian agriculture is almost entirely irrigated, with the Nile being the single source of the country's water supply. Increasingly, agriculture must compete with urban and industrial demand for water.

Land productivity can be increased in several ways. One is to achieve higher yields on "old" lands in the Nile valley. Although yields are already high, additional gains could be achieved for wheat, rice and corn with improved seed quality, greater mechanization, strengthened extension support and better land and soil management. The privatization of input distribution is expected to improve the quality and timeliness of input supplies.

Some of the increase in land productivity is expected to come from increasing productivity on the reclaimed "new" lands. These lands, reclaimed from desert land and from marginal areas near agricultural and some coastal areas, account for about 25 percent of Egypt's total farmland area. Performance on new lands has been below expectation, leaving room for increased productivity through better extension support and selection criteria for settlers.

Measures for improving water efficiency in agriculture include the application of water-saving technologies that are technically and economically feasible. The introduction of water fees is also under consideration. These would provide some cost recovery from farmers to finance the maintenance costs of an increasingly capital-intensive irrigation system. Water fees would also create price incentives to encourage more efficient water use and prevent the degradation of natural resources. In the

delta region, for example, yields have been reduced by increased salinization resulting from the overuse of free irrigation water. In the long term, the sustainability of agriculture's reliance on water resources will require more emphasis on reducing pollution, which is partly caused by pesticide use.

Despite the substantial price liberalization that has occurred in Egyptian agriculture since 1986, important price distortions remained in 1992. The most important of these were free irrigation water and regulated land rents. These increase the profitability of irrigated crops such as sugar and rice, while the low producer price for cotton provides insufficient incentives for increased plantings or the adoption of improved inputs.

Additional changes in price signals in input and product markets are expected to provide the right incentives for replacing existing crops with those that are characterized by a high contribution to agricultural value added, compared with their utilization of scarce land and water resources. Wheat, cotton and vegetables make a high contribution to agricultural value added relative to their resource consumption. In contrast, the contribution of sugar, rice and berseem clover is relatively low. Wheat, for example, accounts for 17 percent of land area and 9 percent of water resources and contributes 17 percent of total value added in Egyptian agriculture. Sugar cane, on the other hand, accounts for 4 percent of land area, uses 9 percent of water resources and contributes 4 percent of total value added in agriculture.

Crop and livestock production in Egypt is integrated, and 85 percent of livestock are raised on small farms. Since natural pastures are limited, most animals are confined and fed berseem clover as well as a variety of other crops and by-products. The 1990s' agricultural strategy seeks to increase productivity in the livestock sector through better genetic selection and disease control. Furthermore, the use of fodder crops and crop residues as feed is to be encouraged, since the cultivation of feed crops competes directly with food crop production.

Agricultural production policies are influenced by consumption policies. Until the late 1980s, one objective of Egyptian farm policy was to ensure cheap food for the urban population. Ninety percent of Egypt's population participated in a ration system, which

provided those eligible with sugar, vegetable oils, rice, tea and other basic items. Egypt also provided subsidized bread, flour, fish, meat, eggs, cheese and other items through government outlets. During 1991 and 1992, the government moved to reduce and target its food subsidies. Some items were eliminated from the ration programme. Prices for bread and other basic foods were increased in 1991. In December 1992, the government increased the prices of sugar and edible oils and freed the market price of higher-quality wheat flour. The government continues to subsidize *baladi* bread, a coarse wheat bread which is a dietary staple.

Implications for agricultural performance
Egypt's main crops are wheat, maize, rice, berseem clover and cotton which, combined, account for more than 80 percent of cultivated land area. Other important crops are broad beans, sugar cane, fruits and vegetables. Since 1986, Egyptian agriculture has undergone a substantial modification in crop mix in response to changing price signals and the removal of planting and procurement requirements.

Wheat area expanded by over 75 percent between 1985 and 1992 while output increased by 150 percent as a result of both increased area and rising yields. In 1992, Egypt harvested its sixth consecutive record wheat crop, causing wheat imports to decline by 14 percent to 6 million tonnes during the period 1985-1992. Wheat flour imports were liberalized in 1992 to allow importation by the private sector, and flour prices were to be determined by the market.

The area planted to coarse grains and rice rose by 11 and 16 percent, respectively, while the area planted to cotton and beans declined by 17 and 13 percent, respectively.

Poultry and livestock became less profitable under market liberalization. The government reduced corn imports in 1986 and removed feed subsidies in 1988. Poultry production in particular began to decline as input prices rose. Output had grown at an average annual rate of 16 percent between 1980 and 1988, mainly because of government subsidies on feedgrains and equipment. Between 1988 and 1992, poultry meat production fell by 21 percent as nearly one-half of the producers were forced out of the industry. Currently, chicken imports are banned to protect the remaining

producers, with plans to replace the bans with tariffs in 1993. Beef imports were banned in 1989 but liberalized again in 1992. In the long term, livestock and poultry output is expected to recover as efficiency gains in production restore profitability.

Agricultural policy reforms to be implemented in the short term include the removal of fertilizer and pesticide subsidies, except for cotton, by November 1993. Price and area controls on cotton are planned to be removed in 1994. A floor price for cotton will be set, with the market price to be determined in a planned cotton exchange. Wheat imports are to be liberalized in mid-1993 and land rental rates are to be market-determined by 1997.

SYRIAN ARAB REPUBLIC
Economic overview

After struggling throughout much of the 1980s, the Syrian economy has performed well in recent years. Real GDP grew by more than 5 percent every year between 1990 and 1992. (Nonetheless, with one of the highest population growth rates in the world – estimated to be 3.5 percent – the country's per caput GDP increased by much less.) Preliminary estimates for 1993 suggest further strong growth in GDP – about 6 percent. This welcome period of solid economic performance follows a decade of stagnating and even declining incomes. Per caput GDP fell from around $1 800 in the mid-1980s to $880 in 1989.

A number of external events and internal policy changes contributed to this performance reversal. One significant external event was the 1990 Persian Gulf conflict, which ended a period of relative isolation and resulted in renewed access to development assistance funds and foreign investment. In 1991 and 1992, Syrian public sector agencies issued a record number of tenders, mostly directed at rehabilitating infrastructure and expanding public sector activities.

Another important external event was the end of a two-year drought, which allowed agriculture and agro-industries to recover in 1991 and 1992. During the drought, the government was forced to import large quantities of wheat and barley, draining foreign exchange reserves. Low water levels meant a reduction in hydropower generation, hampering both manu-facturers and agricultural producers using electric pumps for irrigation. Reduced hydropower generation also increased the need for thermal power, thus lowering crude oil exports.

These external forces coincided with a number of economic policy changes designed to take better advantage of private sector activity and improve public sector performance. In 1991, the Syrian Arab Republic established a new investment law, Law No. 10, to promote both foreign and domestic investment in private and domestic sector companies.

This new law, combined with a more favourable official exchange rate set in 1991, led to expanded trade and investment. Private sector exports now account for around 50 percent of total export trade compared with about 10 percent in the mid-1980s. Since 1990, the

country has recorded trade surpluses. Law No. 10 is also credited with increased investment: the Syrian Investment Bureau reports that, between May 1991 and December 1992, more than $2 billion of new investment (foreign and domestic) was approved.

Over the last few years, the government has also eased trade restrictions, allowed free internal trade of various commodities and encouraged more mixed and privately owned factories and businesses. These policy changes reflect a gradual transition towards more market-oriented economic activity. In the past, the public sector dominated the economy; even today, the government still owns and manages the mining, large manufacturing, energy, banking and insurance sectors. Moreover, the government controls most prices, credit and international trade. The public sector employs approximately half the labour force.

The government also provides the country's 13 million inhabitants with health care services and education. Nutrition levels are comparable with high-income economies and infant mortality has declined by two-thirds over the past 20 years.

The role of agriculture
Even though rapidly expanding petroleum-based industries generate over one-half of export earnings and account for one-fifth of GDP, agriculture remains the most important sector in the economy. Agriculture employs approximately 30 percent of the labour force, accounts for nearly 30 percent of GDP and contributes over 60 percent of non-oil exports. In addition, fast-growing agro-industries, such as textiles, leather, tobacco and food processing, contribute 25 percent of the country's output and account for an estimated 50 percent of jobs in the manufacturing sector.

The cropped area in the Syrian Arab Republic averages 4.8 million ha and has increased only marginally in the past decade. The principal staple, wheat, and the primary feedgrain, barley, occupy 70 to 75 percent of the cropped area. Cotton is the country's most important export crop, accounting for 20 to 25 percent of agricultural exports. Farmers also raise livestock and produce a wide variety of fruit, vegetables, tree crops and legumes. Livestock production accounts for one-third of agricultural output value and sheep exports have surpassed cotton as the most important

agricultural export. Extensive sheep grazing is carried out on marginal rain-fed pasture land and steppe.

Two of the country's major national development objectives are: to achieve food self-sufficiency so as to reduce dependency on imports; and to expand agricultural exports to earn more foreign exchange. Food imports are a significant drain on the country's foreign exchange, accounting for 20 to 30 percent of total imports during the 1980s. To support these objectives, the government has directed a large portion of its spending into agriculture and irrigation. In 1993, public spending on agriculture accounted for approximately 25 percent of total spending.

The government also promotes food self-sufficiency and exports through its trade, production and pricing policies. For example, to influence cropping decisions (and to enhance rural incomes), the government establishes procurement prices for wheat, barley and the major industrial crops – cotton, tobacco and sugar beet. Because interest rates, seeds, fertilizers, pesticides, transport and energy prices are also controlled, the government strongly influences cropping patterns, production levels and input use.

Input and procurement prices are designed to increase total production, to encourage the planting of one crop over another (or, in the case of wheat, to encourage soft wheat over hard wheat varieties) and to increase the amount sold to official purchasing agencies. At times, additional ad hoc measures may be used. For instance, public purchasing agencies offered both a delivery bonus and a bulk delivery bonus to capture additional wheat supplies in 1992.

The government also controls the prices of bread, rice (all rice is imported), sugar and tea. Many other commodity prices are being gradually liberalized. Fruits and vegetables are now market-dependent for both producers and consumers. Likewise, vegetable oils are no longer part of the government's ration card system and private traders are now allowed to import maize and rice. Approximately 200 000 tonnes of maize were imported in 1992, all by private poultry producers and businesses.

Other recent reforms influencing production of agricultural exports include new trade policies which allow private exporters to retain 100 percent of foreign exchange earnings from agricultural exports (75 percent

for industrial products). The export earnings are restricted to purchasing agricultural inputs and basic commodities such as tea, sugar and rice. The government maintains its monopoly on wheat and flour imports. As of 1992, agricultural exporters may use up to 75 percent of export earnings to import agricultural trucks.

Irrigation development

Within agriculture, irrigation development is the major area for public investment and spending. Over the past ten years, some 60 to 75 percent of the entire agricultural budget has been invested in irrigation. Several factors explain this focus. First, while the irrigated area comprises only 15 percent of the cultivated land, it produces over 50 percent of the total value of agricultural production. All cotton, sugar beet, tobacco and sesame crops are produced exclusively under irrigation. Cotton and textile products account for 25 percent of total exports and more than 50 percent of all non-oil exports. In recent years, fruits, vegetables and wheat have been brought increasingly under irrigation.

The second reason for focusing on irrigation development is that production on rain-fed area, which represents 85 percent of the total area, varies greatly from year to year. Since 1988, annual production has fluctuated by 35 percent on average. While good rainfall years mean lower agricultural imports, a drought year entails substantial food and animal feed imports.

Syrian public investment in irrigation focuses primarily on relatively large projects, particularly those in the Euphrates River basin. Public sector projects provide water to private farms, state farms and tenant farmers on state lands. The private irrigation sector includes farmers who drill wells to extract groundwater and pump water from lakes, rivers and springs.

Available data suggest that around 1.25 million ha are potentially irrigable from surface water. In 1992, the total irrigated area from surface water and groundwater was approximately 900 000 ha. Farmers irrigated 415 000 ha from wells in 1991.

The Euphrates River, whose waters are shared by Turkey, the Syrian Arab Republic and Iraq, is the country's principal source of irrigation water and, while Syrian water development projects have been designed to irrigate about 650 000 ha in the Euphrates River

basin, the area currently irrigated is much less because of salinity, waterlogging and reduced river flows.

At present, efforts are under way to reclaim land damaged from waterlogging and salinity during the 1960s. At the same time, water resource development projects in Turkey during the last decade have reduced the Euphrates' mean flow by about one-third.

While surface irrigation has been expanding slowly over the past five years, pumping groundwater to irrigate has been increasing rapidly. Wells account for 80 percent of the newly irrigated land since 1987. More than 60 percent of the increase in total irrigated area from groundwater has occurred in the northeast of the country.

This rapid expansion in the use of groundwater is a serious concern for the Syrian Government. While the increased irrigated area is making important short-term contributions to economic growth, the current rate of uncontrolled groundwater exploitation is likely to have long-term social, economic and environmental consequences. Significant drops in groundwater levels have already been documented in the Damascus, Aassi and Aleppo basins, among others. This diminishing supply, coupled with growing competition from industrial and domestic water users, is adding urgency to government concern.

Irrigation efficiency is another concern: most studies and observers agree that farm-level irrigation efficiency ranges from 35 to 50 percent. The Ministry of Irrigation, Public Works and Water Resources and the Ministry of Agriculture and Agrarian Reform are searching for appropriate methods to improve and enhance irrigation system efficiency and farm-level water management on farms receiving public sector irrigation.

At present, agriculture accounts for around 85 percent of the country's water consumption, but competition from other users is increasing. During the 1980s, industrial water demand rose by nearly 900 percent. Current projections suggest that domestic water requirements will be two to three times greater by 2010. Moreover, as the population and industrial capacity continue to grow, agriculture is likely to face greater water quality problems from waste water and industrial pollution. Agricultural producers in Damascus, Homs and Aleppo have already experienced pollution-related problems.

With irrigation, farmers obtain higher yields, more stable production and greater profit. Since 1989, farmers have been required to pay set fees per irrigated hectare each year. This flat rate only partially covers operation, maintenance and delivery costs. However, it does not encourage efficient water use since the fee is the same irrespective of the amount of water used by the farmer. Recent estimates suggest that one irrigation per hectare on government projects costs approximately four times the annual fee; some crops require from five to ten irrigations per season.

The only expenses required for irrigating with groundwater are the digging of the well and the pumping gear – a one-time fixed investment cost. Before operating a well, farmers must obtain two licences from the Ministry of Irrigation, Public Works and Water Resources: one to dig the well and the other to withdraw the water. The licences specify the extent of water use and must be renewed every ten years. In practice, a large share of wells, both old and new, are not licensed.

These economic incentives are not the only factor contributing to the increase in wells. A second reason is the large number of farmers with smallholdings. Approximately 80 percent of Syrian farmers have holdings of less than 10 ha; the average farm size ranges from 3 ha in high rainfall areas to 45 ha in low rainfall areas. Moreover, these farms are characterized by fragmentation. An average farm consists of four plots, with even 1 ha holdings averaging three separate parcels. Because most farmers want timely, secure access to water, they drill separate wells on each parcel whenever it is practical. Over time, as holdings are divided among heirs, even more wells may be drilled.

In addition, the Syrian Arab Republic's agrarian reform law establishes maximum sizes for irrigated holdings: 16 ha for holdings under government irrigation and a range of 15 to 45 ha for privately irrigated farms, depending on the location and type of irrigation method. The law provides a strong incentive for larger farms to subdivide below the maximum limit and then drill wells on each new individual property. Over the past several years, the favourable pricing structure for many agricultural crops has also encouraged large landowners to subdivide among family members.

Other economic pressures are also influencing farmers' decisions to dig wells and expand irrigation. For

example, as incomes in urban areas increase, consumers are demanding more fruit and vegetables. At the same time, recent changes in trade and exchange rate policies are making Syrian agricultural products more competitive in regional markets. Farmers who initially planned only supplementary irrigation for winter wheat are finding summer vegetables and irrigated fruit production increasingly profitable.

Identifying and implementing policies, programmes, projects and techniques to improve farm-level efficiency and control surface and groundwater exploitation more effectively are two important challenges facing Syrian policy-makers. The growing water scarcity is likely to have important short- and long-term implications for the country's overall social and economic development. Some of the important water-related issues that the government is currently addressing include: better public sector management of irrigation systems; the introduction of water conservation techniques at the system and farm levels; the implementation of water reuse techniques and water harvesting systems; and the reduction of losses in water supply networks in towns.

REGIONAL REVIEW
II. Developed country regions

CENTRAL AND EASTERN EUROPE

This section reviews the status of economic and agricultural reform in Central and Eastern Europe and focuses more specifically on the experiences of Bulgaria, Romania and the Russian Federation.

ECONOMIES IN TRANSITION

The year 1992 saw further contractions in overall output in the transition economies of Central and Eastern Europe. However, there were significant variations in economic performance between countries, largely reflecting differences in the pace and stage of their economic reform process.

According to the IMF,[39] real GDP in the Central European countries[40] in 1992 declined by 7.5 percent, following a 13.5 percent fall in 1991. Forecasts point to a further 1.5 percent decline in GDP in 1993 and a resumption of positive growth from 1994, initially at a rate of 2.6 percent. Within this average, individual country positions differ markedly, however. On the one hand, former Czechoslovakia, Hungary and Poland are already showing signs of economic recovery, although the breakup of highly economically integrated Czechoslovakia into two independent states, the Czech Republic and Slovakia, has created additional uncertainty. On the other hand, economic activity in Bulgaria and Romania continued to decline significantly in 1992, although at a slower rate than the previous year. The civil strife in former Yugoslavia, SFR, a source of immeasurable human suffering, is at the same time seriously disrupting the local economy and negatively affecting the economies of neighbouring countries, especially Albania, Bulgaria and Romania. The first of these is particularly vulnerable to destabilizing influences since it only recently initiated economic reforms.

---

[39] IMF. *World Economic Outlook,* April 1993.

[40] Albania, Bulgaria, the Czech Republic, Hungary, Poland, Romania, Slovakia and former Yugoslavia, SFR.

CENTRAL AND EASTERN EUROPE

The recent economic performance and short- to medium-term prospects in the newly independent states of the former USSR generally appear bleaker than those of the Central European countries. According to the IMF, real GDP in the area (including the three newly independent Baltic republics) contracted by no less than 18.5 percent in 1992, compared with a decline of 9 percent in 1991 and 2.2 percent in 1990. GDP is expected to continue declining, although at a decelerating rate: 11.8 percent in 1993 and 3.5 percent in 1994.

In most Central and East European countries, the agricultural sector continues to be affected by the negative short-term impacts of reform and the uncertainty surrounding privatization and future property rights. However, a severe drought is probably the most important single factor behind the 12 percent drop in Central Europe's agricultural production in 1992, which followed a decline of 4 percent in 1991 and of 3 percent in 1990. In the former USSR, on the other hand, the decline in agricultural production in 1992 was limited to 4 percent, compared with 13 percent in 1991. A partial recovery in cereal production, following the 28 percent drop recorded in 1991, almost offset further declines in other crops and in livestock products.

As reported in *The State of Food and Agriculture 1992*, the major policy areas affecting agriculture in Central Europe and the former USSR include price and market liberalization, land reform, privatization and demonopolization and trade liberalization.

The liberalization of prices is still the policy area in which most progress has been made. Virtually all countries have taken significant steps. Following measures already undertaken in this area by the Central European countries, a price liberalization programme was carried out in 1992 in Belarus, the Russian Federation and Ukraine, soon followed by Kazakhstan and then the other newly independent states of the former USSR. In spite of these efforts, complete liberalization has not been achieved and, in many cases, price controls are still in place on a number of products, including some agricultural and food products. In most countries, price liberalization, together with the elimination or reduction of subsidies on farm inputs and products, has resulted in a deterioration in agricultural terms of trade, as input prices have risen at a quicker

TABLE 5

Indices of agricultural production in Central Europe and the former USSR

	1985-89 Average	1989	1990	1991	1992
CENTRAL EUROPE					
Crops	110.3	112.5	106.1	103.8	83.9
Livestock	103.7	102.5	104.0	95.6	90.0
Agriculture	108.9	110.0	106.5	102.6	90.6
FORMER USSR					
Crops	111.1	114.5	116.7	94.2	104.8
Livestock	118.6	125.6	125.8	116.9	101.7
Agriculture	116.4	120.6	120.2	105.1	100.6

Note: 1979-81=100.
Source: FAO.

pace than farmgate prices. This tendency reportedly continued in 1992. The significant shifts in relative prices following price liberalization as well as the increased cost of and reduced access to credit following credit market reform put pressure on the farm sector to increase productivity through better resource use.

Progress has been slower in land reform because of the complex legal and administrative procedures involved. Most Central European countries already have the necessary legislation in place for reforming landownership patterns and are in different stages of implementing it. The same applies to the three Baltic republics. In most cases, the implementation phase has proved longer than generally anticipated and the process of restructuring and consolidation of landholdings is likely to be spread out over a number of years. In the other newly independent states of the former USSR, progress is less advanced and policy directions less clear but, in the Russian Federation, a reorganization of state and collective farms was begun in 1992, involving both changes in their legal status and the redistribution of land to private farming. By 1 January 1993, there were reportedly about 400 000 private farms in the newly independent states, of which about 180 000 were in the Russian Federation.

Likewise, in the field of privatization and

demonopolization, which has a bearing on the upstream and downstream sectors of agriculture, progress has been uneven. Significant steps have been taken, particularly in former Czechoslovakia, Hungary and Poland, while other countries are progressing at varying speeds and by different methods. Thus, in the Russian Federation a voucher privatization scheme similar to the one applied in former Czechoslovakia was introduced in 1992 and the distribution of vouchers to citizens was begun, although subsequent progress has been slow. No less important than the privatization of existing state enterprises, however, is the creation of new private enterprises at all levels, a spontaneous process that has gained ground in all the transitional economies. Available statistics point to steady increases in the contribution of the private sector to GDP.

One serious problem emerging from the disruption of traditional trading patterns is the risk of creating new barriers to intraregional trade. The experience that followed the breakdown of the Council for Mutual Economic Assistance (CMEA) risks repeating itself with the breakup of former Czechoslovakia into two independent republics and with the disintegration of economic relations between republics of the former USSR. Indeed, the future role of the Commonwealth of Independent States (CIS) appears uncertain and, in addition, the three Baltic republics and Georgia have opted not to join the CIS. There are signs, however, that at least some of the transitional countries are attempting to counter these negative developments and strengthen regional trade relations. Thus, in 1992 the Czech Republic, Hungary, Poland and Slovakia decided to constitute the Central European Free Trade Area, with effect from March 1993. This constitutes a politically significant development, although the agreement is not as far-reaching as originally hoped. Furthermore, trade restrictions for agricultural products are set to be removed much more slowly than for industrial goods.

BULGARIA
The agricultural sector

Agriculture is a moderately important sector of the Bulgarian economy. It accounts for about 12 percent of GDP and employs 17 percent of the labour force. Agricultural and food products account for about 20 percent of exports and 7 percent of imports. Major crop products are grains (mainly wheat and corn), sunflowerseed, tobacco, fruit (apples, grapes, peaches, plums, cherries and others) and vegetables (tomatoes, peppers, onions, potatoes, cucumbers). Major livestock products are pork, dairy products – mainly cheese and yoghurt – and wool.

Throughout its history, Bulgaria has been a net exporter of agricultural products. In a typical year, it exports wheat, tobacco, sunflower oil, fresh and processed fruits and vegetables, wine and livestock products. It imports oilseed meal, cotton and, in some years, maize. However, during the communist period, about 80 percent of Bulgaria's exports went to the former CMEA countries, with some 70 percent going to the former USSR. These export markets have all but collapsed with the dissolution of CMEA trading arrangements and the breakup of the USSR.

Under communism, almost 99 percent of Bulgaria's agricultural land was organized into state and cooperative farms. In theory, state farms were state-owned enterprises and the workers had the status of employees working for fixed wages, while workers on cooperative farms were members and shared in the profits of the farm. However, the distinction became blurred as the farm structure was reorganized several times over the 40 years of communist rule. During the 1970s the state and cooperative farms were consolidated into huge agro-industrial complexes averaging 24 000 ha in size. Beginning in 1986, these were broken up into smaller units and, during the final years of the communist regime, the agro-industrial complexes were dissolved and the original cooperative farms were reconstituted. The other type of farm organization is the state-owned hog and poultry complexes.

The private sector consisted of plots, usually 0.5 ha in size, which were allotted to cooperative farm members for personal cultivation. Such plots accounted for about 16 percent of arable land. However, the private sector accounted for about 25 percent of total gross output and

as much as 40 percent of total meat, fruit and vegetable production.

Both suppliers of inputs and purchasers of output were state-owned monopolies, a typical feature of all communist regimes.

Policy reform

Retail prices. The government removed most retail price controls in February 1991 but began a system of "monitoring" the prices of 14 basic food items. These included flour, bread, four types of meat, certain sausages and other processed meats, vegetable oil and sugar.

In August 1991, the system of price monitoring was transformed into retail price controls. Projected prices for the 14 food items were set to cover costs and a "normative" profit margin was established at 12 percent for processors and 3 percent for retailers. In April 1992, the list of monitored foods was reduced to six: bread, flour, milk, yoghurt, white cheese and fresh meat. The projected prices were raised at the same time.

Producer prices. Most producer prices were also liberalized in February 1991. However, prices of wheat, pork, poultry meat, calves and milk have continued to be under some form of control. In 1991, with a view to monitoring prices, projected prices for these commodities were established, covering costs plus a 20 percent normative profit. In April 1992, this was replaced with a system of minimum prices for the same products. In theory, both state-owned and private purchasing companies were required to pay these minimum prices to producers. However, these prices were not so rigorously enforced in the case of private firms.

Even the minimum prices established in 1992 are well below world levels and the fact that average 1992 procurement prices were very close to the minimum prices suggests that these are in fact being treated as price ceilings. Furthermore, average 1992 prices of uncontrolled commodities such as maize and barley are also well below world prices. Some of the reasons for these low prices are:

- The monopsonistic structure of the state-owned purchasing and processing enterprises. These are technologically inefficient with high costs but, in the absence of competition, they have no incentive to

cut costs. Rather, they maintain their profit margins by squeezing producers.

- The system of export quotas and bans which are periodically in effect tend to hold down producer prices.
- Because of the need to repay credit and the lack of farmer-owned storage, producers are under pressure to sell their crop immediately after harvest when prices are at their seasonal low.

Trade policy. Trade liberalization began in 1990, when the government removed the monopoly status of foreign trade organizations, allowing private companies to engage in trade. Major reform took place in 1991. In February a unified, floating exchange rate mechanism was established, based on interbank bids for hard currency. Under this new system, firms can retain all hard currency earnings which they may use for future imports. In early 1991 all quantitative restrictions on imports were removed and import licensing restrictions eased. The large number of export bans introduced in 1990 was reduced to 21 items in March 1991 (mostly affecting basic food items to prevent domestic shortages).

Despite the overall movement away from non-tariff barriers, the government has introduced a series of temporary licensing and quantitative restrictions on certain commodities, motivated by concerns about possible food shortages. For most of 1992, exports of grain, sunflowerseed oil and other strategic commodities were subject to quotas. In August, these quotas were abolished and replaced with a system of export taxes, set to capture the difference between domestic and international prices. Initially, these taxes were 8 percent for barley, 12 percent for wheat and corn and 15 percent for wheat flour. In January 1993, these were raised to 15, 20 and 25 percent, respectively.

The result of the lifting of the export quotas was a dramatic surge in exports. At least 600 000 tonnes of grain, including 313 000 tonnes of wheat and flour, were exported in the last quarter of 1992, as traders took advantage of the gap between domestic and world prices. These exports led to fears of possible shortages. While there appear to be adequate supplies of bread grains, there are signs of very tight supplies of feedgrains. In response to such fears, the government

imposed a ban on grain exports in March 1993, which was to remain in effect until the end of September 1993.

Land restitution. The Law for Agricultural Land Ownership and Use was passed in February 1991 and a series of amendments were enacted in April 1992. The main provision of the law is to return land to the pre-1946 owners or their heirs. According to the amended law, reinstatement will take place within the boundaries of the original piece of land wherever possible; in other cases, former owners will receive plots equivalent in size and quality. The amended law allows land sales (the original law prohibited land sales for three years following restitution) but imposes a maximum of 30 ha on land acquired through either restitution or purchase. There are no restrictions on leasing, however.

The process of land restitution is proceeding rather slowly, as the municipal land commissions who are in charge of the restitution are facing shortages of technically qualified personnel. As of April 1993, 22 percent of applicants had received temporary certificates of ownership, covering about 15 percent of agricultural land. In spite of the difficulties, the government hopes to be able to restitute 50 percent of the land within 1993 and to finish the process by the end of 1994.

The amended land law also calls for the liquidation of cooperatives. For each cooperative, municipal authorities have appointed a liquidation council responsible for the valuation and physical distribution of non-land assets to former owners and members and for the management of the cooperative until its liquidation. For the valuation it must rely on the services of individuals or companies authorized by the Privatization Agency or the Ministry of Agriculture. Once members receive their share of cooperative assets, they are free to pool those assets to form new cooperatives.

Privatization and demonopolization. The process of demonopolization began in 1990 and accelerated in May 1991 when the Law for the Protection of Competition was passed. In November 1990, most of the state trusts responsible for purchasing and processing agricultural products were split up into a number of independent enterprises which could compete with one another. The actual effect of this action, at least for agriculture, was to set up regional, rather than central, monopolies. Although all legal restrictions on the formation of new private firms have been removed, few

private firms have in fact emerged to compete with the state enterprises to date. Thus, the market power they hold in the upstream and downstream agricultural sectors remains.

The May 1991 law extended the monopoly breakup across most sectors and provided definitions for monopolies. It provides for price controls on monopolies and bans acquisitions or mergers resulting in a monopoly. The price controls are effected through regulations defining "normative profit margins" for enterprises identified as monopolies.

The state-owned enterprises are to be transformed into commercial companies, after which shares are to be sold through auctions or tenders. The privatization process as such is, however, only in its initial phase. Under the Ministry of Agriculture, 461 agro-industrial state enterprises are destined for privatization. By June 1993, only a handful of auctions or tenders for these companies had taken place.

Credit markets. Two major constraints facing both private and cooperative producers are the difficulty of obtaining credit and the high real cost of credit to farmers in view of the unfavourable relative price movements they have experienced. While below the inflation rate, the current nominal interest rate is still prohibitive for most producers, whose net returns are increasing at a much slower rate than inflation. Banks are also reluctant to lend in the current climate of uncertainty about future landownership.

The government has attempted to alleviate the situation through several programmes, but without much success. In the autumn of 1992, it offered to guarantee credit to finance planting costs, but no interest subsidy was offered and producers were required to repay the loans immediately after harvest, which forced them to market their crop at a time when prices were at their seasonal low.

In May 1993, another bill was passed authorizing low-interest credit to help finance the costs of spring planting. Banks that are still under more than 50 percent state ownership are obliged to offer this low-interest credit; the programme is voluntary for private banks. Even though the interest subsidy is financed by the government, banks – including the state-owned banks – are reluctant to participate because the credit is not guaranteed.

The impact of agricultural reform

The immediate effect of reform has been to plunge
Bulgaria into a deep recession. GDP fell 17 percent in
1991 and another 10 percent in 1992. Further, a big
external debt, estimated to be $13.5 billion, has been
left over from the pre-reform regime. In addition,
Bulgaria was hit particularly hard by the collapse of its
important trade with the former USSR as well as by the
trade embargoes imposed on Iraq and later Serbia and
Montenegro. Consumer prices rose by 334 percent in
1991, mainly reflecting the February price liberalization
and administrative increases in energy prices. Inflation
abated in 1992 but remained extremely high at 110
percent. Unemployment in 1992 was estimated to be
15 percent as compared with 11.7 percent in 1991 and
1.6 percent in 1990.

The impact on agriculture. Since 1990, there have
been significant supply-side adjustments in the crop and
livestock sector. Bulgarian agriculture has suffered the
same deterioration in terms of trade as the other Central
European countries: input prices rose by between four
and eight times in 1991, while output prices merely
doubled. This has been compounded by the uncertainty
surrounding land restitution and the liquidation of the
cooperatives. The other main factor affecting agriculture
is the collapse of the Soviet market.

The most dramatic adjustments have been in the
livestock sector. Between 1989 and 1992, cattle
inventories declined by 38 percent, hogs also by 38
percent and poultry by 51 percent. Livestock production
has become extremely unprofitable, as feed costs have
risen while government policies have combined with
reduced consumer demand to hold down producer
prices. The problems have been greatest in the state-
owned hog and poultry complexes, which continue to
depend on very expensive compound feed. Private
livestock producers have been quicker to adjust their
feeding practices to the new economic reality, feeding
from their own grain production.

The livestock situation has also been deeply affected
by the liquidation of the cooperatives. Cattle have been
affected by this process more than other animals
because the majority of cattle were on cooperatives
rather than state livestock complexes. The first
cooperative assets to be disposed of tend to be the
animals. As a result, a large number of private

individuals have found themselves the owners of two or three cows. Many of the new owners have not been able to provide proper housing or adequate feed. At the same time, large-scale livestock facilities on the cooperatives lie abandoned. The result has been a severe liquidation of herds.

There has been less of a visible adjustment in the crop sector. Grain yields have fallen as a result of a decline in input use, the use of low-quality seeds, drought and delays in planting. Wheat area, after falling in 1992/93, should be back to its previous levels in 1993/94, despite continuing low prices.

Maize area, after an increase in 1992/93, is expected to decline significantly this spring, mainly because sunflowerseed has proved to be more profitable. Sunflowerseed prices are higher and sunflowers are also easier to cultivate. Bulgaria is subject to frequent droughts, causing a substantial variation in maize yields. Much of the maize traditionally grown in Bulgaria is in irrigated areas. As water and irrigation services have grown significantly more expensive, producers have become reluctant to plant maize.

Fruit and vegetable production has suffered greater shocks from the transition. Over half of Bulgaria's fruit and vegetable output went to the processing industry while 80 percent of its processed production was exported, mostly to the former USSR. With the loss of the Soviet market, processing plants are working at one-tenth of their former capacity, leading to a virtual collapse of fruit and vegetable marketing. The most evident result of this situation is a 36 percent drop in vegetable production between 1989 and 1992, including a 53 percent drop in tomato output.

The negative impact on fruit production has so far been less evident but a very negative trend is expected to emerge in 1993 and 1994. Much of the land occupied by the orchards is in the southern part of Bulgaria where restitution has proceeded quickest. As this land is restituted, the new owners do not have the funds to apply optimal levels of pesticides or irrigation.

Prospects and policy issues
It will probably be a long time before the shape of Bulgaria's future farm structure becomes clear. A whole set of institutions is needed to support the new private farmers. In the meantime, the government is under

pressure from the short-term negative effects of reform to slow down the pace of reform and implement more interventionist policies. Bulgarian agriculture has the potential to become a significant source of hard currency export earnings but major obstacles remain.

Particularly pressing are the interrelated issues of land restitution and liquidation of the cooperatives. It is feared that the thrust of the current law will take Bulgaria back to its pre-Second World War farm structure, dominated by tiny and fragmented farms. The average size of new plots at the national level is about 0.5 to 0.7 ha. In the immediate future, it is expected that the majority of landowners will want to form new and smaller voluntary production cooperatives which will allow the pooling of fragmented plots. In the long term, the problem of fragmentation should disappear with the development of land markets. However, efficient land markets are hindered by the lack of institutions needed to provide financing, brokerage services, surveying and recording of transactions and by the lack of an information system. Land sales are also slow because of the currently low profitability of agriculture.

The liquidation of cooperatives is also creating great uncertainty. There have been technical difficulties connected with the valuation of assets and legal disputes about the allocation of assets to former owners and cooperative members. Liquidation councils have been accused of incompetence and negligence, resulting in poor preparations for sowing and planting delays.

In the past, the cooperatives were responsible for many essential services to agriculture, such as maintaining the irrigation systems and ensuring phytosanitary controls on marketed produce. In addition, they were the primary marketing channel for private sector production. As the cooperatives are liquidated, no alternative channels are being developed to provide these services. There is also an insufficient system of extension services to help private producers make their production decisions, seek alternative marketing options or form new cooperatives which might manage the irrigation system or provide veterinary or other services.

Bulgaria has the potential to become a surplus producer of wheat and livestock products. However, world market conditions could make it difficult for the country to expand its exports. Even in 1992, the former USSR was still the largest purchaser of Bulgarian grain

(purchased under barter arrangements for oil and natural gas). Bulgaria may have to continue to rely on this market as the main customer for its wheat and livestock products, and these exports will depend crucially on developments in the republics. If incomes begin to rise, this market could expand. On the other hand, with successful economic reform, the Russian Federation, Ukraine and Kazakhstan could emerge as serious competitors for Bulgaria in the world wheat market.

Fruit and vegetables, the other major source of export earnings, has been battered by the collapse of the Soviet market. Exports of field tomatoes, unpeeled canned tomatoes and apples have fallen to a fraction of their previous level. At the same time, exports of early tomatoes, greenhouse tomatoes and green peppers have remained strong, with exports going mainly to Germany and Austria as well as Poland, former Czechoslovakia and former Yugoslavia, SFR. Markets could be developed for other greenhouse vegetables. However, this potential is gravely threatened by the current difficulties of the sector. The greenhouses are slated for privatization and are suffering the same financial difficulties faced by state-owned firms. It is entirely conceivable that some of the greenhouses could end up abandoned or destroyed.

The processing industry is in a particularly depressed state. Plants are technologically outdated, they are often working at a fraction of their capacity and they need a large infusion of capital to finance the renovation needed to meet the quality standards of Western markets.

ROMANIA
The agricultural sector

Agriculture accounted for 19 percent of Romania's GDP in 1991 and employed 29 percent of the workforce. By far the most important crops grown in Romania are cereals, with wheat and maize covering about one-third of the country's arable land. During the period 1986-90, wheat production averaged 7.3 million tonnes while maize production averaged 9.8 million tonnes. Other important crops are oilseeds: sunflowerseed production averaged 700 000 tonnes during 1986-90 while soybean production was typically around 300 000 tonnes per year. The country's most important livestock product is pork.

Romania was for some time a significant net agricultural exporter, exporting significant amounts of wheat and, in some years, maize. Other major exports have been livestock products, sunflower oil, fruit and vegetables. Throughout most of the communist period, Romania imported large amounts of soybean and, in some years, maize. However, during the final years of communist rule, the Romanian Government's drive to eliminate the country's foreign debt led to greatly reduced imports of feedstuffs and the vigorous promotion of agricultural exports. The result was severe domestic shortages of most basic foods.

During the communist period, Romania's farm structure was dominated by state and cooperative farms. State farms, averaging 5 000 ha, covered 20 percent of agricultural land and 16 percent of arable land. These were state-owned enterprises in which the workers had the status of employees. Cooperative farms averaged 2 000 ha. Workers on cooperatives had the status of "members" rather than employees and their income was theoretically linked to the cooperative's performance. In practice, there was little difference in the operation and management of these two types of farm. However, privatization of the two types of organization is proceeding in different ways.

There was a significant private sector during the communist period, however. About 9 percent of the agricultural land continued to be privately owned, although this land was mainly in mountainous regions that were unsuitable for large-scale collectivized agriculture. Another 8 percent of the land was in 0.5 ha plots allotted to cooperative farm members for their

personal use. The private sector contributed close to 40 percent of the meat, fruit and vegetable output.

Policy reform

Compared with other transitional countries in Central Europe, the Romanian reform process has been characterized by a high degree of gradualism and caution in an attempt to protect the population and limit the recessionary impact of the structural reforms.

Retail prices. A first round of liberalization took place in November 1990, when price controls were removed for all but a list of 22 essential items whose prices were fixed by the government and subject to subsidies. Thus, staple foods, together with energy and communications, remained under a price control system. In a series of steps during 1991 and 1992, administrative price ceilings were raised, food subsidies paid to processors to cover losses incurred through retail price ceilings were cut and the number of products subject to price ceilings was reduced. From September 1992, formal price ceilings persisted only for bread, butter, milk and milk powder. On 1 May 1993, the remaining formal retail price ceilings were lifted, leading to a more than fourfold increase in bread prices. Yet food subsidies remain for beef, pork, poultry and milk. These subsidies are paid to state-owned processors who respect the government-established minimum farmgate prices.

Producer prices. Prices in peasant markets were freed soon after the 1989 revolution, but the government has set minimum prices for basic commodities to be paid by all state-owned purchasing enterprises. These prices have been raised a number of times but, in general, have not risen as fast as the rate of inflation. From 1 May 1993, minimum prices remained in force for wheat, maize, pork, beef, poultry and milk. The continued de facto monopoly power of the state purchasing enterprises tends to keep prices close to the minimum levels. Privatization has been slow in the downstream sector and producers still have very few alternatives to selling to state purchasing agencies. The low profit margins of the state-owned companies and their preferential access to state subsidies allows them to advance inputs and financing to farmers in exchange for forward purchasing contracts; however, this has resulted in de facto barriers to the entry of new private agents in agricultural supply and marketing.

Trade policy. The government's first act following the revolution was to ban all agricultural and food exports, reversing previous policies of maximizing exports regardless of the effects on domestic food supplies. At the same time, imports of crucial inputs were authorized. These imports were initially possible because of the hard currency reserves that had been built up during the previous year.

In 1991 most imports and exports were liberalized, although export bans and quotas continued to be applied for many agricultural products. The leu was devalued and made partially convertible, hard currency auctions were authorized and the state monopoly on foreign trade was abolished. Beginning in January 1992, exporters were allowed to retain their hard currency earnings.

From 31 May 1993, export bans on agricultural products were lifted, except for wheat and butter. Agricultural imports are subject to rather high tariffs, although these are frequently waived for "emergency imports" in response to perceived shortages.

Non-agricultural privatization. Small-scale privatization began in February 1990 when a decree was passed that allowed the formation of private businesses employing up to 20 people. The Commercial Societies Law, passed in November 1990, removed most restrictions on the establishment of new businesses. Also from this date, the leasing of state-owned assets has been pursued. By the end of 1992, outside the farming sector, there were over 200 000 private businesses in Romania (including both new private firms and privately managed state-owned units) employing some 1.4 million people.

Large-scale privatization began with an August 1990 law which called for the reorganization of all state enterprises into either commercial companies, in which the government continued to hold all the shares but which are destined for privatization, or so-called *regies autonomes*, which were to remain state property. Theoretically, the *regies autonomes* were to be located in perceived strategic industries (defence, energy, mining, public utilities). A law passed in August 1991 established the target of privatizing the state-owned commercial companies within seven years. For this purpose, the law created five private ownership funds, holding some 30 percent of the shares of the commercial

companies, and one state ownership fund, holding the remaining 70 percent. The state ownership fund will develop and implement annual privatization programmes leading to complete privatization over seven years. The five private ownership funds are joint stock companies in which Romanian citizens hold share certificates. The funds are supposed to develop methods whereby shareholders can exchange their certificates for actual shares in the companies themselves.

The process of privatization itself is only in its initial phase. In agriculture, the large-scale privatization programme will apply to both state farms and companies in the upstream and downstream sectors, affecting a total of 2 200 commercial companies. For 1993, 500 of these have been proposed for privatization.

Land restitution. The redistribution of land began spontaneously soon after the revolution, as cooperatives disbanded and members divided their assets among themselves. Formal land legislation was passed in February 1991, according to which cooperative members who contributed land, as well as members who did not, are entitled to claim up to 10 ha, a quota constrained by the availability of land. In areas with excess land, up to 10 ha may be given to landless families from other localities who would then be obligated to take up residence and cultivate the land. Most citizens are free to buy and sell land, but no one may own more than 100 ha. There is a ten-year ban on land sales by new owners who did not own land in the past. Foreign citizens may inherit land but must sell it within one year.

Former owners whose land is now in state farms may not reobtain that land. Instead, the 176 000 owners whose land was expropriated by state farms have become shareholders in the state farms.

Romania's land restitution has proceeded more quickly than in any other Central or East European country. By June 1993, 90 percent of claimants had received land. Privately owned land increased from 1.4 million ha in 1989 to 10.3 million ha in 1991 and now accounts for more than 70 percent of Romania's agricultural land (80 percent of arable land). However, the process has caused a return to the pre-Second World War farm structure which was dominated by small, fragmented holdings. The average size of new private holdings is about 2 ha, often consisting of two or more

non-contiguous plots, which is also a reflection of the pre-war farm structure. The return to this fragmented farm structure has had a very negative short-term impact on Romania's agricultural performance.

In the longer term, the consolidation of these holdings could be accomplished through a land market. The sale or transfer of land requires the seller to have the final title to his land, and the process of titling has been very slow. Of the approximately five million new landowners, by mid-1993 only 300 000 had received final titles. The government expects that about 700 000 more will receive titles within 1993 and that, by 1995, 80 percent of new owners will have final titles to their land. Would-be purchasers of land also find it very difficult to obtain financing. Mortgages are offered at high interest rates with a five-year repayment period.

Another serious problem faced by new landowners is the lack of suitable machinery. Most of the country's tractors are still owned by the state machinery stations known as "Agromecs". The 611 Agromecs own 70 000 tractors and 27 000 combines, while there are only 36 000 tractors in the private sector. The government has introduced a soft loan programme, offering low-interest credit to producers who want to buy tractors from the Agromecs. However, the fact remains that many of the current tractors are too large to be used on small private farms.

The formation of new cooperatives. To counter the negative effects of land fragmentation, the government has actively encouraged new private farmers to join associations. There are two types of association: loosely organized groups, ranging from small "family associations" (typically with three, four or five families) to somewhat larger but still informal groupings and more formally structured, legally registered associations. In several cases, farmers with several non-contiguous plots belong to two or more such associations, which allow the pooling of adjacent pieces of land for joint cultivation.

Agricultural credit. The government has undertaken several initiatives to help farmers obtain credit, which continues to present difficulties for most. Market interest rates of 70 percent or more are prohibitive for most producers, given the low rate of increase in agricultural prices. Most agricultural credit is provided by Agrobank. Before the revolution, Agrobank had just 10 000 clients;

now it has 150 000. It has also become increasingly independent of the National Bank of Romania, on which it now depends for only 27 percent of its resources. However, 80 percent of Agrobank's loans are short-term and 60 percent are to Romcereal, the state grain company. Agrobank also administers a soft loan programme on behalf of the National Bank of Romania. These loans carry an interest rate of 15 percent and can be used by producers to buy inputs. However, demand for these loans greatly exceeds the supply: 23 billion lei were made available for this programme while applications have been submitted for 250 billion lei.

The impact of economic reform
Romania has seen a decline in most economic indicators that is no less severe than that of most other Central European countries. GDP declined by 14 percent in 1991 and a further 15 percent in 1992. The inflation rate accelerated from 161 percent in 1991 to 210 percent in 1992. Unemployment rose from 2.7 percent in 1991 to 6 percent in 1992 and is still on the rise.

The impact on agriculture. Agricultural output declined by 14 percent in 1992 as a result of confusion regarding land distribution, lower input use and the severe drought in the summer of 1992. Declines were registered in most crops and livestock products. The cumulative decline in agricultural production from 1989 to 1992 amounts to 25 percent.

Total grain production in 1992 was down by 38 percent. With wheat area declining from 2.1 million to 1.5 million ha, production declined by 42 percent. Wheat was less affected by the summer drought – yields were down only slightly from 1991 – than by disruptions caused by land redistribution. Maize output, severely affected by the drought, declined by 35 percent. Planted area increased by almost one-third, as the new private producers sought to produce the feed necessary for their animals, but yields declined by 50 percent.

Oilseed production has undergone major structural shifts. Sunflower area increased by 56 percent between 1990 and 1992, while soybean area declined by 13 percent in the same period. As in Bulgaria, private producers have found sunflowers easy to cultivate and they are relatively drought-resistant. The communist government had strived for an increased soybean output

in order to come closer to self-sufficiency in feed production, but yields remained low. Once freed from government directives, producers have clearly lost interest in soybean.

The initial negative effects of land redistribution may now have passed. Wheat area for 1993/94 is estimated to be 2.3 million ha, which is back to historical levels. Maize area is expected to be very close to that of 1992/93 and sunflower area slightly higher.

Romania has suffered dislocations in its livestock sector similar to those of Bulgaria. Cattle herds, being more difficult to keep on small private farms, have declined the most – by 31 percent between 1990 and 1992. Hog numbers declined by 16 percent in the same period because of the country's inability to import sufficient maize or soybean meal. Milk production declined by 14 percent from 1990 to 1992.

Prospects and policy issues

Romania may be suffering some of the worst disruptions compared with any country in Central Europe, with the exception of Albania. The fact that Romania, once a major exporter, had to import more than 1 million tonnes of cereals in 1990, 1991 and 1992 is an indicator of the magnitude of the problems it is facing. At the same time, inflation continues to be high, large-scale privatization is proceeding slowly and the government seems to be more hesitant than others in the region to implement reform fully. Still, such a cautious approach has not spared Romania the disruptions and severe, immediate recessionary impact also experienced by the region's other reforming countries.

Romania has the potential to become a significant exporter of several agricultural products but the realization of that potential will depend on the government carrying its reform programme through completely. Romania clearly illustrates the problems involved in rapid privatization without the simultaneous creation of the institutional infrastructure needed to support the new private sector. One of the most pressing needs appears to be an acceleration of granting final titles to restituted land. Without permanent title, landowners are unable to sell their land and contribute to the consolidation of landholding.

Another important need would be the development of a greater diversity of marketing and input supply

alternatives. Most purchasing and input supply is still in the hands of costly and inefficient state-owned monopolies which maintain their profit margins by holding down prices paid to producers. In this context, an important contribution could be the development of a more extensive network of cooperatives. The associations currently being encouraged are production cooperatives, which pool adjacent pieces of land to achieve more efficient cultivation. These associations, however, are still at a serious disadvantage when dealing with input suppliers or procurement organizations. There appears to be a need for marketing and input cooperatives in addition to the current production cooperatives.

The development of better extension and information systems would also play a positive role in improving the prospects of Romanian agriculture. Present efforts are aimed at improving the structure of information transmission as regards channels of distribution, market information and agricultural production forecasts.

The development of Romanian agriculture could also be greatly enhanced by the removal of remaining export restrictions, which hold down producer prices and ultimately inhibit supply. If Romania wishes to reduce or turn around its negative trade balance, it will eventually have to encourage exports. Agriculture is one of the sectors with the greatest potential to generate export earnings in the short term.

THE RUSSIAN FEDERATION
Food supply

During the 1980s the growth in agricultural production was double that of population, with the livestock sector showing particular dynamism. Average incomes, however, increased even faster than agricultural production with the result that, although average per caput consumption grew, food demand – especially for animal products – continued to exceed supply. This prompted leaders of the former USSR to put increased food production high on their economic policy agenda. However, the inefficiencies of the production and marketing systems necessitated high and increasing subsidization and rendered evident the need for reform.

The urgency of reform became imperative by 1990 when agricultural production began to shrink, accentuating the supply/demand imbalance and rendering even more manifest the shortcomings of the country's marketing and distribution systems. The excess demand situation persisted through 1991 but was reversed in 1992 when consumer prices rapidly increased following partial liberalization, causing a contraction in the demand for foods. In the case of animal products, the reaction of the processing industry was to reduce meat and milk purchases from farms instead of lowering their sales prices. Underlying the increasingly precarious overall food demand/supply balance was a significant reduction in consumption, particulary of livestock products.

A parallel phenomenon that may have mitigated the imbalance of the food economy to a certain extent was the slowing in population growth which, from 0.7 percent annually up to the late 1980s, was expected to turn negative by 1992. This reversal was linked to the deterioration of living conditions and fears and uncertainties arising from the recent economic and political transformations.

As regards food consumption patterns, official estimates for the first quarter of 1993 indicate declines in per caput consumption below the level of the period January-March 1989 (the most favourable among recent years) of 21 percent for meat products, 34 percent for milk products, 7 percent for eggs, 5 percent for fish products, 13 percent for sugar and confectionary and 32 percent for fruit. On the other hand, consumption increased by 22 percent for grain products, 4 percent for

potatoes and 8 percent for other vegetables during the same period.

Consumption of animal proteins, which had already fallen slightly in 1990 from the levels of 1989, seems to have declined further by about 20 percent during 1991-92. These were proteins partially substituted by starchy foods. Overall, per caput calorie intake fell to about the level of the 1970s, although other estimates point to even lower figures.

Although average food intakes still appear relatively high, considerable pockets of malnutrition emerged among less favoured regions and population groups. Food access problems were accentuated by the reduced control on farm marketing operations and barter deals as well as by the regionally and locally different systems of fixing and/or subsidizing consumer prices for some foods (the latter measure having been legalized by a presidential decree of 27 March 1993). Price differentials among cities remained wide, despite some reduction over time which was probably caused by the response of economic agents to the opportunities for arbitrage that such a situation offered. By the end of March 1993 the discrepancies between the highest and lowest levels of consumer prices among cities were 1:70 for bread, 1:34 for milk, 1:16 for beef and 1:10 for vegetable oil, potatoes and other vegetables. Even those groups of the population that were less affected by the unequal distribution of food supply still experienced a deeply felt qualitative deterioration in their diets.

The overall situation may nevertheless be less gloomy than suggested by the official statistics to the extent that these do not comprise the unknown quantities of food that is privately produced and sold outside the official sphere in more or less legal ways.

Agricultural production in 1992/93

Agricultural production was estimated to have fallen by about 6 percent in 1992, with meat, milk and egg output decreasing by as much as 12 to 15 percent.

Among individual crops, only cereals, pulses and potatoes recovered substantially from the setback of the previous year. The area under grain expanded slightly in 1992 to 62.4 million ha and still further in 1993. Of significant bearing on animal feed supplies was the decline in pasture, from 28.8 million ha in 1986 to 23.3 million ha in 1992.

One of the factors limiting the growth of crop yields is the degradation of soils. This process has been going on for more than 100 years but Russian soil scientists point out that it has greatly accelerated during the past ten to 20 years.

The explanatory factors include widespread neglect of anti-erosion techniques, insufficient crop rotation, soil compaction through overuse of heavy machinery, an unbalanced use of mineral fertilizer and salinization through excess irrigation and insufficient drainage. The detrimental effects are difficult to quantify but are commonly recognized to weigh heavily on potential yield growth.

In 1992 total livestock numbers declined by 5 percent for cows, 6 percent for other cattle, 11 percent for pigs and 9 percent for sheep and goats. The decline on collective and state farms was only partially offset by increases in private farms. Up to 1991, the rate of decrease in the overall herd was smaller than that of meat and milk output, thereby implying slowly rising animal productivity. For 1992, however, the official statistics report diminished productivity.

Herd numbers and animal production further declined during the period January-March 1993 and will most likely continue falling for the rest of the year, although perhaps at a slower pace than in 1992 thanks to higher government procurement prices. Shortages and/or high prices of feed remain the major reason for this decline.

The 1992/93 agricultural year started with autumn ploughing and sowing being reduced by one-fifth compared with normal rates, but with moderate frost-lifting of grain. Depending on summer and autumn weather, crop production in 1993 could improve slightly over the results of 1992 yet will not compensate for the decline in livestock production. Overall, agricultural production is likely to decrease by 5 percent or more.

Agricultural policies

Agrarian reform is generally perceived to be a prerequisite for enhancing growth of agricultural production, balancing demand and supply, raising nutrition standards and improving the performance of downstream activities linked to agriculture.

The conceptual and operational implications of reform are loosely defined by such slogans as restructuring, marketization and plurality of socio-economic

formations. There are strong divergencies of opinion as to the nature, speed and depth of the process.

The institutional instability surrounding agrarian affairs is illustrated by the fact that the Centre of Land and Agro-industrial Reform was created in June 1992 and subsequently abolished in May 1993. Various government agencies and regional authorities are influential in implementing reform laws and decrees in their own ways. Another actor, represented in most provinces and counties, is the Association of Peasant Farms and Cooperatives of Russia (AKKOR).

Reorganized and new farms. There is general agreement that, in the foreseeable future, the bulk of primary food products will have to be generated by the collective and state farms, whether in their traditional form or after reorganization. In 1992, their share in gross output was some 60 percent and that in marketed output even larger. However, a new sector of family and private "peasant farms" is coming into existence, although it still accounts for a minor part of the country's agricultural output.

Yet, how fast should private farming expand and what should be its relationship with collective and state farms? Should the latter remain as huge as in the past or be broken into smaller but still large (by Western standards) units? The farmers remaining on the reorganized state or collective farms shall be awarded shares in assets and land, but should such shares be assigned in physical or in value terms? Although a number of laws, decrees and ordinances have been issued on these and other questions, they are still disputed and implemented locally in different ways.

In principle, private full ownership is already granted by law, but the selling or buying of privately owned farmland for non-agricultural purposes remains prohibited by law and constitution. In late 1992, full private ownership was finally granted by law only for garden and household plots, and two corresponding constitutional amendments were also approved.

Reforming and privatizing the huge public farms while minimizing losses and disruptions is no less important than setting up new individual farms. Disagreements exist as to the speed, depth and form that these parallel processes should take.

Up to the end of 1992, out of a total 25 609 collective

and state farms, 19 719 were "reregistered". Thirty-five percent of these kept their previous status while 65 percent reorganized in "other forms of ownership". The majority of the latter (8 551) became "societies" with limited liability or "mixed societies", while another 2 410 formed "agricultural (production) cooperatives" and "associations of peasant farms". Some split into smaller cooperative units, among which a number evolved into what can be considered wholly independent peasant farms. Overall, the extent to which the reorganized farms can be considered private is a question of definition.

During 1992, 134 700 new family and private, small group farms came into existence, bringing the total to 183 700 by the end of the year. As most of them were set up after spring 1992, their contribution to that year's agricultural output was only 2 to 2.5 percent. Up to mid-1993, their number grew to more than 250 000 and they farmed about 10.4 million ha or 5 percent of the Russian Federation's agricultural land. The average area per farm was 43 ha. Family and private farms have begun to organize cooperatives for buying, leasing and servicing machinery as well as for processing, marketing and banking. Forming such cooperatives is often made difficult by the absence of relevant legislation, which leaves them in a semi-legal status. Moreover, the small number of private farms that usually exists in a given locality is not sufficient to support viable cooperation.

The sector of household plots and gardens has greatly expanded in recent years in terms of quantity and value of output. Including the rural "personal" plots, this private sector as a whole accounted for 80 percent of the total output of potatoes (produced on 73 percent of their plantations) and 55 percent of the other vegetable output. Some reformers hope that the rural household plot farming will expand, as it is a less costly and more realistic way of establishing genuine family farms.

Price parity. Another major economic as well as political bone of contention in 1992/93 was price policy. Advocates of intersectoral equality want agricultural producer prices to rise at a similar pace to those of the industrial inputs. Nevertheless, the prices for such inputs are estimated to represent only 25 to 40 percent of agriculture's production costs. Labour, intrafarm or interfarm inputs, land, management (or

organization of farming) account for the greater part of these costs.[41] In any event, it is unlikely that an alignment of price increases between agricultural output and industrial input would by itself greatly help agriculture or reduce the need for greater efficiency within the sector.

During 1991, the state roughly doubled the industrial input prices for agriculture and the practice of applying contractual prices expanded; at the same time, prices received by farmers rose by one-half and more.

On the whole, domestic terms of trade developments in 1991 and the first nine months of 1992 did not appear to penalize agriculture unduly. Indeed, industrially produced inputs had previously been supplied at extremely low costs.

The issue became worrisome only in late 1992 when prices of industrially produced inputs and services were largely liberalized. During the last three months of that year input prices rose 3.3 times faster than agricultural output. The wholesale prices for industrially produced inputs rose 1.9 times during the first quarter of 1993, with a 2.1-fold increase for trucks and tractors and a 2.4-fold increase for mineral fertilizer and feeds.

No less detrimental to farmers than the increases in input prices as such were the delays (frequently extended over several months) in payments for agricultural products as well as in credits and inflation compensations. More recently, these delays were somewhat shortened by all payments being made through the country's central bank. Still, given the above price increases, a one-month delay alone means roughly a 25 percent value decline of the money available for input purchases. However, in most cases industry and services demanded immediate or even advance payment.

In early 1993, the Russian Federation Government made an effort to re-establish "price parity" and to compensate at least partly for the effect of payment delays. A decree of 23 January 1993 provided for several forms of financial support for the food economy, including compensations of 30 percent on input cost rises. Following the decree, the government sharply raised the 1993 procurement prices for all categories of farmers producing grain, oilseeds and sugar beet.

Procurement prices for grain which, in August 1992, were fortyfold more than the average prices for 1990,

---

[41] Land, long denied as a cost factor, was at last indirectly assigned a price, although a low one, with the introduction of land taxes, rents and limited selling and buying of land in 1991.

were again more than doubled in February 1993 and raised slightly further in March. The new prices are to be revised every three months in the light of changes in input prices and production costs on the basis of negotiations between the Ministry of Agriculture, the state purchasing organization and the "Agricultural Union". Moreover, half of the price will be paid in advance on conclusion of a sales contract. By April 1993, milk was paid roughly twice, and meat about ten times, the price of grain.

State purchases now only account for the smaller part of the marketed farm output and their importance varies greatly by region. Even so, they may help maintain minimum price levels in the case of excessive declines in market prices. Whether budgetary constraints will allow the state to honour its purchasing commitments fully is a different question.

From the late 1980s, the state began reducing its role in food marketing and distribution. Even though 1992 was a relatively good harvest year, state procurement of the main crops was much smaller than during the period 1986-1990. Nevertheless, procurements exceeded planned targets for most major products except grain and potatoes. A decree of 17 December 1992 requires that each region should aim at creating its own grain fund and subsidizing the consumer price of bread. For 1993 planned purchases through the central fund are only 12.6 million tonnes of grain, 2.6 million tonnes of potatoes, slightly more than 1 million tonnes of meat and 6 million tonnes of milk.

Since 1991, collective and state farms have been permitted to sell part of their livestock products through their own marketing organizations. Such sales were small in 1991 but, by 1992, amounted to roughly 20 percent of total meat output. Another 30 percent is produced privately with only a small part sold to state agencies, mainly through the collective and state farms. Thus, about half of the meat output is self-consumed or marketed outside the official trade system. The corresponding percentages are smaller for eggs and milk and larger for potatoes and vegetables.

By a decree of 12 February 1993, the state president requested that central and regional public food funds should guarantee adequate food supplies to some zones which, because of adverse climatic conditions or population size, are not self-sufficient. Beneficiaries are

Moscow and St Petersburg, a number of northern and industrial zones, the army and some other state organizations. Purchases to this end are to be effected on the basis of voluntary contracts, partly through privatized trade organizations on behalf of the state. Purchases abroad and from states of the former USSR are also to contribute to the central fund.

Barter operations and foreign trade

The reduced role of central purchases has not yet given way to a functioning market, but a primitive form of market is operating under galloping inflation and with some remnants of the former command economy. In 1992 food processing was still largely a monopoly of state-owned firms. Sugar is a special case: part of the refined sugar output is returned to the beet producers on the basis of contracts while another smaller part is retained by the refineries, thus being consumed and marketed outside the state system. Similar practices are observed for mixed feed.

The volume of free grain trade in 1992 is estimated to be around 15 percent of production, with 2 percent going through the commodity exchanges (*birzhy*). Barter trade among farms, non-industrial enterprises and territorial administrations has expanded. An example is the "barter fund" of Vologda province, which exchanges metal, timber and machines for animal feeds and other foods from Kazakhstan and some Russian provinces. Throughout the Russian Federation, many farms barter meat and other farm products in exchange for needed inputs. About 30 percent of industrial farm inputs are estimated to be acquired outside the parastatal AGROSNAB system, and this share is expected to reach 45 to 50 percent in 1993 and subsequent years. Such transactions, even where legal, are only officially recorded in part.

Up to autumn 1991, food trade among the republics of the former USSR was only recorded for individual republics and was not published systematically. The first statistical yearbook, published by the Russian Federation, contained data on main food commodity imports and exports from former Soviet republics without a breakdown by trading partners. Most likely, these data only cover exchanges through state-owned firms and the procurement system using public funds. Apart from grain, former Russia's agricultural imports

from other republics in 1989 consisted mainly of meat and meat products (876 000 tonnes), milk and milk products (4.5 million tonnes), 847 million eggs, 3 million tonnes of vegetables, fruit, grapes and melons and 2.6 million tonnes of sugar. On the other hand, former Russia's deliveries of these products to other republics were negligible, except for eggs and potatoes. Since then, the quantities (including those from Georgia and Baltic states) have greatly declined. Even the reduced agreements concluded for 1991 were not fulfilled.

The main suppliers of meat and milk were Ukraine, the Baltic states and former Belarus. Ukraine also supplied most of the eggs and former Belarus most of the potatoes. Central Asia, Ukraine and Moldavia were the main suppliers of vegetables, fruit and melons. The main supplier of grain from within the former USSR to Russia was and still is Kazakhstan.

The above refers to the so-called "near abroad" as distinct from "far abroad" trade, the latter referring to trade *vis-à-vis* countries outside the former USSR, which now include the three Baltic states. For grain, the Russian Federation heavily depends on imports from far abroad, the other most important import items being sugar, meat, vegetable oil and oilseed meal. According to official data, far abroad wheat imports in 1992 increased from 12.4 million tonnes in 1991 to 20.6 million tonnes, but maize imports were more than halved from 11.8 million tonnes to 5 million tonnes. Far abroad imports of meat in 1992 decreased to 380 000 tonnes (in 1991 they were 693 000 tonnes) while those of vegetable oil increased fourfold, from 108 000 to 452 000 tonnes, and those of sugar from 3.6 million to 4 million tonnes.

Barter trade operations are also reported between territorial administrations and partners far abroad, e.g. between St Petersburg and Poland or Hungary; or the Ufa oil and Vorkuta coal *vis-à-vis* Lithuanian meat.

Prospects for agriculture
It will not be before two or three years, perhaps even more, that the 1986-1990 farm production levels can be expected to be reached again. This applies more to the livestock sector where rebuilding the animal herds will take time. One may even question whether regaining earlier output levels should be a primary goal. Rather,

the emphasis may be shifted to: *i)* better integration of downstream activities linked to the food sector; and *ii)* adjusting to the changes in consumer demand that may be expected when real incomes recover – although regaining their previous level may be an even lengthier process.

Renewed growth in agricultural output will probably be sought by increasing productivity without raising capital and labour costs per unit of output. Cost reduction, even more than physical growth objectives, could become the main contribution of the new individual farms. The collective and state farms and their reorganized successors still have to prove their ability to render this service to the food economy, all the more so since direct and indirect subsidization of agriculture is growing again. To this must be added the cost of higher state purchase prices and the subsidies on livestock products in 1993 as well as central and local consumer subsidies. If agriculture does not reduce its production costs, it will remain a major factor of inflation and, thereby, become increasingly a factor of economic distortions itself.

The solution of these problems in the long term will require the settlement of currently conflicting views among policy-makers, from top to local levels. Political and economic uncertainty are the greatest obstacles to the reform and recovery of the Russian Federation's agriculture.

OECD COUNTRIES

OVERVIEW

The OECD countries' policy actions in agricultural trade and the macroeconomy affect the welfare of the developing countries often as much as or more than these countries' own policies. The combined macroeconomic policies of the developed countries have a heavy influence on the global economic growth and inflation rates, interest rates, exchange rate structure and, therefore, the levels of trade and capital flows among countries. The domestic agricultural and agricultural trade policies of the developed countries also strongly influence the well-being of developing countries' agricultural sectors and rural communities. For these reasons, *The State of Food and Agriculture* reports each year on changes in the world economic environment in its World review, and on changes in the agricultural and trade policies of OECD countries in its Regional review.

The State of Food and Agriculture 1993 highlights some of the likely impacts of the reform of the Common Agricultural Policy (CAP) of the European Economic Community (EEC), having reported on the CAP reform measures in 1992. With a new administration and agricultural legislation (which expires in 1995) in the United States, the relevant section raises some of the major issues and likely options that will be considered in adjusting United States agricultural policy to changing realities. Finally, as the world's largest net importer of agricultural products, Japan has announced a sweeping agricultural policy reform package. The section on Japan highlights the changes taking place in the country's agricultural sector, both as part of and apart from the announced reforms.

UNITED STATES
The budget deficit and its impact on agricultural policy

A new administration, committed to increased economic growth and a phasing out of the budget deficit has taken over in Washington, DC. The major preoccupation has been how the new austerity programmes to reduce the budget deficit will affect different societal and economic groups, including agriculture. The changes and shifts in direction of agricultural policy that are likely to occur over the next several years are important to United States agriculture but they are no less important to the global community, since that country's agriculture plays a predominant role in the global agricultural arena. Following is a brief analysis of the general consequences of possible changes in United States agricultural policy in the coming months and years.

A desire to reduce the government's budgetary deficit has led the United States administration to propose a package of measures to Congress, aimed primarily at cutting government expenditures and increasing revenues. Some of the measures would modify existing agricultural programmes, while other more general actions, such as those proposed in the area of tax policy, would affect agriculture as part of the overall economy. The administration proposed phasing in the agricultural reforms from FY 1994 to 1997 and requested legislation to make some of the changes immediately while leaving others until the 1995 farm bill.

The administration's agricultural proposals represent an adjustment of programme mechanisms rather than a fundamental change in the form of farm programmes. Even the measures proposed for inclusion in the 1995 farm bill do not imply a radical change in structure, although they conceivably could prompt consideration of more fundamental reforms. Under the current proposals, the target price/deficiency payment mechanism for supporting farm incomes remains in place, as do the loan rate and production control mechanisms for supporting prices. The administration explicitly ruled out an early reduction in export subsidies on the grounds that it would not be appropriate to "disarm" unilaterally before the issue was resolved in GATT's stalled MTNs.

The two changes that would have the greatest budgetary and programme impact, and which would become effective for 1996 crops, are: an increase in the

mandatory area from which production is *not* eligible for support payments under the so-called "triple base" programme[42] from 15 to 25 percent of base acreage; and the elimination of the so-called 0/92 and 50/92 programmes. Under the 0/92 programme for wheat and feedgrains, producers may plant from 0 to 100 percent of their acreage eligible for production support (payment acreage) but still receive deficiency payments on 92 percent of that payment acreage without suffering a reduction in the farm's future programme acreage base. The benefits are calculated in the same way for rice and upland cotton, except that farmers must plant at least 50 percent of their payment acreage (50/92).

Eliminating the 0/92 and 50/92 programmes would require farmers to return the acreage currently under these programmes to production in order to receive programme benefits. This would reduce the partial decoupling accomplished by the 0/92 and 50/92 programmes and the resulting increase in production may need to be offset by increases in Acreage Reduction Program (ARP) levels.

Eliminating these programmes may also affect farmers' decisions concerning the Conservation Reserve Program (CRP). Many CRP contracts will begin to expire in 1996. What will owners do with this land then? Until now, the likely choices have included a renewal of the CRP contracts; the continued idling of some or all of that land, but under the 0/92 and 50/92 programmes; or the return of the idled land (for which farmers retain a base) to production. Elimination of the 0/92 and 50/92 programmes would remove one option, and there is uncertainty about the CRP renewal option.

It is unclear whether or not Congress will honour the new administration's request for funding in 1994 and 1995 to enrol the additional 1 million ha in the CRP to meet the target set by the 1990 Food, Agriculture, Conservation and Trade Act (FACT). How it may deal with reauthorization of the CRP when its authority expires at the end of 1995 is also a question to be considered. Some critics of the CRP have suggested that the $1.8 billion now spent annually on CRP rental payments could be put to better use in other approaches to conservation. The increased output which could result from the elimination of these options might be offset by increases in the ARPs for programme crops.

Other policy changes proposed by the administration

[42] See *The State of Food and Agriculture 1992*, p. 119.

with the aim of achieving budget savings include: directing subsidies to farmers with an off-farm income below $100 000; increasing loan origination fees and assessments for certain programme crops; reforming crop insurance and disaster assistance programmes; and phasing out subsidized sales of timber from public lands.

The long-term implications of these proposals to cut the United States federal budget may make the farm programmes less attractive to potential participants. As programme benefits for farmers are further reduced by the increase in mandatory flexible acres and the possible required increase in ARPs (if the CRP and 0/92 and 50/92 programmes are eliminated), some farmers may find it is to their advantage not to participate in the programmes. They would still be able to take advantage of higher domestic prices for commodities as a result of the programmes but, at the same time, they would be able to produce whatever amount of any commodity they chose. The government would be less effective in controlling the supply of a commodity, which is the mechanism used in the commodity programmes to maintain price levels.

The CRP and other conservation measures in the farm programmes have also provided a means for the United States Government to help control soil erosion and pesticide runoff on farms. Participating farmers must meet certain conservation requirements to be eligible for programme payments. With reduced programme participation, the farm programme would be less effective in this role. Without these measures to control the adverse environmental effects of agriculture, the government would need to find new ways of responding to the general public's growing pressure to regulate such issues. One likely result would be new laws enacted by individual states as a means of control. Such laws would vary by state and would therefore affect farmers differently depending on the location of their farms.

Farmers still participating in the programmes may also be adversely affected if increasing numbers of farmers choose not to participate in the farm programmes. If supplies increase, programme pressure may be placed on participating farmers to reduce their production further as a means of controlling supply. Such control would be effected by increasing the level of the ARP, which would further reduce the programme payments that a farmer could receive and thus also reduce the

incentives for participating in the programme. The cuts may also have the opposite budget effect to that intended, since they may actually increase government spending on farm programmes. An increased supply resulting from programme changes would lower the market price for a commodity while deficiency payments would rise as the difference between the market price and the target price widened. The higher payments to participating farmers would increase government expenditures, depending on how many farmers remain in the programme and on the amount of increase in the payments.

The United States Government is committed to its export programmes as long as similar programmes exist in other major agricultural producer countries. Levels of assistance, provided under schemes such as Public Law (PL) 480 and the credit guarantee programmes, are mandated by Congress and will remain in effect through 1995.

If further increases in acreage ineligible for support under the triple base were to reduce the number of farms participating in farm programmes, a major challenge for the United States Government would be to maintain levels of commodity stock in the Commodity Credit Corporation (CCC), which is used to provide food assistance.

The long-term outlook for export programmes will depend on budgetary issues facing the United States Government when the present farm act expires in 1995. The amount of money appropriated to different export programmes and food aid will depend on what pressures exist at this time with regard to government spending. Programmes such as PL 480 are likely to continue at similar levels. However, export programmes such as the Market Promotion Program may be reduced. The future of the Export Enhancement Program (EEP) is more likely to be determined by what happens at the GATT negotiations and by perceived competition from other developed countries rather than by the budget.

The effect of the contemplated programme changes on decoupling and market liberalization is unclear. Elimination of the 0/92 and 50/92 programmes would be a retrenchment from decoupling while the increase in mandatory flexible acres ineligible for support payments from 15 to 25 percent would enhance the decoupling process. Increased supply, including for export, from

OECD COUNTRIES

lower programme participation would lower prices in world markets and, to the extent that this would precipitate further government intervention to control supplies, the earlier movement towards market liberalization would be reversed.

The recent situation and policy developments

Situation. Relatively strong prices at planting time, a relaxation of government planting restrictions and generally favourable weather conditions led to larger harvests of nearly all major United States programme crops, particularly maize, in 1992. Despite stronger exports, privately held stocks of nearly all cereals (especially maize) – including the Farmer-Owned Reserve (FOR) – grew during the 1992/93 marketing year. Government-held stocks remained near the minimum needed to maintain the 4 million tonne Food Security Wheat Reserve (FSWR) and to operate food relief programmes.

Export assistance. It was proposed that the level of export credit guarantees be maintained at the same level in FY 1994 as in 1993 – $5 billion for short-term guarantees, $500 million for medium-term guarantees and $200 million for guarantees of sales to emerging democracies. The administration's budget proposal assumes as much as $1 billion in EEP bonuses in 1994 compared with an estimated $1.2 billion in 1993 and $968 million in 1992.

Food aid. PL 480 food assistance was estimated to be $1 698.9 million in FY 1993 compared with $ 1 604.5 million in 1992. A reduction to $1 618.1 million was proposed for 1994 as part of the administration's deficit-reduction programme. The proposal for 1994 would finance an estimated 6.3 million tonnes of commodities, about the same amount as in 1992 but approximately 200 000 tonnes less than was estimated for 1993. East European countries are increasingly becoming recipients of United States food aid under PL 480 Title I credit sales, accounting for 37 percent of the 2.5 million tonnes of commodities that had been allocated as of mid-May 1993. In addition, the United States in April 1993 pledged $700 million (including $200 million for transport costs) to the Russian Federation: this was to finance $433.5 million in credit sales of agricultural commodities and $66.5 million in donations under the Food For Progress (FFP) programme. An additional

OECD COUNTRIES

$194 million is to be used for direct food aid donations provided under the Section 416(b) surplus disposal programme and FFP programme.

EUROPEAN ECONOMIC COMMUNITY
Common Agricultural Policy reform

The State of Food and Agriculture 1992 presented an overview of the main elements of the Common Agricultural Policy (CAP) reform, approved in June 1992. This section views the reform package in the context of the problems it intends to address and the effects it is expected to have in the coming years.

The reform of the CAP constitutes a response to a series of problems that had been building up within the European Economic Community (EEC) over a number of years. The price-driven support system was leading increasingly to overproduction, as a continuously expanding farm output was outstripping demand. The budgetary costs associated with the disposal of increasing surpluses through stockpiling and export subsidies had continued to grow steadily in spite of virtually static producer prices since 1985. Attempts to cut costs and curb surpluses throughout the 1980s had proved insufficient. Furthermore, in spite of the high budgetary costs of maintaining the price support system in addition to the costs borne by consumers through higher prices, it was felt that the CAP no longer provided the desired support to farmers, particularly small farmers and those in less favoured regions, who were unable to take full advantage of more intensive production methods and, therefore, to benefit from the price support mechanisms in the same way as larger farming units. Indeed, prior to reform, more than 80 percent of EEC spending on agricultural support went to less than 20 percent of the Community's farmers. An additional problem in many areas of the EEC was the overexploitation of land with intensive fertilizer use.

The specific elements of the reform package agreed in 1992 were presented in greater detail in *The State of Food and Agriculture 1992*. The agreed reforms will be phased in gradually over the marketing years 1993/94, 1994/95 and 1995/96. When fully implemented, the reforms should have a major impact on EEC agriculture, at once affecting production, farm incomes, farm structures and the environment.

Farm production

Farm production will be affected by the various changes in the market regimes as well as by some of the accompanying measures such as the afforestation and

environmental programmes. For *arable crops* (cereals, oilseeds and protein plants), various elements in the reform package will have a limiting effect on production. This should be the case for the significant cereal price cuts, which will bring the intervention price down to 100 ECU per tonne by 1995/96, and the abolition of guaranteed prices for protein crops from 1993/94 (guaranteed prices for oilseeds were already abolished from the marketing year 1992/93).

In addition, the set-aside requirements for producers to qualify for the direct payments designed to compensate for the price cuts will have a limiting effect on the production of arable crops. The initial set-aside requirement has been fixed at 15 percent of arable cropland on a rotational basis, but this can be modified yearly in the light of the market situation. Small farmers who produce less than 92 tonnes of cereals will, however, be exempt from the set-aside obligation and will still qualify for compensatory direct payments. Land devoted to arable crops may also be reduced through the absorption of land by forestry as a result of the afforestation programme.

The production of arable crops may be further reduced by some of the elements in the new environmental programme; namely, measures to promote extensive of crop production, long-term set-aside for environmental reasons and the conversion of arable land into extensive pasture.

Although the total effect of all the above measures on arable crops is very difficult to quantify, the Commission of the European Communities (CEC) has attempted to estimate production for 1999. For *cereals,* production estimates for 1999 were based on a hypothetical set-aside rate of 15 percent and the absorption of 1 million ha of arable land by the long-term set-aside and afforestation schemes.

These assumptions signify a drop in total EEC cereal area from 36 million ha in 1991/92 and 35.7 million ha in 1992/93 to 33.3 million in 1999/2000. On the further assumption of yields stabilizing at the levels of 1991/92, total EEC cereal production in 1999/2000 is projected to be 167 million tonnes compared with 181 million tonnes in 1991/92 and 166 million tonnes in the drought-affected crop year 1992/93. If yields are assumed to continue increasing at 1 percent per year (somewhat lower than the 1.8 percent annual increase

recorded over the last five years), production in 1999/2000 should reach 177 million tonnes.

Meat production will be affected mainly by the changes in the beef regime and the decrease in feed prices following the cereal price cuts. *Beef* producers will be directly affected by the 15 percent cut in intervention prices but this will be counterbalanced by the decrease in feed prices following the price cuts for arable crops. Farmers raising beef cattle on grazing land will be compensated through direct payments in the form of increases in the various premiums paid for livestock units. However, to encourage extensive production, premiums will only be awarded for livestock units not exceeding established maximum density limits (livestock units per hectare of forage area). Smallholdings with less than 15 livestock units will, however, be exempted from these limits. The impact of density requirements on production may be somewhat limited, since exceeding the maximum density does not imply forfeiting premiums on the entire herd, but only on the livestock units in excess of the maximum density limit. As for *other animal products*, no changes have been introduced to the marketing regimes for pork, poultry and eggs, the producers of which, on the other hand, will benefit from the lower feed prices. This should tend to stimulate production of these products and make EEC producers more competitive.

Overall, CEC projections of *meat* production in 1999 reflect the expected impact of the reform on various products. Indeed, a reduction is forecast for beef production, which should drop to 8.1 million tonnes in 1999 from 8.7 million tonnes in 1991 and 8.4 million tonnes in 1992. Pork production, on the other hand, is projected to reach 15.3 million tonnes in 1999 compared with 14.3 million and 14.2 million tonnes in 1991 and 1992, respectively, while poultry production is projected to increase from 6.7 million tonnes in 1991 and 6.9 million tonnes in 1992 to 7.8 million tonnes in 1999.

Milk production in the EEC is largely determined by milk quotas, which are to be reduced by 2 percent if required by market conditions. At the same time, the butter price will be cut by 5 percent. Consequently, a shift is to be expected from butter production towards cheese and fresh dairy products in line with present trends in the consumption of dairy products.

OECD COUNTRIES

Farm incomes and farm structures

As for *farm incomes*, the impact of the price cuts in the reform package will be offset by direct payments to farmers in the form of compensatory amounts or premiums not related to current production. For arable crops, the price cuts are designed to be offset by direct payments, provided farmers comply with the annual set-aside requirements for land devoted to arable crops. The compensatory payment, granted on a per hectare basis, will be calculated regionally on the basis of the average of certain past yields (tonnes per hectare) which will be multiplied by the compensatory amount (ECU per tonne). Thus, per hectare compensation payments will vary between regions.

The compensatory payment is designed to deliver, on average, full compensation for the price cuts (or for the abolition of guaranteed prices). However, compensation within each region will be biased in favour of producers with yields below the regional average and who will be more than compensated for the loss in their income caused by the price cuts. More efficient producers with higher yields will suffer a loss. As for animal production, the cuts in beef prices will be compensated by the reduction in feed prices and by premium increases. The maximum density limits for premiums will favour producers practising less intensive cattle production, while limits on the total number of animals per herd eligible for premiums will limit payments made to large producers. With no changes introduced in the market regimes for pork, poultry and eggs, the lower feed prices may have a positive impact on producers' incomes for these products, although increased production may lead to lower margins.

Based on representative samples of holdings from the European Communities' Farm Accountancy Data Network,[43] the Commission has simulated the effect of the reform on arable crop producers as well as beef and dairy farmers.

The simulations are static: they assess the impact of all adopted measures at the end of the transition period when all measures are fully operational and they assume that farmers do not adapt resource use and production plans to the new incentives provided by the policy reforms. The simulations indicate that, for all the considered types of dairy and cattle farms, farm incomes expressed as farm net value added will increase as a

---

[43] *Agra Europe*, 5 March 1993.

result of the reform. For arable holdings, the impact will differ according to the farm size and small- and medium-sized producers will actually see farm incomes increase. This should be true to a larger extent for small producers, with a cereal production below 92 tonnes, than for medium-sized producers. On the other hand, the largest farms, producing more than 230 tonnes of cereal, will experience a drop in farm net value added.

In general terms, the reform of the CAP implies a closer direction of farm support towards the smaller and less efficient producers, although this effect is significantly less pronounced than it would have been with the original reform proposals submitted by the CEC in 1991.

The effect of the reform on *farm structures* is not clear-cut. Generally, one of the aims of the reform is to maintain the viability of small family-based farms and to slow down the rural exodus. The somewhat improved targeting of support towards this type of farm and more extensive forms of agriculture will work to such an effect. However, the reform of the market regimes is accompanied, *inter alia,* by an early retirement scheme which aims at releasing land either for the enlargement of holdings to improve their economic viability or for non-farm purposes.

CAP reform and the environment
The reform of the CAP is designed (and is expected) to have a positive impact on the environment. Positive effects should be derived from both the reform of the market regimes and the afforestation and the agro-environmental action programme accompanying the market reforms. As far as the reform of the market regimes is concerned, the price cuts will reduce the incentives to increase production through intensification. In addition, there are specific incentives to adopt less intensive production practices.

The *afforestation programme* in its turn will provide financial aid to farmers who wish to use agricultural land for the development of forestry. The financial support can cover: aid for afforestation costs; a per hectare allowance to cover maintenance costs for afforested areas during the first five years; an annual allowance to cover income losses resulting from afforestation of agricultural land; and investment aid for the improvement of woodlands. The precise impact of the

programme is difficult to foresee and will depend in part on implementation at the national level.

The *agro-environmental programme* has a broader scope and will provide financial assistance for a series of measures aimed at improving the rural environment. These include:

- the adoption of farming practices that reduce agricultural pollution;
- the "extensification" of both crop and livestock farming;
- land use that is compatible with the protection of the environment, soil and landscapes;
- the preservation of local breeds;
- the upkeep of abandoned farmland and woodlands where necessary for ecological and safety reasons;
- long-term set-aside of land for environmental reasons;
- the training of farmers in environmentally friendly farming and in the upkeep of the countryside.

As in the case of the afforestation programme, the precise impact of the agro-environmental programme is also difficult to assess and will depend on national implementation.

What the CAP reform does not do
Although the reform approved in 1992 will introduce far-reaching changes to the CAP, it will not change some of its basic principles and mechanisms such as common prices decided by the European Council of Ministers, common protection against agricultural imports by the use of variable levies, the use of export subsidies to render EEC products competitive on world markets and public intervention in agricultural markets. Thus, the reform may serve to reduce production and internal surpluses for some products as well as levels of export refunds. However, because of reduced feed prices, the production of pork, poultry and eggs will probably be stimulated.

Generally, however, the reform will not change the rules of access for agricultural imports to the EEC market or for EEC agricultural exports to the world market. For most products the preferential treatment of EEC producers *vis-à-vis* importers on the internal market remains. Insofar as the double pricing system stays in place, i.e. internal guaranteed agricultural prices are set

OECD COUNTRIES

independently of world market prices, EEC farm producers and consumers will continue to be largely isolated from price changes on the world market as long as world market prices do not rise above the internal guaranteed price levels.

JAPAN
An agriculture in transition

For the past couple of decades Japanese agriculture has been undergoing a quiet revolution and the forces of change, both internal and external, have been intensifying. In recognition of this mounting pressure, in May 1991 the Ministry of Agriculture, Forestry and Fisheries set up a task force to develop new basic policy directions to meet the changing situation and challenges in the food and agricultural sector and in rural areas. In June 1992, the ministry issued the task force's report, *The Basic Direction of New Policies for Food, Agriculture and Rural Areas*, which it then adopted as its future policy guidelines, submitting several bills and budgetary proposals to the 1993 session of the Diet.

This section of *The State of Food and Agriculture 1993* reports on the current situation of Japanese agriculture, the forces being exerted both for and against change and the problems that must be faced and overcome as Japanese agriculture is further integrated into the international trade and economic system leading up to the twenty-first century.

Setting. With a total land area of 378 000 km², Japan is larger than Italy but smaller than Sweden and Thailand. It is largely mountainous and abundantly forested, more rugged and precipitous than most of western Europe and has rivers that flow more rapidly. Situated in the southern part of the temperate zone, the climate ranges from subtropical in the south to much colder conditions on the northern Hokkaido Island where severe winters are common. Approximately 70 percent of Japan is mountainous with only 14 percent of the total land area devoted to agriculture, of which slightly more than half is paddy field for rice production. With 124 million people, Japan has the fourth largest population in Asia and the Pacific.

The Japanese political system is a bicameral parliamentary democracy. The government is highly centralized with executive power vested in the Cabinet headed by the prime minister, the leader of the parliamentary majority. The Liberal-Democratic Party, which had held the majority in the Diet from the postwar period until July 1993, had come under serious political pressure from Japanese voters, including business and labour union leaders, who wanted a drastic

political reform, and farm groups who opposed liberalization of the domestic agricultural market.

After decades of being the miracle economy of the industrialized world, Japan is in the midst of a serious economic slow-down. According to the *World Bank Atlas 1992,* GNP real growth for the period 1980-1991 averaged a strong 4.3 percent annually. Per caput income growth averaged 3.7 percent annually during the same period. The weakening of the economy, which began in the last quarter of 1991, led to a decline in GDP growth to 1.8 percent in 1992 from 4.4 percent in 1991 and 5.2 percent in 1990. However, estimated unemployment and inflation remained low at 1.9 percent and 2.2 percent, respectively.

Agriculture accounted for 2 percent of GDP in 1991, while 5.9 percent of the total population was counted as agricultural. Since 1988, Japan has been the largest net importer of agricultural products, importing a value of $29 billion in 1991.

The agricultural sector

Total agricultural land in Japan in 1991 was 5 204 000 ha, of which 2 825 000 ha, or 54 percent, was paddy field. Since 1975, agricultural land has been declining in favour of non-farm uses at an average annual rate of about 22 000 ha, almost all of which has been taken out of paddy production. The number of farm households dropped from six million in 1960 to 3.7 million in 1992 (9 percent of total Japanese households) and is expected to decline further to less than three million by the year 2000.

Another distinguishing characteristic of Japanese agriculture is the small size of landholdings per farm household. Of all commercial farms in 1991, fully 58 percent were less than 1 ha while only 13 percent were more than 2 ha in size. But the size of holdings tells only part of the story. Landholdings are also very fragmented, with a single household's landholdings scattered around a farm village in a complicated system of cross-holding to reduce the risk of total crop failure. For example, of the country's 2.7 million ha of paddy land, while 50 percent are consolidated in plots of 0.3 ha or more, only 3 percent are in plots of 0.5 ha or more. The target is to enlarge their size to an average of 1 ha or more during the next ten years. In effecting land consolidation and restructuring, the removal of berms and the

reconstruction and levelling of paddy fields into larger sizes is a labour- and investment-intensive operation.

Of the 3.7 million farm households in Japan, 23 percent are classified as non-commercial, with the remaining 77 percent classified as commercial. Of the 2.9 million commercial farm households, only 16 percent are full-time farm households, while the remaining 84 percent are classified as part-time. Part-time farm households fall into two categories: Type I households, which receive more than 50 percent of their income from farming, and Type II households, which receive less than 50 percent of their income from farming. Type I farm households account for 19 percent and Type II for 81 percent of part-time farms. Thus, of the 3.7 million farm households in 1992, only 897 000 were commercial, engaged either full time or part time in farming and with more than 50 percent of their income (Type I) derived from farming. Moreover, only about 7 percent of the income of Type II farm households comes from farming, with the rest coming from non-farm sources. This means that the actual amount of labour devoted to farming has declined much more dramatically than the decline in the number of farm households would suggest.

Some basic trends related to the agricultural sector include the decline of agriculture as a portion of total GNP; continued rural-urban migration; an ageing population of farmers with few new entrants; and a relatively slow increase in average farm size. In fact, the labour shortage in agriculture has become acute. Today, 4 to 5 percent of the land classified as agricultural is idle, mainly because of a lack of labour. New graduate entrants to agriculture have declined rapidly and, at present, number only about 2 000 per year. The reasons are lower per caput income in agriculture; harder work and more onerous working conditions, including longer hours than those of urban counterparts; and the uncertain outlook for agriculture, exacerbated by the GATT talks and external pressures to liberalize. In addition, in the more remote areas young women tend to migrate to the city, making it difficult for the young men who remain to find wives. While farm household disposable income is 133 percent of non-farm household disposable income, per caput disposable income is only 92 percent, since farm households comprise more members than non-farm households.

Agricultural marketing policy

One of the main instruments of Japanese agricultural policy is the Staple Food Control System, administered by the Food Agency of the Ministry of Agriculture, Forestry and Fisheries. The objective of the Staple Food Control System is to control the supply, based on estimated demand, and the price of rice, wheat and barley. Although the bulk of staple grains are sold through collectors and agricultural cooperatives directly to wholesalers rather than to the government, the whole system is controlled by the Food Agency.

The mechanisms for controlling rice differ from those for wheat and barley. Japan is self-sufficient in rice, its major staple food, whereas it is far from self-sufficient in wheat and barley. Direct quantitative control of supply is applied to rice. Under the Food Control Law, an annual basic plan is drawn up to project the next year's rice demand, and supply is then adjusted to meet that demand through the use of production controls, including crop diversion. Each producer must then sell a specified quantity of rice to the government for the purpose of stabilizing volume and price. Standard-priced rice is government rice sold through registered wholesalers and retailers, with the government setting the maximum price that can be charged to the consumer. Standard-priced rice is a standard-quality rice sold at a lower price than voluntary marketed rice (VMR) to meet market demand.

VMR, which was instituted in 1969, still comes under government control. While the government sets the price for its rice purchases, the price for VMR is negotiated between national collectors' organizations and wholesale organizations. In order to overcome the lack of transparency and the rigidity of the pricing mechanism, VMR exchanges were established in August 1990 in two locations (Tokyo and Osaka), and the rice marketed through those exchanges is sold by tender.

Annual rice consumption in Japan is approximately 10 million tonnes. As 3.5 million tonnes are consumed by producers, 6.5 million tonnes are sold into the market and 2 million of these are purchased by the government as standard rice and for market control. The remaining 4.5 million tonnes are sold as VMR, of which 1 million tonnes are sold by auction at the Tokyo and Osaka exchanges. The auction price is allowed to fluctuate by approximately 7 percent between established maximum

and minimum prices. This is the VMR price discovery mechanism. Rice distributors estimate that 2 to 3 million tonnes of rice flow through the "open under-the-table market", or open black market, with most of the remainder flowing through the agricultural cooperatives directly to rice wholesalers and on to the retail market.

A growing market economy in rice distribution has been exerting its power in many ways, even though the food control law is still in force. In the face of a declining demand for rice, growers are increasingly producing high-quality rice for regional brand names and high-quality products. Organic rice, i.e. rice produced without chemicals, whether they be pesticides or mineral fertilizers, can be sold directly by farmers to consumer groups under contract. In addition, private mail order systems have been developed to deliver rice directly from farmers to consumers in remote cities.

Since rice carryover stocks have declined in recent years, the government has relaxed the production adjustment control scheme in order to obtain sufficient stocks for market control and provide enough standard-quality rice to the retail shops.

The mechanism for controlling the wheat and barley markets is indirect with a guaranteed minimum producer price. While it is not a requirement, domestic producers sell virtually all their wheat and barley to the government. The government sets the purchase and sale prices and agricultural cooperatives are encouraged to negotiate quantity distribution contracts with end-users. The Food Agency purchases domestically produced wheat at a subsidized producer price that is substantially higher then the price it charges to processors. Based on projections of requirements, each week the government issues licences through the Food Agency for wheat and barley imports, thus maintaining market stability. The Agency is the sole buyer of imported wheat and barley.

Agricultural cooperatives. Agricultural cooperatives are pervasive in the lives of Japanese farmers. There are two types of agricultural cooperative: the multipurpose type which engages in marketing farm products, input supply, credit, mutual insurance, processing, advisory and other services; and the single-purpose type which concentrates on marketing the products of certain specialized sectors such as fruit, vegetables and livestock products.

There are three tiers to the organization of these cooperatives: the local-level cooperatives; the prefectural cooperative federations, which specialize in various kinds of services such as credit, savings, marketing, purchasing and insurance; and the national cooperative federations.

The national tier includes: the Norinchukin Bank which, with 50 percent of farmer savings, ranks number one in deposits and credits; the Zenkyoren National Mutual Insurance Federation of Agricultural Cooperatives; a medium-sized insurance company; an import and export trading firm; a national medical and welfare federation; a national press and information federation; a publishing house; a tourist corporation which ranks sixth in the country; and the National Federation of Agricultural Cooperative Associations (ZEN-NOH), a conglomerate which ranks eighth among Japanese trading companies and involves about 140 companies and affiliates with annual sales of around $60 billion, as well as the federation's policy-making body and political lobbying arm, the Central Union of Agricultural Cooperatives (ZENCHU). The agricultural cooperative structure has been described as giving cradle-to-grave service to its members as well as having a powerful political influence via the ruling party over government policies affecting agriculture.

Farmers constitute the regular members of the cooperatives who have voting rights. There is also a non-voting associate member class for non-farmers who want to take advantage of cooperative services. While almost all farmers are members of the cooperatives, associate members number about one-third of total membership. Farmer members have declined (from 5.9 million in 1970 to 5.5 million in 1990) while associate members have increased (from 1.3 million in 1970 to 2.9 million in 1990). Employees of the multipurpose cooperatives number about 300 000; that is, one employee for every 18 farmer members.

The government implements much of its agricultural policy through the cooperative system. When agricultural products are covered by government price support subsidies, the subsidies are paid to the producers through the cooperatives. In addition, the rice land diversion programme (through which one-third of paddy land has been diverted to other crops, since the per caput consumption of rice fell from a high of 118 kg

in 1962 to 70 kg in 1989) is implemented at the local level by the cooperative system together with the administrative authorities. In 1989, about 95 percent of rice, 96 percent of wheat, more than 90 percent of barley and more than 50 percent of fruit, vegetables, beef cattle and milk was marketed through the agricultural cooperative system. In addition, on the input supply side, more than 90 percent of fertilizer, 70 percent of farm chemicals, 64 percent of petroleum used on farms, 50 percent of farm machinery and 40 percent of feed was purchased from the cooperative system.

The cooperatives do not compete with each other at the local level and the system operates according to egalitarian principles. Farmers often have little alternative but to sell to the local agricultural cooperative and are likewise pressed to buy inputs from the cooperative. Given the egalitarianism, large farmers cannot receive significant favourable returns from their cooperatives, such as volume discounts for inputs or volume premiums for sale of their products, which they usually expect from rural commercial firms. Thus, they cannot benefit from economies of size in their marketing or input purchasing activities.

The agricultural cooperative system is having to adjust rapidly to a new set of realities. In addition to financial problems related to the slowing of the general economy and financial deregulation, the volume of agricultural products flowing through the cooperatives is declining. There is a tendency for larger producer members to shift from their traditional marketing channels through cooperatives to others, including direct marketing to consumers.

Local cooperatives are being merged and consolidated with the aim of reducing the number of general purpose cooperatives to about 1 000, less than one-third of the present number, by the year 2000. In addition, integration of the prefectural federations with the national federations is being considered as local-level cooperatives are consolidated.

Beef market liberalization. After protracted negotiations, Japan decided to end the quota system on beef imports in 1988. The quota system was replaced by tariffs which began in 1991 at 70 percent *ad valorem*, dropping to 60 percent on 1 April 1992 and to 50 percent on 1 April

1993. Beef stocks increased because supplies, including imports, exceeded demand in 1989 and 1990 before returning to 1988 levels by early 1992. During this period, the price of high-grade beef, including Wagyu beef, remained relatively stable while the low-grade price, that is for dairy beef, dropped by about 25 to 35 percent, depending on the grade. In addition, there was a dramatic shift in demand from frozen to fresh and chilled beef. The high-grade beef price has dropped recently, mainly because of the tightening of the economy.

Since the major impact of liberalization was on the relatively low-grade beef coming from the dairy herds, dairy farmers were the most severely hurt. While milk prices were unaffected, the price of dairy beef calves sold to feeders dropped significantly.

To help compensate for the dairy producers' losses, the government provides deficiency payments to cattle feeders. Feeders are expected to pass these payments back to dairy producers by paying higher prices for their feeder calves. Still, since the liberalization of the beef market, the number of dairy farms has decreased by 20 percent. Interestingly, however, the size of the national dairy herd has not been reduced, so a considerable consolidation of dairy herds has been achieved in the process.

The liberalization of the beef market has lowered domestic prices and introduced a market competitiveness to which Japanese farmers have responded by aiming for quality. Dairy beef feeders welcome the lower calf prices, while the government subsidizes the calf prices paid to dairy farmers by the feeders with deficiency payments.

Per caput beef consumption in Japan now stands at 6.2 kg per year, with the rate of increase having slowed from 10.9 percent in 1989 and 1990 to 1.6 percent in 1991.

Agriculture and the environment

Throughout Japan's history there has been a close relationship between water management and agriculture. Japan has rapidly flowing rivers because of its very steep mountains and there is consequently little pollution buildup in the rivers. However, at the outlets of the rivers, pollution is beginning to appear in the sea. Agricultural pollution comes mainly from agricultural

chemicals and fertilizers and animal husbandry wastes. Paddy comprises just over half of the total cultivated area and acts as a reservoir, filtering water to the groundwater level. On uplands, nitrogen fertilizer becomes nitric acid. On paddy, there is no oxygen so nitrogen fertilizer is transformed into ammonium which is fixed in the soil while some nitrogen is released as gas. Thus, there is noticeably more chemical- and fertilizer-induced pollution of groundwater in upland areas than in paddy areas.

Japanese Government policy first addressed sustainable agriculture in FY 1992. Sustainable agriculture is defined by the country's Ministry of Agriculture, Forestry and Fisheries as agriculture using lower than normal inputs of chemicals and fertilizer. It must meet two basic criteria: sustainable yields and quality; and the reduced use of chemicals and mineral fertilizer.

Two major technologies introduced to encourage sustainable agriculture are time-release fertilizers and biological and integrated pest management. Another means of insect control that has been used in Japan is to lure male insects into a concentrated area by using the scent or sound of the female insect and then disposing of them in that limited area.

Another programme being promoted by the Ministry of Agriculture, Forestry and Fisheries is the recycling of animal waste. Animal waste is processed into fertilizer under contracts between crop and livestock farmers. The ministry helps by establishing facilities to process the manure, by establishing demonstration farms and by providing extension services.

The incentive for farmers to engage in sustainable agriculture at present is not so much an economic factor but rather more an altruistic caring for future generations. There is technology evolving that should reduce input use and costs. For example, there is now a rice transplanter with a chemical applicator that puts the chemicals and fertilizer in close proximity to the seedling, thereby reducing overall use.

The ministry is now concentrating on fruit and vegetable farms where chemical use is the largest. In general, however, it instructs prefecture governments to review and revise their fertilizer application and pest control standards for the purpose of maintaining environmental quality.

New policy directions

Several factors and trends are converging at present and leading to major structural changes in Japanese agriculture as well as to a rethinking of agricultural policy. The more important of these factors are the following:

- The strengthening of the Japanese yen, which means that agricultural imports are less expensive and will continue to increase.
- The depopulation of rural areas, the deterioration of rural infrastructure and the loss of amenities as the number of farm successors and new entrants decline and the ageing of the farm population accelerates because of lower incomes, hard work and long working hours as well as more favourable job opportunities outside farming.
- The declining demand for rice, resulting in the conversion and abandonment of paddy fields which, in turn, has a deleterious impact on water quality and the environment.
- The small and fragmented structure of agricultural holdings, which reduces or prevents farmers from introducing cost-saving technology such as direct rice planting.
- The need to liberalize the agricultural import markets further as the internationalization of agriculture continues.
- The declining food self-sufficiency ratio in terms of national calories supplied, which stood at 46 percent in 1991.

It is widely recognized that many current trends are unfavourable to agriculture and rural areas. In view of the urgency of the situation facing Japanese agriculture, the Ministry of Agriculture, Forestry and Fisheries has begun a process of sectoral reform with a task force which, after exchanging views with people and organizations nationwide, submitted its report, *The Basic Direction of New Policies for Food, Agriculture and Rural Areas*, in June 1992. The report spells out structural targets and, as previously stated, provides broad guidelines for the reform of the agricultural sector and the transformation of rural areas. New laws and budgets are being proposed to achieve a comprehensive reform over a ten-year period.

Under the new policy, the structural targets – which

constitute the heart of the plan to make Japanese agriculture more efficient and competitive – relate to the size of holdings and the form of management. At the end of ten years, the target is to have 300 000 to 400 000 individual farm management bodies (single farm households), 150 000 of which will be engaged in rice cultivation, including 50 000 in single-crop rice farming with 10 to 20 ha and 100 000 in multiple-crop farming (including rice) with 5 to 10 ha. In addition, there would be 40 000 to 50 000 organized farm management bodies (management associations of several types, including agricultural producer cooperatives, small-scale corporations and agricultural production associations) managing single-crop rice holdings of 30 to 50 ha.

As part of the implementation of the new policy, new laws that were passed in 1993 provide for each community to set its goals for agricultural reform under the policy and to determine how to organize itself, e.g. into an individual cooperative or a limited partnership, in order to increase the size of farm management holdings. In the end, more than 3 000 municipalities will govern the reform along the lines of their own objectives, with the national government supporting their decisions with price and structure policies. The necessary budget has been appropriated in FY 1993 for carrying out this policy at national, prefectural and municipal levels.

The future envisioned for Japanese agriculture and rural communities will require enormous investments, and many difficult problems will have to be solved. The price of farmland in the area covered by the Urban Planning Law is extremely high. The law concerning reserved farmland in the urbanization promotion area was revised in 1991 and aims at promoting the conversion of farmland for urbanization and at easing the pressure on land prices and on the housing market. Formerly, farmland was protected from urbanization and was valued for tax purposes as agricultural land, thereby giving farmers a major tax break. Under the new law, farmers in the urban fringe can declare their land either agricultural or ready for urban development. If they declare their land agricultural, they must do so for 30 years, in which case they are eligible for the lower agricultural tax rates. If they declare the land ready for urban development, they will be taxed based on the higher urban market price. This should ease farmland

OECD COUNTRIES

prices and rental values, at least for the 1 percent of total farmland affected by the law.

The tradition of ownership and cross-holding is also a constraint to increasing the size of farms. Prefectural corporations for land aggregation and farmland development purchase land and rent or sell that land to other farmers in an effort to accelerate land consolidation and the increase in farm sizes. These corporations are likely to be used by the Ministry of Agriculture, Forestry and Fisheries to help implement the new policy. This would mean that the ministry would infuse the corporations with rather large amounts of funding in order to accelerate their ability to purchase and resell or rent agricultural properties.

Some analysts suggest that the government plan to incorporate a number of farms into a single legal entity, such as a limited partnership, may meet with limited success, even though there are already 3 800 agricultural production corporations in existence. If all of the shareholders are family members, it may work – at least for the first generation – but non-family members may not be willing to subject themselves to others managing their property. However, there is an agricultural committee system responsible for the administration of farmlands under ministerial direction. There are committees in each of the prefectures which, in turn, have a network of committees at the municipal level. These agricultural committees appear to have a major function in observing the terms of sale and rental of farmland in each of the various municipalities and communities in Japan. The agricultural committees, the technical advisors in the agricultural cooperatives and the agricultural extension officers are likely to be consolidated into a comprehensive system in each jurisdiction. This system would then become the focal point for the promotion of family and non-family corporations or limited partnership farms and for promoting the full use of agricultural land. The latter will obviously be an attempt to incorporate the land that is now held by Type II part-time farmers into more serious production units.

Progress made in achieving the objectives of the new policy would help Japanese agriculture operate in a global economy. The enlargement and consolidation of paddy fields would lower labour inputs and improve rice production efficiency. The direct seeding of rice rather

than transplanting would allow a huge decrease in labour input, from 50 hours to produce 0.1 ha of rice down to five hours. This, along with other economies of size that could be realized under the new policy directions, could reduce production costs by more than 50 percent.

However, some large and powerful political forces are resistant to change. Past attempts to decentralize government activities and to reduce the role of government, including in the agricultural sector, have been opposed by state employee labour unions. The cooperative system's employee labour union also views the status quo as the best protection of their own interests. The strong resistance to change in Japanese agriculture amounts, in part, to a labour issue involving both government and agricultural cooperative employees as well as farmers. This issue will need to be resolved in order for the full reforms visualized in *The Basic Direction of New Policies for Food Agriculture and Rural Areas* to be achieved.

Having begun the reform of its agriculture during a period of weakened general economic activity, the necessary steps for reform will be more difficult to implement than they would have been when the economy was booming. The recent slowing of the general economy will at least make the allocation of the necessary investment funds for agricultural reform more difficult. The reforms suggested in the new policy report represent a massive undertaking for the planned ten-year period but the Japanese Government has taken the initial legal and budgetary steps to effect the indicated reforms and appears committed to seeing them through.

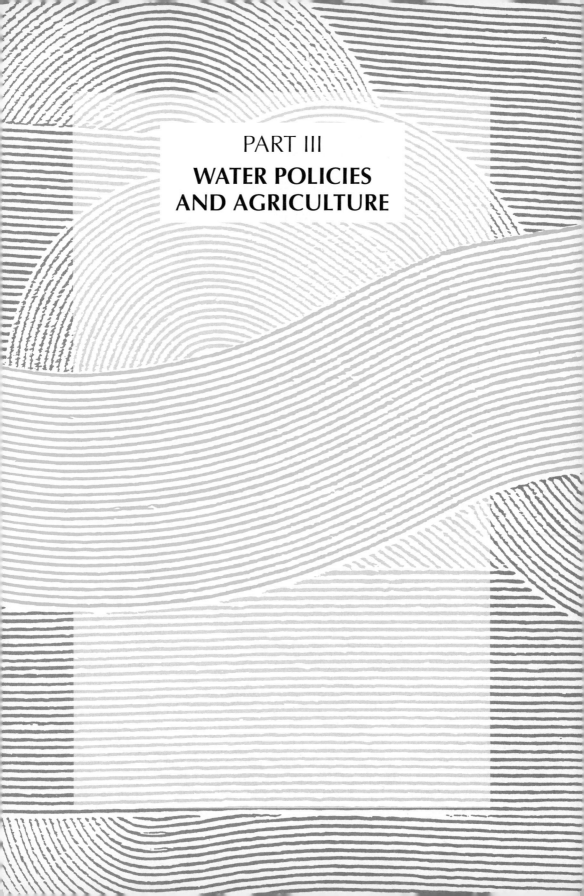

PART III
WATER POLICIES
AND AGRICULTURE

BOX 7
GLOSSARY: WATER TERMS

Aquifer
An underground stratum that is saturated with water and transmits water readily.

Command and control
A system of water supply or quality management based on administrative allocations (in contrast to incentive or price-based allocations).

Cost recovery
Fee structures to cover the cost of providing a service.

Demand management
The use of economic, legal, institutional and other policy interventions to influence the demand for water.

Drip irrigation
Localized drop-by-drop application of water that uses pipes, tubes, filters, emitters and ancillary devices to deliver water to specific sites at a point or grid on the soil surface.

Ecosystem
A complex system formed by the interaction of a community of organisms with its environment.

Externality
The uncompensated, unintended side-effects of one party's actions on another party.

Gravity irrigation
A system that depends on sloping canals and fields for the transportation of water to the irrigated site.

Groundwater table
The level of water storage (above mean sea level) in an aquifer; hence, the point at which the soil is fully saturated with water.

Irrigated area
i) **Gross irrigated area.** The area of land irrigated in a year (land having two irrigation seasons is counted twice).
ii) **Net irrigated area.** The area of land surface that receives irrigation water in a year (two irrigation seasons are counted as one).

Irrigation
Human intervention to modify the distribution of water in natural channels, depressions, drainageways or aquifers and to manipulate this water for improving the production of agricultural crops or enhancing the growth of other desirable plants.

Riparian state
A state through or along which a portion of a river flows or in which a lake lies.

River basin
A geographical area determined by the watershed limits of a system of waters, including surface and underground waters, flowing into a common terminus.

Seepage
The infiltration of water downwards or laterally into soil or substrata from a source of supply such as a reservoir, irrigation canal or channel.

Sewage
Liquid refuse or waste matter carried off by surface water via sewers.

Sewerage
The removal and disposal of sewage and surface water by sewer systems.

Sustainable development
The management and conservation of the natural resource base and the orientation of technological and institutional change in such a manner as to ensure the attainment and continued satisfaction of human needs for the present and future generations. Such sustainable development (in the agricultural, forestry and fisheries sectors) conserves land, water, plant and animal genetic resources and is

environmentally non-degrading, technically appropriate, economically viable and socially acceptable.

Tube wells
Wells consisting of perforated tubes or pipes placed in holes bored into the ground to tap groundwater supplies from one or more aquifers.

Underflow
The underground flow or movement of water in an aquifer.

Underground transmission
Water distribution by means of underflows within an aquifer system.

Water quality
This is defined by the level of dissolved salts and/or other contaminants. Acceptability may vary with the intended use, i.e. drinking-water requires higher-quality water than irrigation.

Waterlogging and salinization
Unproductive soil conditions that occur when the water table is very near the surface. Waterlogging is caused by overwatering and a lack of proper drainage. Salinity is caused by a combination of poor drainage and high evaporation rates that concentrate salts on irrigated land.

Watershed
An area drained by a river or stream system.

Watershed management
A process of formulating and implementing a course of action that involves natural and human resources, taking into account social, political, economic, environmental and institutional factors that operate within the watershed, the surrounding river basin and other relevant regions, to achieve desired social objectives.

Wetlands
Areas of marsh, fen, peat land or water that include natural, artificial, permanent or temporary areas with either static or flowing fresh, brackish or marine water.

WATER POLICIES AND AGRICULTURE
I. Water resource issues and agriculture

INTRODUCTION AND OVERVIEW

An interesting observation arising from the preparation of this year's special chapter on water and agriculture is how difficult it is to generalize about water. Almost any statement requires qualification. For example, while we can say that water is one of the most abundant resources on earth, we know that less than 1 percent of the total supply is reliably available for human consumption. Water is a liquid for the most part, but it can also be a solid and a vapour. Drinking-water is certainly essential for human survival but water-related illnesses are the most common health threat in the developing world. An estimated 25 000 people die every day as a result of water-related sicknesses.[1]

One statement, however, needs no qualification: human existence depends on water. The geosphere, the atmosphere and the biosphere are all linked to water. Water interacts with solar energy to determine climate and it transforms and transports the physical and chemical substances necessary for all life on earth.

In recent years, water issues have been the focus of increasing international concern and debate. From 26 to 31 January 1992, the UN system sponsored the International

---

[1] UNEP. 1991. *Freshwater pollution.* UNEP/ GEMS Environmental Library. No. 6. Nairobi.

Conference on Water and the Environment (ICWE) in Dublin, Ireland. The ICWE called for innovative approaches to the assessment, development and management of freshwater resources. In addition, the ICWE provided policy guidance for the United Nations Conference on Environment and Development (UNCED) in Rio de Janeiro in June 1992. UNCED highlighted the need for water sector reforms throughout the world.

In 1993, the World Bank issued a comprehensive policy paper defining its new objectives for the water sector. FAO recently established an International Action Programme on Water and Sustainable Agricultural Development (IAP-WASAD). Likewise, the UNDP, WHO, UNICEF, WMO, Unesco and UNEP are all coordinating or participating in special programmes related to water resources.

Other international, national and local organizations are becoming more active in water issues. The 1990 Montreal meeting, "NGOs Working Together", focused attention on drinking-water supply and sanitation. The Canadian International Development Agency, the French Ministry of Cooperation and Development, the German Agency for Technical Cooperation (GTZ), the United Kingdom's Overseas Development Administration and the United States Agency for International Development (USAID) have recently developed water resource strategies for foreign assistance.

The message highlighted by all these efforts is that water is an increasingly scarce and valuable resource. Of principal concern is our failure to recognize and accept that there is a finite supply of water. The consensus is that the growing water scarcity and misuse of freshwater pose serious threats to sustainable development.

Competition among agriculture, industry and cities for limited water supplies is already constraining development efforts in many countries. As populations expand and economies grow, the competition for limited supplies will intensify and so will conflicts among water users.

Despite water shortages, misuse of water is widespread. Small communities and large cities, farmers and industries, developing countries and industrialized economies are all mismanaging water resources. Surface water quality is deteriorating in key basins from urban and industrial wastes.

Groundwater is polluted from surface sources and irreversibly damaged by the intrusion of salt water. Overexploited aquifers are losing their capacity to hold water and lands are subsiding. Cities are unable to provide adequate drinking-water and sanitation facilities. Waterlogging and salinization are diminishing the productivity of irrigated lands. Decreasing water flows are reducing hydroelectric power generation, pollution assimilation and fish and wildlife habitats.

At first glance, most of these water problems do not appear to be directly related to the agricultural sector. Yet, by far the largest demand for the world's water comes from agriculture. More than two-thirds of the water withdrawn from the earth's rivers, lakes and aquifers is used for irrigation. As competition, conflicts, shortages, waste, overuse and degradation of water resources grow, policy-makers look increasingly to agriculture as the system's safety valve.

Agriculture is not only the world's largest water user in terms of volume, it is also a relatively low-value, low-efficiency and highly subsidized water user. These facts are forcing governments and donors to rethink the economic, social and environmental implications of large publicly funded and operated irrigation projects. In the past, domestic spending for irrigation dominated agricultural budgets in countries throughout the world. For instance, since 1940, 80 percent of Mexico's public expenditures in agriculture have been for irrigation projects. In China, Indonesia and Pakistan, irrigation has absorbed more than half of agricultural investment. In India, about 30 percent of all public investment has gone into irrigation.[2]

A significant portion of international development assistance has also been used to establish irrigation systems. Irrigation received nearly 30 percent of World Bank agricultural lending during the 1980s. Spending commitments for irrigation by all aid agencies exceeded $2 billion per year in the past decade.

Once established, irrigation projects become some of the most heavily subsidized economic activities in the world. In the mid-1980s, Repetto [3] estimated that average subsidies to

irrigation in six Asian countries covered 90 percent of the total operating and maintenance costs. Case-studies indicate that irrigation fees are, on average, less than 8 percent of the value of benefits derived from irrigation.

Despite these huge investments and subsidies, irrigation performance indicators are falling short of expectations for yield increases, area irrigated and technical efficiency in water use. As much as 60 percent of the water diverted or pumped for irrigation is wasted.[4] Although some losses are inevitable, in too many cases this excess water seeps back into the ground, causing waterlogging and salinity. As much as one-quarter of all irrigated land in developing countries suffers from varying degrees of salinization.[5] Moreover, stagnant water and poor irrigation drainage escalate the incidence of water-related diseases, resulting in human suffering and increased health costs.

Today, agriculture is often unable to compete economically for scarce water. Cities and industries can afford to pay more for water and earn a higher economic rate of return from a unit of water than does agriculture. (For economists, water flows uphill to money.) For the first time in many countries, agriculture is being obliged to give up water for higher-value uses in cities and industries. Irrigators in some areas are now asked to pay for the water they receive, including the full cost of water delivery. In other

[2] R. Bhatia and M. Falkenmark. 1992. *Water resource policies and the urban poor: innovative approaches and policy imperatives.* Background paper for the ICWE, Dublin, Ireland.

[3] R. Repetto. 1986. *Skimming the water: rent-seeking and the performance of public irrigation systems.* Research Report No. 4. Washington, DC, WRI.

[4] FAO. 1990. *An International Action Programme on Water and Sustainable Agricultural Development.* Rome.

[5] Ibid.

areas, new regulations require farmers to pay for polluting streams, lakes and aquifers.

The irony is that irrigated agriculture is expected to produce much more in the future while using less water than it uses today. At present, 2.4 billion people depend on irrigated agriculture for jobs, food and income (some 55 percent of all wheat and rice output is irrigated). Over the next 30 years, an estimated 80 percent of the additional food supplies required to feed the world will depend on irrigation.[6]

These developments are placing enormous pressure on agricultural policy-makers and farmers. Throughout the world, governments assume the prime responsibility for ensuring food security and, because food depends increasingly on irrigation, food security is closely linked with water security. Between 30 and 40 percent of the world's food comes from the irrigated 16 percent of the total cultivated land; around one-fifth of the total value of fish production comes from freshwater aquaculture; and current global livestock drinking-water requirements are 60 billion litres per day (forecasts estimate an increase of 0.4 billion litres per year). Food security in the next century will be closely allied to success in irrigation.

Irrigation can help make yield-increasing innovations a more attractive investment proposition but it does not guarantee crop yield increases. The overall performance of

many irrigation projects has been disappointing because of poor scheme conception, inadequate construction and implementation or ineffective management. The mediocre performance of the irrigation sector is also contributing to many socio-economic and environmental problems, but these problems are neither inherent in the technology nor inevitable, as is sometimes argued.

Irrigation projects can contribute greatly to increased incomes and agricultural production compared with rain-fed agriculture. In addition, irrigation is more reliable and allows for a wider and more diversified choice of cropping patterns as well as the production of higher-value crops. Irrigation's contribution to food security in China, Egypt, India, Morocco and Pakistan is widely recognized. For example, in India, 55 percent of agricultural output is from irrigated land. Moreover, average farm incomes have increased from 80 to 100 percent as a result of irrigation, while yields have doubled compared with those achieved under the former rain-fed conditions; incremental labour days used per hectare have increased by 50 to 100 percent. In Mexico, half the value of agriculture production and two-thirds of the value of agricultural exports is from the one-third of arable land that is irrigated.

Irrigation is a key component of the technical package needed to achieve productivity gains. In the future, as high levels of costly inputs are added to cropland to sustain yield increases, the security and efficiency of irrigated production will become even more important to world farming. Water will no longer be plentiful and cheap. It will be scarce, expensive to develop

---

[6] International Irrigation Management Institute. 1992. *Developing environmentally sound and lasting improvements in irrigation management: the role of international research.* Colombo, Sri Lanka, IIMI.

and maintain and valuable in use. The prospect of high-cost water may at first seem to be another problem looming for low-income economies. However, the high cost will be an incentive to use water more efficiently. The single most important factor limiting the adoption of proven irrigation and drainage technology is the low cost of water. Moreover, if farmers have opportunities for higher-value uses and can make profits, both governments and farmers will invest in irrigation.

This water dilemma – to produce more in a sustainable way with less water – points to the need for demand management mechanisms to reallocate existing supplies, encourage more efficient use and promote more equitable access. Policy-makers need to establish a structure of incentives, regulations, permits, restrictions and penalties that will help guide, influence and coordinate how people use water while encouraging innovations in water-saving technologies.

In the past, supply-side approaches dominated water resource management practices. Water itself was physically managed through technical and engineering means that captured, stored, delivered and treated water. However, the era of meeting growing demand by developing new supplies is ending. In our present-day water economy, resource management is shifting away from the goal of capturing more water towards that of designing demand- and user-focused approaches that influence behaviour.

PURPOSE AND SCOPE

This special chapter is primarily intended for agricultural policy-makers, water managers, researchers, students, development planners and agricultural project donors. It is meant to help us reflect on the way water resources are managed at present; to contribute to the discussion on sustainable water use; and to stimulate thinking, research and change. Decisions made in this decade regarding how water is used will have a profound effect on our future supplies.

This first section gives an overview of world water resources and briefly discusses the key issues: scarcity, quality and health.

The second section stresses the need to integrate the water sector with the national economy and analyses the physical, economic and social aspects of water. It then provides a conceptual foundation for understanding the circumstances under which water policies either work or fail. Section II also assesses the advantages and disadvantages of broad alternative approaches to public water policy.

Section III examines how policy analysis is applied to water resource planning, including both supply-side (physical and hydrological) and demand-side considerations. It discusses the advantages and disadvantages of various policy options for urgent water policy issues related to surface water and groundwater.

The fourth and final section reviews three specific policy issues in irrigated agriculture: declining growth and investment trends; the difficulties imposed by irrigation-induced environmental degradation; and efforts to reform managerial and administrative systems.

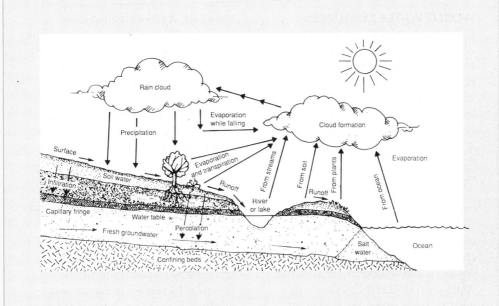

BOX 8

THE HYDROLOGICAL CYCLE

Water continuously circulates on the planet. The hydrological cycle has no beginning or end but we can describe it as starting with the waters of the oceans, which cover about three-quarters of the earth. Radiation from the sun and wind energy, which is itself indirectly derived from solar energy, cause evaporation of water which rises as a vapour and forms clouds. In turn, if conditions are right, these condense and fall back to earth as rain, hail or snow.

Some of this precipitation evaporates from leaves and soil, some runs over the surface and forms streams and some percolates into the soil where it may be drawn on by plants and transpired back into the atmosphere or returned to the surface by soil capillarity. Some soil moisture evaporates and some soaks down below the root zone to join the groundwater reservoir. Groundwater percolates through pores in the soil and rocks and may reappear on the surface at lower elevations as a spring or as seepage into streams and rivers which eventually re-enter the ocean. Still some lies in the groundwater reservoir or aquifer and may be tapped by a mechanical tube well or an open well.

The hydrological cycle illustrated in the Figure is the system by which water circulates from the oceans through the atmosphere and back to the ocean overland and underground. Available freshwater is a rare form of water, for 99 percent is either saline (97 percent of all water is in the ocean) or frozen (2 percent in the ice caps and glaciers). Most of the remainder (1 percent) is groundwater with minute proportions in freshwater lakes, soil moisture, rivers and biological systems.

WORLD WATER RESOURCES

Every day the hydrological cycle renews the world's freshwater resources through evaporation and precipitation (see Box 8). The average annual rainfall over land is 110 000 km^3, but some 70 000 km^3 evaporate before reaching the sea. The remaining 40 000 km^3 are potentially available for human use. Global freshwater consumption is currently around 4 000 km^3, only 10 percent of the annual renewable supply.

These numbers suggest that plenty of water is available for human use but a closer look reveals a more complicated situation. The 40 000 km^3 of available water are distributed very unevenly and two-thirds of it runs off in floods. That leaves around 14 000 km^3 as a relatively stable supply. A substantial share of this supply should be left to follow its natural course in order to safeguard wetlands, deltas, lakes and rivers.[7] For example, 6 000 km^3 of water is needed to dilute and transport the estimated 450 km^3 of waste water now entering the world's rivers each year.[8] Without substantial investment in waste water treatment and more effective regulation, even more water will have to be diverted to dilute and transport wastes.

Precipitation, withdrawals and availability of water vary widely around the world. Table 6 demonstrates regional changes in per caput water availability since 1950 and shows forecasts for 2000. Per caput availability is highest in Latin America and lowest in North Africa and the Near East, while withdrawals are highest in North America and lowest in Africa. Per caput water availability in Europe and North America is not expected to change greatly by 2000, while Asians, Africans and Latin Americans will face less per caput water availability as their populations continue to grow.

At present, Asia accounts for over one-half of the world's water withdrawals. Figure 11 illustrates regional water consumption during the past century. Forecasts to the year 2000 suggest that Asia will consume 60 percent of the world's water, followed by 15 percent in North America, 13 percent in Europe and less than 7 percent in Africa. Latin America's share of world water consumption is forecast to be less than 5 percent in 2000, although the region's consumption has nearly quadrupled since 1950.

Water scarcity

Human actions bring about water scarcity in three ways: through population growth, misuse and inequitable access.[9] Population growth contributes to scarcity simply because the available water supply must be divided among more and more people. Every country has a more or less fixed amount of internal water resources, defined as the average annual flow of rivers and aquifers generated from precipitation. Over time, this internal renewable supply must be divided among more and more people, eventually resulting in water scarcity.

---

[7] S. Postel. 1992. *Last oasis: facing water scarcity.* New York, Norton.

[8] See footnote 1, p. 230.

[9] T.F. Homer-Dixon, J.H. Boutwell and G.W. Rathjens. 1993. Environmental change and violent conflict. *Sci. Am.* (February).

TABLE 6

Per caput water availability by region, 1950-2000

Region	1950	1960	1970	1980	2000
	(.. '000 m³ ....)				
Africa	20.6	16.5	12.7	9.4	5.1
Asia	9.6	7.9	6.1	5.1	3.3
Latin America	105.0	80.2	61.7	48.8	28.3
Europe	5.9	5.4	4.9	4.4	4.1
North America	37.2	30.2	25.2	21.3	17.5

Source: N.B. Ayibotele. 1992. *The world's water: assessing the resource.* Keynote paper at the ICWE, Dublin, Ireland.

When annual internal renewable water resources are less than 1 000 m³ per caput, water availability is considered a severe constraint on socio-economic development and environmental protection. Table 7 lists the countries where per caput internal renewable water availability will fall below 1 000 m³ by the end of this decade. Most countries facing chronic water scarcity problems are in North Africa, the Near East and sub-Saharan Africa. Countries with less than 2 000 m³ per caput face a serious marginal water scarcity situation, with major problems occurring in drought years. By the end of the 1990s, water availability is expected to fall below 2 000 m³ per caput in more than 40 countries.

In many countries, while scarcity is less of a problem at a national level, serious water shortages are causing difficulties in specific regions and watersheds. Notable examples include northern China, western and southern India and parts of Mexico.

People also bring about water scarcity by polluting and overusing existing supplies. Box 9 describes some of the pressing water pollution issues. This type of scarcity can be regarded as the consumption of the resource's "capital". For instance, an aquifer represents resource capital, providing what is generally a renewable source of water "income" that can be tapped for human consumption. Sustainable use of the aquifer leaves the capital intact so that future generations can continuously use the renewable portion or income. If pumping is greater than recharge, the aquifer is depleted and the capital is consumed.

Overuse of groundwater has become a major problem in China, India, Indonesia, Mexico, the Near East, North Africa, Thailand, the western United States and many island countries where seawater intrusion results.

The overpumping of aquifers not only results in a water source that is too depleted to serve as a supply, it may also cause the land above the aquifer to settle or subside, resulting in widespread structural damage in extreme cases. Bangkok and Mexico City are well-known examples.

Finally, a shift in access or distribution patterns may concentrate

TABLE 7

Countries predicted to have scarce water resources in 2000

Country[1]	Population in 2000	Water availability	
		Internal renewable water resources	Water resources including river flows from other countries
	(millions)	*(.... m³ per caput ....)*	
Egypt	62.4	29	934
Saudi Arabia	21.3	103	103
Libyan Arab Jamahiriya	6.5	108	108
United Arab Emirates	2.0	152	152
Jordan	4.6	153	240
Mauritania	2.6	154	2 843
Yemen	16.2	155	155
Israel	6.4	260	335
Tunisia	9.8	384	445
Syrian Arab Republic	17.7	430	2 008
Kenya	34.0	436	436
Burundi	7.4	487	487
Algeria	33.1	570	576
Hungary	10.1	591	11 326
Rwanda	10.4	604	604
Botswana	1.6	622	11 187
Malawi	11.8	760	760
Oman	2.3	880	880
Sudan	33.1	905	3 923
Morocco	31.8	943	943
Somalia	10.6	1 086	1 086

[1] A number of other countries with smaller populations, e.g. Barbados, Cape Verde, Djibouti, Malta, Qatar and Singapore, are also included in the water-scarce category. *Source*: FAO calculations based on World Bank/WRI data.

TABLE 8

Ratio of prices charged by vendors to prices charged by public utilities in selected cities

Country	City	Ratio
Bangladesh	Dacca	12-25
Colombia	Cali	10
Côte d'Ivoire	Abidjan	5
Ecuador	Guayaquil	20
Haiti	Port-au-Prince	17-100
Honduras	Tegucigalpa	16-34
Indonesia	Jakarta	4-60
	Surabaja	20-60
Kenya	Nairobi	7-11
Mauritania	Nouakchott	100
Nigeria	Lagos	4-10
	Onitsha	6-38
Pakistan	Karachi	28-83
Peru	Lima	17
Togo	Lomé	7-10
Turkey	Istanbul	10
Uganda	Kampala	4-9

Source: R. Bhatia and M. Falkenmark. 1992. *Water resource policies and the urban poor: innovative approaches and policy imperatives.* Background paper for the ICWE, Dublin, Ireland.

water resources among one group and subject others to extreme scarcity. In many cities of the developing world, large numbers of people depend on water vendors and may pay 100 times as much as the rate of public utilities (see Table 8). Numerous recent studies document that large numbers of urban poor pay much higher prices and a much larger share of their income for water than families with access to a city water system.[10] Poor families in some large cities spend up to 20 percent of their income on water. When the cost is so high, they use little water for washing and bathing, which results in serious health problems.

---

[10] See footnote 2, p. 232.

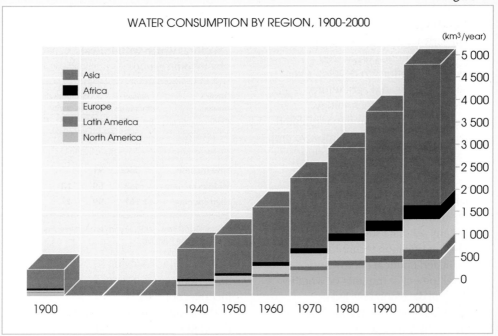

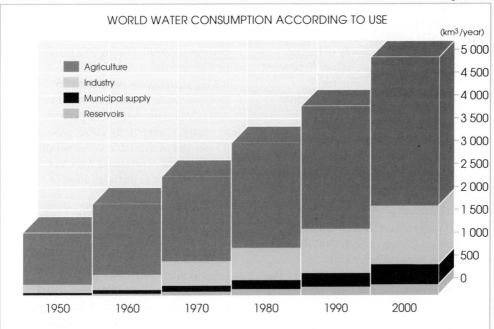

Source: I.A. Shiklomanov. 1990. Global water resources.
Nat. Resour., 26: 34-43

Note: Consumption by reservoirs
is through evaporation

World water use

The early civilizations of Asia, Africa and Latin America organized cooperative efforts to develop river valleys for irrigated agriculture. Through irrigation technology, societies controlled and manipulated natural water supplies to improve crop production. The result was often reliable and ample food supplies which led to the creation of stable agricultural villages, the division of labour and economic surpluses.

Many scholars still argue over whether irrigation technology facilitated political control and development of the state or whether political developments led to advancement of the technology. No matter the direction of cause and effect, no one disputes the association of development with control over water use.

In today's world, agriculture still accounts for the majority of human water use. Globally, around 70 percent of water withdrawals are for agriculture. Domestic and industrial uses consume the remaining 30 percent.[11]

Water uses differ greatly depending on access, quantity, quality and socio-economic conditions. For example, Table 9 illustrates that agricultural water use is higher as a proportion of total water use in the low-income countries (91 percent) than in the high-income group (39 percent). Nevertheless, on a per caput basis, the high-income countries use more water

TABLE 9

Sectoral water withdrawals, by income group

Country income group	Annual withdrawals per caput	Withdrawals by sector		
		Agric.	Ind.	Dom.
	(... m³...)	(............... %.................)		
Low-income	386	91	5	4
Middle-income	453	69	18	13
High-income	1 167	39	47	14

Source: World Bank. 1992. World Development Report 1992, based on WRI data.

for agricultural purposes than the low-income countries.

The trends in world water use during this century are presented in Figure 12. Overall, global water consumption has increased almost tenfold. Agriculture's share, which was 90 percent in 1900, will have dropped to an estimated 62 percent by 2000. During this same period, industrial consumption will have grown from 6 percent to 25 percent, while consumption by cities will have increased from 2 percent to nearly 9 percent. By 2000, around 35 percent of available water supplies will be in use, compared with less than 5 percent at the beginning of the century.

Water quantity and quality requirements also differ widely depending on the type of use. Net agricultural requirements are especially large in relation to other uses. For instance, around 15 000 m³ of water are normally sufficient to irrigate 1 ha of rice. This same amount of water can supply: 100 nomads and 450 head of stock for three years; or 100 rural families through house connections for four years; or 100 urban families for

---

[11] Domestic uses include drinking-water supplies, private homes, commercial establishments, public services and municipal supplies.

BOX 9
WATER AND POLLUTION

The quality of water from different sources varies widely. Precipitation absorbs gases from the atmosphere and removes particles from the air. When the precipitation strikes the ground it becomes surface water runoff or enters the ground. The surface water flows into larger and larger channels, ponds, lakes and rivers until some of it reaches the sea. Along its course, surface water picks up both organic and mineral particles, bacteria and other organisms as well as salts and other soluble substances. The water in lakes and swamps sometimes acquires odours, tastes and colours from algae and other organisms and from decaying vegetation.

Since ancient times, heavy metals from mining and pathogens from cities have caused serious, although localized, contamination. Since the industrial revolution, water pollution problems have become first regional, then continental and now global in nature. Much water is polluted when it is used in industry and agriculture or for domestic purposes. Mining is the major cause of metal contamination, whereas other industries contribute to acidification. The intensification of agricultural activities has led to the contamination of groundwater by fertilizers and other chemicals. Moreover, irrigation projects often cause a rapid rise in the level of groundwater, which leads to waterlogging and soil salinity.

Since 1977, the UNEP/WHO Global Environment Monitoring System (GEMS) has been working with Unesco and WMO to develop a global water quality monitoring network. More than 50 water variables are monitored to provide information on the suitability of water for human consumption and for agricultural, commercial and industrial use. Recent assessments have found that the main water pollutants are: sewage, nutrients, toxic metals and industrial as well as agricultural chemicals.

Conclusions drawn from the GEMS assessment include: the nature and level of freshwater pollution strongly depends on socio-economic development; the most common water pollutant is organic material from domestic sewage, municipal waste and agro-industrial effluent; and the high water nitrate levels found in Western Europe and the United States are a result of the nitrogen fertilizers and manure used for intensive agriculture. The GEMS assessment also noted a dramatic increase in the use of fertilizers in developing countries, particularly where intensive irrigation allows for double or triple cropping.

Other conditions highlighted in the GEMS report include deforestation, eutrophication, suspended particulate matter (SM) and salinity.

Deforestation, i.e. the clearing of land for agriculture and urban development, often leads to water contamination. When the soil is stripped of its protective vegetative covering, it becomes prone to erosion. This in turn leads to higher water turbidity, because of the increased amounts of suspended matter, to nutrient leaching and to a decreased water-retention capacity of the soil. There is also concern about the destruction of wetlands, which destroys the habitat of many species and removes natural filter mechanisms, permitting many common pollutants to reach water supplies.

Eutrophication is the enrichment of waters with nutrients, especially phosphorus and nitrogen. It can lead to enhanced plant growth and depleted oxygen levels as this plant material decays. It is not always a human-induced problem, but is often linked to organic waste and agricultural runoff. Today 30 to 40 percent of the world's lakes and reservoirs are eutrophic. Not all interventions have proved successful, but

eutrophication can be reversible if mid- and long-term strategies are enacted. Laws and measures introduced to reduce tripolyphosphates (used mostly in detergents) and to remove phosphorus from waste water have had positive effects.

SM consists of materials that float in suspension in water. There are three main sources of SM: natural soil erosion, matter formed organically within a water body and material produced as a by-product of human activity. SM settles on the sediment bed and forms deposits in rivers, lakes, deltas and estuaries. Evidence of human-induced SM from Roman and Mayan times has been discovered in lake beds, implying that this was one of the first types of water pollution. River damming affects the amount of SM flowing from rivers to the oceans because reservoirs act as effective sinks for SM. An estimated 10 percent of the global SM discharge to the sea is trapped in reservoirs. Approximately 25 percent of the water currently flowing to the oceans has been previously stored in a reservoir. Damming can also greatly modify water quality; waters flowing out of reservoirs not only have reduced SM quantities, they are also depleted of nutrients and are often more saline,

which consequently has detrimental effects on downstream agriculture and fisheries.

Salinity is a significant and widespread form of freshwater pollution, particularly in arid, semi-arid and some coastal regions. The primary cause of salinization is a combination of poor drainage and high evaporation rates which concentrate salts on irrigated land. Salinity can adversely affect the productivity of irrigated crops and is also detrimental to industrial and household water users. It is not a new phenomenon; salinization of soil and water in the flood plain of the Tigris and Euphrates Rivers contributed to the decline of the Mesopotamian civilization some 6 000 years ago. The estimated global gross area of irrigated land is 270 million ha. About 20 to 30 million ha are severely affected by salinity while an additional 60 to 80 million ha are affected to some degree. Waterlogged soil, which aggravates the problem of salinity, is usually caused by overwatering and a lack of proper drainage systems. Runoff from agricultural areas fertilized with manure and chemicals pollutes watercourses and groundwater by increasing levels of nutrients.

The present level of water pollution warrants that steps be taken to control further contamination of water resources. More serious action needs to be taken in water resource management, waste water treatment and the provision of safe public water supplies. In developed and developing countries there should be controls and regulations regarding the treatment and recycling of industrial effluents, while efforts must be made to replace harmful products and ban dangerous pesticides.

There is compelling evidence that at least 20 to 30 percent of the water currently used in households and industries can be saved by adopting appropriate regulatory and policy instruments (tariffs, quotas, groundwater extraction charges). The twin benefits of clean water and reduced demand can be obtained if the recycling or reuse of water is encouraged in industries through pollution control legislation and economic incentives (water tariffs based on economic costs, effluent charges and low-interest loans for effluent and sewage treatment plants). Similar savings may be possible in irrigated agriculture by investments in canal lining, by encouraging less water-intensive crops (through relative output prices) and by raising irrigation rates.

Source: UNEP. 1991.
Freshwater pollution. UNEP/
GEMS Environmental Library.
No. 6. Nairobi.

two years; or 100 luxury hotel guests for 55 days.[12]

Industry requires large amounts of water, but most of it is recycled back into the water system. The major problem is that much of this water is returned polluted with wastes, chemicals and heavy metals. Over 85 percent of total withdrawals by industry are recycled as waste water.[13]

Domestic water demand is moderate in comparison with agriculture and industry but its quality requirements are high. Domestic and municipal water uses include drinking, washing, food preparation and sanitation.

Water and health

Two of the most troubling domestic water supply issues for policy-makers are access and health. Nearly one billion people in the world are without clean drinking-water. Providing easier access to safe drinking-water significantly improves health conditions. Personal hygiene increases when water availability rises above 50 litres per day (which generally means that it must be delivered to the house or yard). An estimated 1.7 billion persons contend with inadequate sanitation facilities. The lack of sewage collection and treatment is a major source of surface and groundwater pollution.

Health officials identify five categories of disease related to water: *i)* water-borne diseases (typhoid, cholera, dysentery, gastroenteritis and infectious hepatitis); *ii)* water-washed infections of the skin and eyes (trachoma, scabies, yaws, leprosy, conjunctivitis and ulcers); *iii)* water-based diseases (schistosomiasis and guinea-worm); *iv)* diseases from water-related insect vectors such as mosquitoes and blackflies; and *v)* infections caused by defective sanitation (hookworm).

The World Bank's *World Development Report 1992* estimates that providing access to safe water and adequate sanitation could result in two million fewer deaths from diarrhoea among young children and 200 million fewer episodes of diarrhoeal illnesses each year.

Water as a strategic resource

Water, even when plentiful, is frequently drawn into the realm of politics. Domestic laws and well-established customs can help resolve water-related disputes at national and village levels but international law has not developed fast enough to deal with the growing number of water-related conflicts between many countries and regions. In 1989, Egypt's then Minister of State for Foreign Affairs, Boutros-Ghali, declared: "The national security of Egypt is in the hands of the eight other African countries in the Nile basin."[14] As Postel notes, Boutros-Ghali highlights the importance of water to Egypt's economy as well as the advantage upstream countries have over downstream neighbours.

[12] I. Carruthers and C. Clark. 1983. *The economics of irrigation.* Liverpool, Liverpool University Press.

[13] D.B. Gupta. 1992. The importance of water resources for urban socioeconomic development. In *International Conference on Water and the Environment: Development Issues for the 21st Century.* Keynote Papers. Dublin, Ireland.

[14] See footnote 7, p. 236.

The increasing value of water, concern about water quality and quantity, and problems of access and denial have given rise to the concept of resource geopolitics or "hydropolitics". In this context, water joins petroleum and certain minerals as a strategic resource. Its increasing scarcity and value will only intensify the prevalence of water politics and relevant international conflicts.

Several countries depend heavily on river flows from other countries. Botswana, Bulgaria, Cambodia, the Congo, Egypt, the Gambia, Hungary, Luxembourg, Mauritania, the Netherlands, Romania, the Sudan and the Syrian Arab Republic all receive over 75 percent of their available water supplies from the river flows of upstream neighbours. More than 40 percent of the world's population lives in river basins that are shared by more than one country.

Along with land and energy sources, water has been the focus of disputes and, in extreme cases, even wars. The division of the Indus waters and its tributaries among India and Pakistan provided a salutary warning example. War was only just avoided in the early years of independence by a binding agreement, backed by massive international aid, to build two huge water storage dams and a system of canals. Water could then be channelled to the areas of Pakistan that were deprived of water when some of the Indus tributaries were diverted into Indian territory.

The costs to all parties of this settlement were high but certainly less than the human and financial costs of a conflict. Many other international rivers, including the Nile, Euphrates, Ganges and Mekong, are prospective risk points for disputes. The future of the Jordan waters is already an integral component of regional peace talks and illustrates how complicated hydropolitics can be. The fact that groundwater resources are also involved in the talks adds another dimension of difficulty.

BOX 10
THE INTERNATIONAL CONFERENCE ON WATER AND THE ENVIRONMENT: DEVELOPMENT ISSUES FOR THE 21ST CENTURY

The International Conference on Water and the Environment (ICWE) was held in Dublin, Ireland, from 26 to 31 January 1992. The conference provided the major input on freshwater problems for UNCED, convened in Rio de Janeiro, Brazil, June 1992. The ICWE was attended by 500 participants from 114 countries, 38 NGOs, 14 intergovernmental organizations and 28 UN bodies and agencies.

The major work of the ICWE was undertaken by six working groups which addressed:
• integrated water resources development and management;
• water resources assessment and impacts of climate change on water resources;
• protection of water resources, water quality and aquatic ecosystems;
• water and sustainable urban development and drinking-water supply and sanitation;
• water for sustainable food production and rural development and drinking-water supply and sanitation;
• mechanisms for implementation and coordination at global, national, regional and local levels.

The two main outputs of the conference are the Dublin Statement and Report of the Conference, which set out recommendations for action based on four guiding principles. First, the effective management of water resources demands a holistic approach linking social and economic development with the protection of natural ecosystems, including land and water linkages across catchment areas or groundwater aquifers; second, water development and management should be based on a participatory approach that involves users, planners and policy-makers at all levels; third, women play a central part in the provision, management and safeguarding of water; and, finally, water has an economic value in all its competing uses and should be recognized as an economic good.

THE WATER SECTOR AND NATURAL RESOURCE POLICY

In January 1992, the ICWE concluded that scarcity and misuse of freshwater pose a serious and growing threat to sustainable development and protection of the environment.[15] The conference emphasized that human health and welfare, food security, economic development and ecosystems are all at risk, unless water and land resources are managed more effectively in the future.

To address water problems at local, national and international levels, the ICWE recommended a range of development strategies and policies based on four principles (see Box 10). While the conference participants readily agreed on the wording of the first three principles, the fourth provoked a long and contentious debate. Principle 4 declares that water has an economic value in all its competing uses and should be recognized as an economic good.

For many, it is difficult to reconcile the concept of water as an economic good with the traditional idea of water as a basic necessity and human right. Older elementary economic textbooks explain this conceptual puzzle – why diamonds, which have so little utility, are expensive while freshwater, which is so essential to life, is cheap. More recent texts leave water out of these vignettes. Like fresh air, water was once considered a classic free good; now that it is growing scarce, while not yet expensive, it is at least acknowledged to be valuable.

Scarcity is one of the most important issues in considering the various socio-economic tradeoffs in allocating water among different users. Allocation policies and decisions determine who will have access to water and under what conditions, and what impact this will have on society and the economy.

The cheapness of water is often more apparent than real. It is a free good not because water provision is without cost – obviously this is far from true – but because governments have chosen to charge less than full costs for water services for one or more reasons.[16] These subsidies are now coming under scrutiny. The ICWE's final report acknowledges that failure in the past to recognize water's economic value and the real cost of service provision has led to wasteful and environmentally damaging uses. Moreover, the conference report states that managing water as an economic good is an important way of achieving efficient and equitable use, as well as encouraging the conservation and protection of scarce water resources.

It is in this context that the ICWE and UNCED called for a new approach to the assessment, development and management of freshwater resources. The proposed approach involves the management of freshwater as a finite and vulnerable resource and the integration of sectoral water plans and programmes within the framework of national economic and social policy.[17]

---

[15] *The Dublin Statement and Report of the Conference*. 1992. ICWE, Dublin, Ireland.

[16] Water may be considered a "free" good in the form of rain, but when this free good is captured and delivered to customers by canal, pipe or other means, it becomes a water service. There is generally much less resistance to water service fees than there is to water charges.

BOX 11
FRAGMENTED PLANNING AND WATER RESOURCES IN SOUTHERN INDIA

The World Bank's water resources management policy paper presents several examples from southern India to illustrate the kinds of problem caused by fragmented decision-making. The Chittur River's highly variable flows have traditionally been diverted at many points into small reservoirs to irrigate the main rice crop. The diversion channels are large enough to accommodate flood flows following the monsoon rains. Thus, when a storage dam was constructed, the uppermost channel was able to absorb virtually all the regulated flow. The upper tanks now tend to remain full throughout the year, concentrating benefits and adding to evaporation losses. The more extensive lower areas have reverted to uncertain rain-fed cultivation, and total agricultural value added has decreased. Construction of the storage dam without adequate consideration of downstream users or the existing storage capacity of the basin is one example of how individual project development in isolation can cause significant economic losses.

The construction of the Sathanur Dam on the Ponnani River in Tamil Nadu to serve a left bank command area deprived productive delta areas of irrigation water. While the rights of downstream irrigators are recognized in the dam operating rules, most of the regulated flow is diverted upstream; water losses have greatly increased in the wide sandy bed and no surface water has reached the sea for 20 or more years. Continued spills in about 50 percent of all years were used to justify the subsequent construction of the right bank command, further aggravating shortages in the delta and leading to continual conflicts between the two Sathanur commands. Meanwhile, additional storage dams on upstream tributaries are

A more integrated and broader approach to water sector polices and issues is important because of water's special nature as a unitary resource. Rainwater, rivers, lakes, groundwater and polluted water are all part of the same resource, which means global, national, regional and local actions are highly interdependent.[18] Water use in

[17] UN. 1992. Protection of the quality and supply of freshwater resources: application of integrated approaches to the development, management and use of water resources. Chapter 18, Agenda 21, *Report of the United Nations Conference on Environment and Development*.

[18] P. Rogers. 1992. *Comprehensive water resources management: a concept paper*. Policy Research Working Paper. Washington, DC, World Bank.

adding to evaporation losses in what was already a fully developed basin. Irrigation in the productive delta has declined further and the Sathanur commands in turn are suffering. The high-value crops that were once grown on the main river are being replaced by cultivation on less productive lands, served by tributaries that are more variable than the main river.

The Amaravati River, a tributary of the Cauvery, is the most disputed major river in India. In the absence of a Cauvery agreement, Karnataka (the upstream riparian state) has steadily developed large irrigation schemes, depriving the delta (Tamil Nadu's rice bowl) of its accustomed supplies. Meanwhile, Tamil Nadu has been developing the Amaravati. As at Sathanur, water releases are made from the Amaravati Dam for the traditional areas, but these are far downstream and the substitution of regulated flood flows has encouraged the development of private pumps along the river bank. Even though the new electric connections have now been banned, little can be done to control illegal connections or diesel pumps and, consequently, little water now reaches the lowest commands, let alone the Cauvery. Meanwhile, new storage dams are being constructed on tributaries both in Kerala and Tamil Nadu, further depriving not only the old lands but also the new lands and the pump areas.

Source: World Bank. 1993.
*Water resources management:
a policy paper.*

one part of the system alters the resource base and affects water users in other parts.

Dams built in one country frequently reduce river flows to downstream countries for years afterwards, thereby affecting hydroelectric and irrigation capacity. When a city overpumps a groundwater supply, streamflows may be reduced in surrounding areas; when it contaminates its surface water, it can pollute groundwater supplies as well.

Certain human actions at local levels may contribute to climate change, with long-term implications for the hydrological system worldwide.

Water policies, laws, projects, regulations and administrative actions often overlook these linkages. Governments generally tend to organize and administer water sector activities separately: one department is in charge of irrigation; another oversees water supply and sanitation; a third manages hydropower activities; a fourth supervises transportation; a fifth controls water quality; a sixth directs environmental policy; and so forth.

These fragmented bureaucracies make uncoordinated decisions, reflecting individual agency responsibilities that are independent of each other. Too often, government planners develop the same water source within an interdependent system for different and competing uses (see Box 11). This project-by-project, department-by-department and region-by-region approach is no longer adequate for addressing water issues.

To help resolve the growing number of water resource issues, policy-makers are increasingly being called on to review and explain the conditions, problems and progress in the overall water sector.

This integrated approach requires water managers to understand not only the water cycle (including rainfall, distribution, ecosystem interactions and natural environment and land-use changes), but also the diverse intersectoral development needs for water resources.

The next section further explores this important concept of linking the water sector with the national economy and provides a conceptual basis for understanding the role of economic policy-making.

WATER POLICIES AND AGRICULTURE
II. Water resources: economics and policy

In early civilizations, water played a relatively simple role. It was needed for transportation and drinking and it provided a fishing and hunting source. Over time, sedentary agricultural societies evolved and water use became more important. Families began settling near springs, lakes and rivers to supply livestock and crops with water, gradually developing technologies to divert water for irrigation and domestic purposes. Babylonian, Egyptian, Hittite, Greek, Etruscan, Roman, Chinese, Mayan, Incan and other empires constructed water delivery systems such as long aqueducts to carry water to large cities.[19] In fact, until the middle of the twentieth century, most societies were able to meet their growing water needs by capturing reliable and relatively inexpensive sources.

When water is plentiful relative to demand, water policies, rules and laws tend to be simple and only casually enforced. As populations grow and economies expand, water sectors evolve from an "expansionary" phase to a "mature" phase.[20] At a certain point during the expansionary phase, the financial and environmental costs

---

[19] V. Yevjevich. 1992. *Water Int.,* 17(4): 163-171.

[20] A. Randall. 1981. Property entitlements and pricing policies for a maturing water economy. *Aust. J. Agric. Econ.,* 25: 195-212.

of developing new water supplies begin to exceed the economic benefits in the least productive (marginal) uses of existing supplies. The reallocation of existing supplies, rather than the capture of unclaimed supplies, then becomes the least costly method to maximize benefits.

A water sector in the "mature" phase is characterized by rising marginal costs of providing water and increasing interdependencies among users. In this phase, conflicts over scarcities and external costs arise. (External costs result when one user interferes with another's supply, e.g. when an upstream user pollutes a river and raises costs for downstream users.) These conflicts eventually become so complex that elaborate management systems are needed to resolve disputes and allocate water among different users and economic sectors.

Developing effective water sector policies is troublesome for a number of reasons. First, water has unique physical properties, complex economic characteristics and important cultural features that distinguish it from all other resources.[21] Second, water resource management is administratively complicated because it involves legal, environmental, technological, economic and political considerations.[22] In most societies, political considerations dominate decisions on water resource use. Nonetheless, most policy options are framed and discussed in economic terms.

This section attempts to provide a conceptual basis for understanding water policy interventions while examining the circumstances under which water policies work or fail. It comprises three parts: the first examines the relationship between the water sector and the overall economy; the second explains the social, physical and economic nature of water; the third assesses the advantages and disadvantages of broad alternative approaches to public water policy and also reviews policy issues related to the economic organization of water resource management.

---

[21] R.A. Young and R.H. Haveman. 1985. Economics of water resources: a survey. *In* A.V. Kneese and J.L. Sweeney, eds. *Handbook of natural resources and energy economics*, Vol. II. Amsterdam, Elsevier Science Publishers.

[22] For example, water resource management depends on the government's ability to establish an appropriate legal, regulatory and administrative framework. In fact, markets are based on a system of enforceable private property rights. Private water markets require secure and transferable property rights, including the right to exclude other users.

LINKING THE WATER SECTOR WITH THE NATIONAL ECONOMY

Economic policy-makers tend to confront policy issues one at a time, stating policy objectives in single dimensional terms. This approach presents difficulties because a policy aimed at achieving a single objective usually has unintended and unrecognized consequences. Water managers and policy-makers need to assess the entire range of government interventions to understand fully the economic, social and environmental impacts on a given sector, region or group of people.

Improving water resource management requires recognizing how the overall water sector is linked to the national economy. Equally important is understanding how alternative economic policy instruments influence water use across different economic sectors as well as between local, regional and national levels and among households, farms and firms. For too long, many water managers have failed to recognize the connection between macroeconomic policies and their impact on, for example, technical areas such as irrigation.

Macroeconomic policies and sectoral policies that are not aimed specifically at the water sector can have a strategic impact on resource allocation and aggregate demand in the economy. A country's overall development strategy and use of macroeconomic policies – including fiscal, monetary and trade policies – directly and indirectly affect demand and investment in water-related activities. The most obvious example is government expenditures (fiscal policy) on irrigation, flood control or dams.

A less apparent example is trade and exchange rate policy aimed at promoting exports and earning more foreign exchange. For example, as a result of currency depreciation, exports of high-value, water-consuming crops may increase. If additional policy changes reduce export taxes, farmers are provided with an even greater incentive to invest in export crops as well as in the necessary irrigation (see Box 12).

National development strategies can directly influence water allocation and use in other ways. In the case of a food self-sufficiency strategy, the government may subsidize water-intensive inputs to encourage farmers to produce more rice. By providing financial incentives for rice producers, the government is influencing the demand for water and private irrigation investment through price policies.

Apart from the direct effects on water use resulting from such price policies, the increased demand for irrigation water also has intersectoral, intrasectoral, distributional and environmental implications. The agricultural sector is provided with an economic advantage in access to water *vis-à-vis* the industrial sector (intersectoral); water used for rice gains an economic advantage over water used for other crops (intrasectoral); rice producers with more land and access to water gain over those with less land and water (distributional); and increased pesticide and fertilizer use are likely to affect water quality (environmental).

Sectoral policies affect water use and allocation in non-agricultural sectors in a variety of ways. For example, in the western United States, 70 to 80 percent of the region's water yield results from

BOX 12
ECONOMIC POLICIES AND WATER USE IN THE SYRIAN ARAB REPUBLIC

After struggling throughout the 1980s, the Syrian economy has performed well over the past few years. The end of a two-year drought allowed agriculture and agro-industries to recover in 1991. During the drought, the government was forced to import large quantities of wheat and barley, thereby draining foreign currency reserves. In addition, the lower water levels meant a reduction in hydropower generation, increasing the need for thermal power and, in turn, lowering crude oil exports.

Two of the Syrian Arab Republic's major national development objectives are: achieving food self-sufficiency to reduce dependency on imports; and

expanding agricultural exports to earn more foreign exchange. To support these objectives, the government has invested 60 to 70 percent of the entire agricultural budget in irrigation over the past ten years.

Several factors explain this special attention for irrigation development. The irrigated area comprises only 15 percent of the cultivated land yet produces over 50 percent of the total value of agricultural production. A large part of wheat production as well as all major industrial crops, including cotton, tobacco and sugar beet, are produced on irrigated farms. Production on the remaining rain-fed area, representing

85 percent of the total area, varies greatly from year to year. At present, agriculture accounts for about 85 percent of the country's water consumption, but competition is increasing. During the 1980s, industrial water demand increased by nearly 900 percent. Current projections suggest that water requirements will be two to three times greater by 2010.

The government's effort to promote food self-sufficiency has produced a second generation of water-related problems. To encourage growth in agricultural production and enhance rural incomes, interest rates, seeds, fertilizers, pesticides, transport and energy prices

snowmelt from the high-elevation forests, many of which are under public jurisdiction. Water yields are significantly affected by timber harvest policies on these lands. Rangeland management policies on lower elevations also alter vegetation conditions and thus affect the rate of evapotranspiration, in turn affecting streamflow and groundwater

recharge.[23] In such cases, it is important for downstream city water managers to recognize, understand and become involved in the decisions of

---

[23] B. Saliba, D. Bush, W. Martin and T. Brown. 1987. Do water market prices appropriately measure water values? *Nat. Resour. J.*, 27 (summer).

are subsidized. The government also establishes purchase prices and buys industrial crops, major cereals and feedgrains; e.g. the 1992 domestic wheat price was almost twice the international price.

These policies are contributing to the proliferation of wells in the Syrian Arab Republic. Digging wells to pump groundwater accounts for 80 percent of the newly irrigated land since 1987. With irrigation, farmers obtain higher yields, more stable production and greater profit. Since water is free, the only investment expense required is the well and the pumping gear – a one-time fixed cost. Farmers obtain subsidized credit to purchase subsidized fuel for operating imported pumps purchased with overvalued currency (an implicit subsidy). With these economic opportunities, most farmers want to dig wells or pump surface water.

Other current economic pressures are also influencing farmers' decisions to dig wells and expand irrigation. For example, as incomes in urban areas increase, consumers are demanding more fruit and vegetables. At the same time, recent changes in trade and exchange rate policies are making Syrian agricultural products more competitive in regional markets. Farmers who inititally planned only on supplementary irrigation for winter wheat are finding summer vegetables and irrigated fruit production increasingly profitable.

other sectors such as livestock and forestry.

With the continuing importance of structural adjustment and stabilization programmes, many developing countries are implementing fundamental changes in macroeconomic and sectoral polices. Typical adjustment programmes call for a greater reliance on markets, more open trade, fiscal austerity and a phasing out of producer and consumer subsidies (input and product markets). Budget-reducing measures imply increased competition between and within sectors for funding new water projects. In these situations, the overall economic, social and environmental implications of choices must be carefully addressed. For example, when governments must choose between financing either irrigation projects or hydroelectric power projects, there is an additional social opportunity cost of the irrigation water in countries that are dependent on imported energy sources. At the same time, when water scarcity keeps some farmers on uneconomical lands such as steep watersheds, the country suffers twice: once in terms of reduced production compared with what would be possible with irrigation; and again in terms of erosion and resource depletion, with erosion possibly shortening the life of existing waterworks.[24]

In most countries, pressure has increased not only to modify investment allocations but also to recognize and accommodate new demands for water. The direct implications for water managers include fewer capital investments in new water projects, the elimination of irrigation subsidies, increased efforts to recover its cost and more emphasis on demand management to improve the efficiency of existing supplies.

THE SOCIAL, PHYSICAL AND ECONOMIC NATURE OF WATER

Policy-makers throughout the world treat water as more than a simple economic commodity. Because water is essential to life, they often reject competitive market allocation mechanisms. Many societies believe that water has special cultural, religious and social values. Boulding observed that "the sacredness of water as a symbol of ritual purity exempts it somewhat from the dirty rationality of the market".[25] In many cultures, goals other than economic efficiency play an unusually large role in selecting water management institutions. Some religions, such as Islam, even prohibit water allocation by market forces.

The international community recognizes that access to water is a basic human right. The ICWE asserted that "...it is vital to recognize first the basic right of all human beings to have access to clean water and sanitation at an affordable price".

The connection between water and human life is most dramatic in arid regions, where crop irrigation is essential to food production. In Egypt, little food can be grown without the help of the Nile for irrigation. However, the focus on water's special status tends to obscure the fact that, in most societies, only a tiny fraction of water consumption is actually for drinking and preserving life. In fact, a large portion of urban water is used for convenience and comfort. In the arid

[24] D.W. Bromley, D.C. Taylor and D.E. Parker. 1980. Water reform and economic development: institutional aspects of water management in the developing countries. *Econ. Dev. Cult. Change*, 28(2).

[25] K.E. Boulding. 1980. The implications of improved water allocation policy. *In* M. Duncan, ed. *Western water resources: coming problems and policy alternatives*. Boulder, Colorado, Westview.

western United States, per caput water withdrawal by households frequently exceeds 400 litres per day, about half of which is used to irrigate lawns and gardens. Most of the remainder is for flushing toilets, bathing and washing cars.

Another important influence on water resource policy is societies' partiality for technical solutions. In most countries, water management is typically relegated to the engineering domain. Indeed, most water managers are engineers, who are trained to solve technical problems. As inadequate public policies are increasingly blamed for water-related problems, a strong case is emerging for emphasizing human behaviour as an additional component of water systems.

Physical attributes of water

Water has two additional features that further complicate management efforts: bulkiness and mobility. The value per unit of weight tends to be relatively low (placing water among the commodities that are termed "bulky"). Unlike petroleum, the costs of transporting and storing water are generally high relative to its economic value at the point of use. In crop irrigation, the water applied may yield additional economic values of less than $0.04 per tonne of water. Water is also difficult to identify and measure because it flows, evaporates, seeps and transpires. This evasive nature means that exclusive property rights, which are the basis of a market economy, are hard to establish and enforce.

Many water management problems are site-specific and so elude uniform policy treatment. While water consumption and quality requirements are tied to local populations and development levels, local water availability usually changes with climatic variations throughout the year and over longer cyclical swings. These supplies may be highly variable and unpredictable in time, space and quality. In regions throughout India, for instance, most rainfall is concentrated during a three-month period and there are large year-to-year variations. In addition, forecasts of significant global climate change – attributable to both natural and human causes – raise concerns about longer-term supply trends (see Box 13).

Water projects that attempt to compensate for extreme seasonal variations such as floods and droughts frequently require enormous investments. The economies of size are so large in these cases that unit costs continue to exceed the range of existing demands. This is a classical "natural monopoly" situation in which a single supplying entity is the most economically efficient organizational arrangement.

On the other hand, most economies of size for pumping groundwater are achieved at relatively small outputs and multiple suppliers can therefore operate efficiently. However, aquifers are usually hydraulically linked with rivers or streams – part of a river's volume may come from underground flows and rivers may replenish groundwater stocks. This hydraulic linkage is affected when an aquifer is heavily pumped. A lowered groundwater table may draw water from a connected stream, reducing its flow to surface water users. Box 14 describes the special policy concerns related to aquifers.

Aquifer management is often complicated by the aggregate impact

BOX 13

CLIMATE CHANGE, WATER RESOURCES AND AGRICULTURE

To date, research has not been able to provide clear conclusions about the prospective impacts of climate change and global warning. Among the potential impacts of climate change is its effect on the hydrological cycle and water management systems. For instance, an increase in floods and droughts will increase the frequency and severity of disasters. Relatively small changes can cause severe water resource problems, especially in semi-arid regions and humid areas where demand or pollution has led to water scarcity.

The statement adopted by the Second World Climate Conference, held in Geneva in 1990, concluded that the design of many costly structures to store and convey water, from large dams to small drainage facilities, is based on analyses of past records of climatic and hydrological parameters. Some of these structures are designed to last from 50 to 100 years or even longer. Records of past climate and hydrological conditions may no longer be a reliable guide for the future. The possible effects of climate change should be considered in the design and management of water resource systems.

Data systems and research must be strengthened to predict water resource impacts, detect hydrological changes and improve hydrological parameterization in global climate models.

Agricultural impacts could be significant but researchers are uncertain whether global agricultural potential will increase or decrease. Increases in drought risk are potentially the most serious effect of climate change on agriculture. Disease and pest patterns, raised sea levels and storm surges are additional problems. It also appears that many areas will have increased precipitation, soil moisture and water storage, thus altering patterns of agricultural ecosystems and other water uses.

_____

Source: WMO/UNEP/FAO/ Unesco/ICSU. 1990. Second World Climate Conference. Geneva; and UNEP. 1992. *The state of the environment.*

of the actions of many individuals. Even though each individual may have a negligible impact when taken alone, the sum total can be of major importance. One example is the rapid spread of tube well irrigation in South Asia. One tube well has little effect on the total water supply, but thousands of tube wells can quickly deplete an aquifer. Establishing effective policies to regulate these many small, scattered decision-makers is exceedingly difficult.

Economic attributes of water use

Water provides four types of important economic benefits: commodity benefits; waste assimilation benefits; aesthetic and recreational benefits; and fish and wildlife habitats. Individuals derive commodity benefits from water by using it for drinking, cooking and sanitation. Farms, businesses and industries obtain commodity benefits by using water in productive activities. These commodity benefits represent private good uses of water which are rivals in consumption (e.g. one person's or industry's water use precludes or prevents its use by others). Government policies and regulations that concentrate on improving market access and competition are important means for improving the productive and allocative efficiency of the commodity uses of water.

The second and increasingly important economic benefit of water is waste disposal. Water bodies have a significant, but ultimately limited, assimilative capacity, meaning that they can process, dilute and carry away wastes.

Recreation and aesthetic benefits and fish and wildlife habitats were once regarded as luxury goods outside the concern of governments. Today, these two types of benefit are gaining increased attention. In developed countries, more and more people are focusing their recreational activities around lakes, rivers and seas. In developing nations, as incomes and leisure time grow, water-based recreation is becoming increasingly popular and an adequate supply of good-quality water helps provide a basis for attracting the tourist trade. Examples are cruises on the Nile in Egypt and visits to the Iguazú Falls on the Brazil-Argentina border. Likewise, information and knowledge about how humans have an impact on ecosystems have raised concern about the fish and wildlife benefits provided by water. Fish and wildlife habitats are related to both commodity and recreational uses.

Waste assimilation and recreational and aesthetic values are closer to being public goods than private goods. Public goods are non-rivals in consumption – one person's use does not preclude use by others. For example, the enjoyment of an attractive water body does not deny similar enjoyment to others. Non-rival goods require large amounts of resources to exclude unentitled consumers from using the good. Exclusion costs are frequently very high for water services such as flood control projects and navigation systems. Goods and services that are non-rivals in consumption are normally better suited to public sector interventions, including ownership, provision and regulation.

BOX 14
AQUIFER OVERDRAFT

An aquifer is a geological formation, actually or potentially containing water in its pores and voids. Aquifers consist of the porous rock or soil media (sand, gravel or rock materials) within which water is collected and through which it flows. Moisture from rain or snow that escapes evaporation collects in streams as surface water or seeps into the ground. Soil water not taken up by plants seeps downwards until it reaches the water-saturated zone. Water in aquifers is called groundwater. Groundwater deposits are economical to use for human purposes if they are close to the surface (and thereby inexpensive to pump) and are of good quality.

Aquifers vary greatly in their nature and extent. The quantity, quality and ease of extraction can be determined accurately only after extensive exploration. Underground geology varies widely and is expensive to map. Aquifers may be very thin or hundreds of metres thick; some are local in character, while others extend for hundreds of kilometres. The Ogallala-High Plains Aquifer in the central-western United States underlies more than 10 million ha over six states.

Relative to surface water, groundwater moves very slowly – in some cases only a few metres per year. While aquifers may have accumulated over thousands of years, modern pumping devices can easily exhaust them more rapidly than the natural recharge rate. It is also possible to divert surface water to recharge an existing aquifer artificially and make it available for future use.

Aquifer status reports from many parts of the world suggest that all is not well with our groundwater resources. Symptoms of management problems begin with pumping rates that exceed the natural recharge. Primary symptoms are: an exceedingly rapid exhaustion of groundwater stocks and the consequent increase in pumping costs; the intrusion of poorer-quality water into the deposit being exploited; salt water intrusion from rapid pumping near seacoasts; and mineralized deposits interspersed with better-quality water.

Subsidence of overlying lands is another adverse impact of aquifer overexploitation. As water is withdrawn, the soil and rock particles comprising the aquifer are compressed into a smaller volume and, consequently, crack the earth's surface. This results in damage to buildings, roads, railroads, etc. Another consequence of overpumping may be the interruption of flows in neighbouring wetlands and streams; deprived of their water source, they are reduced in size or may dry up altogether. Other adverse effects from overpumping result when residential or farmers' wells dry up because of the presence of larger and deeper wells.

From a broad perspective, aquifer exploitation can bring about either or both of two types of social dilemma. First, overdraft is an example of a class of resource problems, usually called "common pool" problems.[1] A common pool resource can be defined by two characteristics. The first is subtractibility (meaning that a unit of resource withdrawn by one individual is not available to another individual user). The second is the high cost of excluding potential beneficiaries from exploiting the resource. Fugitive or mobile resources, such as water, petroleum or migratory fish and wildlife, are typical examples of resources with high exclusion costs.

Common pool problems or dilemmas arise when individually rational resource use leads to a non-optimal result from the perspective of the users as a group. Three conditions are necessary to produce a common pool resource dilemma: first, large numbers of users withdraw the resource; second, the actions and characteristics of the individual users and the extraction technology bring about suboptimal outcomes from the group's viewpoint; third, there must be an institutionally feasible strategy for collective resource management that is more efficient than the current situation.[2]

The roots of the problems associated with common pools are found in the inadequate economic and institutional framework within which the resource is exploited.[3] Common pool resources have been typically utilized in an "open access" framework, within which resources are used according to a rule of capture. When no one owns the resource, users have no incentive to conserve for the future and the self-interest of individual users leads them to overexploitation. The characteristics of the economic institutions governing their use is the fundamental issue in managing common pool resources.

The second type of social dilemma associated with groundwater exploitation is the imposition of external costs or externalities. In the presence of significant externalities, the calculation of costs and benefits by exploiters does not yield a collectively optimal rate of exploitation.

---

[1] R. Gardner, E. Ostrom and J.M. Walker. 1990. The nature of common pool resources. *Rationality and Society*, 2: 335-358.

[2] Ibid; and E. Ostrom. 1990. *Governing the commons: evolution of institutions for collective action.* Cambridge, UK, Cambridge University Press.

[3] R.A. Young. 1993. Aquifer overexploitation: economics and policies. *Proc. 23rd Conference of the International Association of Hydrogeologists,* Santa Cruz, Spain.

ECONOMIC ORGANIZATION OF THE WATER SECTOR: MARKETS OR GOVERNMENTS?

Most countries rely on a mix of market policies and direct government interventions to manage water resources. Each system has its own advantages and disadvantages.

A competitive market has the potential to allocate resources (water supplies) efficiently among competing demands. Producers and consumers acting in their own self-interest reach the price at which available supplies are allocated. Private producers, guided by prospective profit, seek to buy inputs as cheaply as possible, combine them in the most efficient form and create products that have the highest value relative to cost.

Consumers' incomes, tastes and preferences influence expenditure patterns, which encourage firms to produce the commodities people are willing and able to buy. Prices are forced upwards for the commodities most desired, and producers allocate resources in the direction of the greatest potential profits. The firms producing desired goods most efficiently are rewarded by profit while the unsuccessful are eliminated, so production occurs at the least cost. However, the needs of potential consumers with limited incomes may either not be met at all or be met only partially.

While the private market has the potential to produce the maximum private-valued bundle of goods and services, the public sector also plays an important role. Public actions incorporate a broader range of social goals than the private sector. The public sector can ameliorate income inequalities, promote development in disadvantaged regions, regulate private activities that harm the environment and control other undesirable effects of a private, profit-oriented monopoly.

Market failures

If water as a commodity, or the economic system in which water is used, meets the preconditions for a market system, government interventions can be minimized. In competitive markets, government's primary role is to emphasize "incentive structures" and to establish "rules". Some of the most important rules are the laws governing the establishment of property rights and the enforcement of contracts.

Market economies experience shortcomings called market failures.[26] Market failures occur when incentives offered to individuals or firms encourage behaviour that does not meet efficiency criteria or, more generally, because efficiency or economic criteria fail to satisfy national social welfare objectives. In these cases, the public sector may intervene to influence water provision and allocation. Market failures affecting water resources include externalities, public goods and natural monopolies. In other cases, even efficient markets may not meet societies' equity criteria so public intervention is necessary to compensate for distributional inequity.

Externalities are inherent in water sector activities. An example is the detrimental effect of saline return water flows (caused by irrigation) on

---

[26] C. Wolf. 1988. *Markets or governments; choosing between imperfect alternatives.* Cambridge, MA, Massachusetts Institute of Technology Press.

downstream water users. Another example is the waterlogging of downslope lands through inefficient irrigation practices. Most irrigators do not normally consider the external costs they impose on others, so governments attempt to protect affected individuals through regulations, taxes, subsidies, fees or technical standards. For instance, irrigation practices can be regulated by setting and enforcing standards to control salinity and waterlogging.

In recent years, the "polluter pays" principle has attracted increased attention in industrialized countries (and to a lesser extent in developing countries). This principle requires producers to pay the "full" cost of their production process, including externalities such as polluting water.

Water storage projects and flood control programmes represent examples of *public goods.* The market does not adequately supply public goods because private entrepreneurs cannot easily exclude non-paying beneficiaries and capture a return on investment. For example, it is not possible to exclude people living along a river from the benefits of a flood protection plan on that river.

A firm that experiences decreasing costs throughout its range of production is easily able to dominate the entire market and become a *natural monopoly* (a common situation in the water sector). Decreasing costs imply increasing returns; thus, the first firm to begin production can always underprice new entrants. Urban water supply systems, hydropower plants and canal irrigation projects are subject to this type of market failure. Unregulated monopolies can restrain production and charge excessive prices; they also

have little incentive to innovate. A water supplier acting as a natural monopoly has the power to impose exorbitant costs – even economic ruin – on its customers.

Public regulation or public ownership can mitigate the undesirable effects of a private, profit-oriented monopoly. When increasing returns exist, the lowest-cost production is that of a single producer. Society is likely to benefit by regulating or owning the monopoly rather than by encouraging competitive suppliers. More than one competitive supplier would present much higher distribution costs.

While free competition is viewed as the most efficient system for allocating resources, potential market imperfections can accentuate income disparities. Societies' public welfare goals often incorporate a broad range of social objectives. Primary among these is ameliorating income inequalities between members of the society and sometimes among political subdivisions or regions. In these situations, the government may direct investment and subsidies towards specific regions or groups. Water projects provide important investment strategies both for human welfare (drinking-water and food supplies) and for infrastructure to support economic development.

Government failures

Even in the event of market failures, public sector interventions or non-market approaches may not lead to the socially optimum solution. In many cases, non-market responses to market failures lead to less than optimal outcomes. In particular, some government agency performance incentives result in a divergence from socially preferable outcomes (both in terms of allocative efficiency and distributional equity criteria). The problem areas relevant to water sector services are:

- *"Products" are hard to define.* The outputs of non-market activities are difficult to define in practice and difficult to measure independently of the inputs that produced them. Flood control or amenity benefits of water storage reservoirs are examples of water system outputs that are hard to measure.
- *Private goals of public agents.* The internal goals, or "internalities", of a public water agency as well as the agency's public aims provide the motivations, rewards and penalties for individual performance. Examples of counterproductive internal goals include budget maximization, expensive and inappropriate "technical-fix" solutions and the outright non-performance of duties. In addition, agencies may adopt high-tech solutions, or "technical quality", as goals in themselves. For example, they may recommend sprinkler or drip irrigation systems when other less expensive but reliable methods are more economical. Finally, irrigation agency personnel may be persuaded, by gifts or other inducements, to violate operating rules for a favoured few.[27]
- *Spillovers from public action.* Public sector projects can also be a major source of externalities.

Salinity and waterlogging of downslope lands can occur just as easily from inappropriately managed public irrigation projects as from private irrigators.

- *Inequitable distribution of power.* Public sector responsibilities, however noble their intent, may not be scrupulously or competently exercised. Yet the monopoly control of water supplies by public agencies provides certain groups or individuals with so much power over the economic welfare of water users that procedures to protect those of limited influence should be of prime importance.

Economic structure and irrigation

For many years, the economic systems in a number of developing countries discriminated against agriculture through policies such as high levels of protection for domestic manufacturing sectors, overvalued exchange rates and taxes on agricultural exports. Most developing countries today are at some stage of structural reform, attempting to adjust and transform their economies towards a more liberal economic trade regime – modifying government involvement and increasing market influence.

The developing world's recent record in consolidating macroeconomic stability with solid economic growth is very mixed. Where success is evident, most of the economic transformation has taken place at the macro level and much remains to be done to effect the consequent adjustments at the micro level, at the level of water users in other words.

Even with widespread acceptance of the need for macroeconomic price

---

[27] R. Wade. 1982. The system of administrative and political corruption: land irrigation in south India. *J. Dev. Stud.*, 18: 287-299.

policy reforms for all other sectors since the early 1980s, the dominant supporting actions for agriculture have been non-price policies. For non-agricultural sectors, the new policy mix includes minimizing state involvement in the pricing and marketing of inputs and outputs, privatization and limiting government borrowing.

Despite the irrigation sector's often being sheltered or even benefiting from the effects of these economic policy reforms, government subsidy cuts are inevitably affecting the scope and efficiency of agricultural support services. In most countries, there is a pressing need to discuss how various policy options, including both public interventions and market-oriented, private sector activities, may assist the irrigation sector in the process of economic reform.

Section III reviews the advantages and disadvantages of some of these policy measures for surface water, groundwater and water quality.

WATER POLICIES AND AGRICULTURE
III. Water policies and demand management

To help select the most appropriate policy option or programme alternative, policy analysts divide the water sector into supply-side and demand-side components. The supply-side approach is structure-oriented; investments in water projects are combined with engineering and technical expertise to capture, store and deliver water and to make systems operate effectively. The supply side focuses on providing water and related services.

For most of the twentieth century, policy-makers have focused their attention on the supply side. Economists have evaluated public water supply and policy options through benefit-cost analysis (BCA). The main purpose of BCA is to assure that scarce resources (such as labour, capital, natural resources and management) are all employed to their best advantage. BCA attempts to quantify the advantages and disadvantages to society of alternative policies or actions in terms of a common monetary unit.[28]

With new water-related problems arising in many parts of the world, policy-makers are increasingly emphasizing non-structural approaches to water management. A non-structural approach encompasses demand management, scientific research,

---

[28] See footnote 21, p. 252.

education and persuasion to coordinate how humans use water. These demand-side policies attempt to address the human causes of water problems such as water quality degradation, overexploitation of aquifers and the decreasing availability of water flows to meet non-consumptive water uses (hydroelectric power, pollution assimilation and fish and wildlife habitats).

In part, this user-focused approach entails coordinating and influencing people through organizations and institutions. This focus on water users aims to promote least-cost, environmentally sound water planning and takes both demand and supply options into account. Voluntary associations, government bureaucracies and private businesses are examples of organizations that operate on both the demand (user) side and the supply (delivery) side of water supply systems. On the supply side, large hierarchical organizations usually control the capture, storage, conveyance and distribution of surface water. Demand-side organizations, for example water user associations, are established to represent the interests of irrigators and to introduce and enforce water allocation rules.

This section examines how water institutions and water allocation systems incorporate a user-focused approach to address surface water, groundwater and water quality issues related to agriculture.

INSTITUTIONS AND WATER POLICY

Institutions are defined more broadly than simply government agencies and private organizations. Institutions are "...sets of ordered relationships among people which define their rights, exposure to rights of others, privileges and responsibilities".[29] In this context, institutions set the "rules of the game" within which the economic system operates. For example, the property rights system is considered a water institution because it includes provisions which determine access to water and land. The property rights structure helps define the incentives, disincentives, rules, rights and duties (including informal customs and formal legal systems) that guide human activities and encourage conformist behaviour.[30] Thus, property rights are part of an institutional arrangement governing economic activities including water use.

Many demand-side policies attempt to coordinate water use through institutions such as property rights and incentive structures such as prices. Altering the institutional system of permissions, restrictions, incentives and penalties can compel consumers to do what they might not otherwise do. For instance, financial inducements (monetary rewards and penalties) can encourage people to use water in a more socially desirable way.

Two factors significantly influence the form of water institutions in a

[29] A.A. Schmid. 1987. *Property, power and public choice*, 2nd ed. New York, Praeger.
[30] D.W. Bromley. 1989. *Economic interests and institutions: the conceptual foundations of public policy*. New York, Blackwell.

society: the relative scarcity of water and the transactions costs required to establish and enforce water rights. While scarcity is both supply- and demand-dependent, the human pressures on the demand side are probably the most important. Transactions costs include the resources required to obtain information, negotiate agreements on property rights and police these agreements. Water supply and demand characteristics make transactions costs for water relatively high and the value of water relatively low compared with other resources or commodities.

Many economists are trying to find ways to improve water-use efficiency through improved institutional performance. Research to date suggests that institutions and technological change are altered in response to the same types of incentives.[31] When water is plentiful relative to demand, laws governing water use tend to be simple and enforced only casually. Where water is scarce, more elaborate institutional systems evolve. Higher population and income levels as well as technological advances are prompting many governments to establish formal water-use and water quality management systems.

Establishing an institutional structure for allocating water is a fundamental role of social policy for any nation. The choice of structure is ultimately a compromise between the physical nature of the resource, human reactions to policies and competing

social objectives. Not surprisingly, different cultures make tradeoffs based on the relative importance of their particular objectives. Countries try various means to balance economic efficiency (obtaining the highest value of output from a given resource base) and fairness (assuring equal treatment).[32] Individual freedom, equity, popular participation, local control and orderly conflict resolution are other important objectives which societies must juggle when choosing a structure for water allocation.[33]

[31] V.W. Ruttan. 1978. Induced institutional change. In H.P. Binswanger and V.W. Ruttan, eds. Induced innovation. Baltimore, The Johns Hopkins University Press.

[32] P. Bohm and C.F. Russell. 1985. Comparative analysis of policy instruments. In A.V. Kneese and J.L. Sweeney, eds. Handbook of natural resources and energy economics, Vol. I. Amsterdam, Elsevier Science Publishers.

[33] See D.A. Stone. 1988. Policy paradox and political reason. Glenview, Illinois, USA, Scott, Foresman; and A. Maass and R.L. Anderson. 1978. ... and the desert shall rejoice: conflict, growth and justice in arid environments. Cambridge, MA, Massachusetts Institute of Technology Press.

WATER ALLOCATION SYSTEMS

In an "ideal" market-based water allocation system, entitlements (water rights) are well defined, enforced and transferable and they confront users with the full social cost of their actions. This type of market-dependent institutional arrangement requires security, flexibility and certainty.[34] Security refers to protection against legal, physical and tenure uncertainties.

The assumption is that users will undertake profitable long-term investments to obtain and use water supplies only if water entitlements are reasonably secure.

A system is flexible if allocations between users, uses, regions and sectors can be changed at a low cost in relation to benefits. Flexibility implies that changes in demand are accommodated easily by reallocating water to higher-valued uses as they emerge. Certainty is also necessary: water-use rules must be easy to discover and to understand.

The three basic types of "water rights" systems are: *i)* riparian – only those owning the land in physical contact with a natural watercourse have a right to use it; *ii)* prior appropriation – based on beneficial and actual use; and *iii)* public administration – a public authority authorizes water distribution and use. Prior appropriation and public administration are the most common systems in use throughout the world.

Property rights systems and surface water allocation

Some water allocation systems are relatively decentralized and based on entitlements or rights to specific quantities of water. Examples of these types of system are found in the western United States and southern Australia. In contrast, France uses a more centralized public utility model of water allocation (see Box 15). Chile is the only country with a comprehensive water allocation system that establishes tradeable property rights.[35]

Chile's water law: allows trade between and among economic sectors; protects third party rights; establishes compulsory water user associations and a national water authority to resolve conflicts; and allows for judiciary solutions to those conflicts not resolved by water user organizations or the water authority.[36] Water transfers require authorization at two levels – those of the local water user associations and the national water authority.

While formal tradeable water rights systems have not been established in other developing countries, Rosegrant and Binswanger[37] document the expansion in surface water and groundwater markets. One recent study on surface water trade in

---

[34] S.V. Ciriacy-Wantrup. 1967. Water economics: relation to law and policy. *In* R.E. Clark, ed. *Waters and water rights: a treatise on the law of waters and related problems*, Vols I-VII. Indianapolis, Allen Smith.

[35] M.W. Rosegrant and H.P. Binswanger. 1993. *Markets in tradeable water rights: potential for efficiency gains in developing country irrigation.* Washington, DC, IFPRI.

[36] R. Gazmuri. 1992. *Chilean water policy experience.* Paper presented at the World Bank's Ninth Annual Irrigation and Drainage Seminar, Annapolis, Maryland, USA.

[37] See footnote 35.

BOX 15
A "PUBLIC UTILITY" MODEL FOR WATER ALLOCATION AND POLLUTION CONTROL

France's model for allocating water could be termed a "public utility" model. Administration is centred in six river basin committees (RBCs) and six river basin financial agencies (AFBs) which control water abstraction, treatment and delivery. The RBCs are the centre for negotiations and policy-making regarding water management at the basin level. The AFBs base action plans on extensive water data (quality and quantity needs) and are the centre of knowledge and technical expertise for the government and other interested water users. The RBCs collect fees, award grants and loans, develop long-term plans, collect and analyse water data, conduct studies and finance research.

The RBCs approve 20- or 25-year water development plans and, every five years, establish action plans to improve water quality. They also set two fees to be paid by water users: one for water consumption and the other for point source pollution. The fees provide incentives for users and also form a fund to encourage better water use through grants or soft loans. The RBCs include representatives from national, regional and local government administrations as well as individuals from industrial, agricultural and urban interests.

Those withdrawing water outside the authority (excluding small units) must measure and pay for it. Costs depend on the source (surface or ground) and how valuable it is in the specific basin. This approach also employs the "polluter pays" principle. While pollution assimilation is recognized as a legitimate water use, the entity causing pollution must pay for the costs of remediating the pollution and must compensate for any damages. Reports indicate that the system is self-financing and that it has performed well over 25 years.

The French approach provides feasible and apparently effective solutions to the major concerns about public water management: water scarcity, pollution and conjunctive use of ground and surface water.

It does, however, appear to rely more on centralized administrative discretion and less on the preferences and initiatives of private individuals. For example, water charges are set without regard for scarcity values based on bids and offers by users.

Source: World Bank. 1993.
Water resources management:
a policy paper.

Pakistan reported active markets in 70 percent of watercourses.[38]

The water allocation system in the western United States originated last century and evolved out of the customs of miners and farmers.[39] This system is called the "prior appropriation" doctrine because water entitlements are granted according to the date on which a person applies the water to a beneficial use. The phrase "first in time, first in right" describes the basic principle, as the date of appropriation establishes the order in which users may draw from the water source.

In the western United States system, the individual's property interest in water is limited to the right to divert and use a specified quantity. Private individuals cannot "own" water but have "usufructuary" rights. The state retains ownership and determines which uses are beneficial. Beneficial uses were originally limited to private sector, off-stream purposes in agriculture, households and industry. More recently, in-stream uses for recreation and for fish and wildlife habitats are being recognized.

Water rights are generally tied to a specific parcel of land. However, in most states these water rights can be sold, without loss of priority, to another individual for use on another parcel. Rights are protected by the state from other appropriators and cannot be taken from an individual by the government without just compensation for the foregone economic value.[40]

In the prior appropriation system, irrigation water rights are administered by private non-profit cooperative organizations or by public districts, under the supervision of the state government. Financing requirements and cost recovery are normally based on area served rather than on a strict volumetric pricing system. Early in the history of western irrigation, private capital was the main source of funds. In the twentieth century, private financing has mostly been replaced by federal subsidies. In contrast, municipal and industrial water supplies are typically financed by the users, with a full-cost pricing rule.

In recent years, southern Australian states have begun to allocate water through a system of transferable water entitlements.[41] The Australian water law is based on a non-priority permit system under state control and ownership. Individuals obtain a right to use water through a licence issued by a state agency; this right is usually for a specified type of use on a designated tract of land. In contrast to the United States doctrine of prior appropriation, all users share equally in supply shortfalls and permits expire after a specified time period. Recent studies indicate the need to base permits on the water system's capacity in proportion to the quantities assigned in the original permit.[42]

---

[40] R.A. Young. 1986. Why are there so few transactions among water users? *Am. J. Agric. Econ.*, 68: 1143-1151.

[41] J.J. Pigram. 1992. *Transferable water entitlements in Australia*. Centre for Water Policy Research, University of New England, Armidale, New South Wales, Australia.

[42] N.J. Dudley and W.F. Musgrave. 1988. Capacity sharing of water reservoirs. *Water Resour. Res.*, 24: 649-658.

---

[38] See footnote 35, p. 269.

[39] D. Getches. 1990. *Water law in a nutshell*, 2nd ed. St Paul, Minnesota, West Publishing.

In southern Australia, the transfer of rights is generally limited to water users in the same watershed, with special conditions imposed to protect supply reliability and to prevent third-party damages. Reports evaluating water market performance highlight two points: first, the system is facilitating reallocation from low-value to higher-value uses; and, second, transferable entitlements should be considered as part of a broad package of decentralized decision-making for the entire water sector.[43]

Prices and surface water allocation

In practice, market forces rarely establish prices for water. Instead, prices are set by publicly owned supply agencies or regulated private utilities. Water prices ("rates" in public utility jargon) have an impact on both efficiency and equity as well as influencing agency revenues. The charging scheme for recovering costs and allocating water is a decision variable for the supplying or regulating agency.

Rate-setting can be evaluated within a multiple objective framework in which allocative efficiency, equity of income distribution and fairness in apportioning costs all play a role in evaluating pricing policies. The secondary criteria of simplicity, administrative feasibility and stability are also taken into account.

The most commonly employed pricing policy for water is a *flat rate charge*, designed primarily to recover costs. Flat rates are not set according to the volume received, although a proxy for volume usually provides the basis for the charge. In agriculture, the most frequent basis for a water charge or service fee is the area irrigated. For residential use in the industrialized world, flat rate charges have been based on the number of residents, the number of rooms, the number and type of water-using fixtures or measures of property value.

Flat rates are criticized because they do not include incentives for rationing water in line with willingness to pay. Such schemes are, however, simple to administer and assure the supplier adequate revenue. The high cost of installing and monitoring meters is suggested as being the main reason for continuing the flat rate approach. This argument is convincing in cases where water is plentiful, supply costs are low and managers doubt the rationing effects of volumetric pricing. In other cases, water managers are turning to volumetric pricing to address water scarcity problems and the high costs of developing new supplies. Box 16 presents evidence from developing countries that pricing does indeed restrict water use.

Policy-makers who are primarily interested in allocative efficiency (maximizing net social product) as the goal for a pricing scheme advocate *marginal cost pricing*. The marginal cost represents the incremental cost of supplying a good or service. The marginal cost is a schedule of costs related to quantity and typically rises as further increments are supplied. When water prices are set at the marginal cost, rational consumers demand additional water only as long

---

[43] For an extended discussion, see K.D. Frederick. 1993. *Balancing water demand with supplies: the role of management in a world of scarcity*. Technical Paper No. 189. Washington, DC, World Bank.

BOX 16
PRICE IMPACTS ON WATER USE

In Australia, Canada, Israel, the United Kingdom and the United States, studies have demonstrated that water demand drops by 3 to 7 percent when prices charged to households rise by 10 percent. While it is difficult to measure elasticity of demand without metering consumption, some research in developing countries indicates how prices, combined with other policy efforts, affect water use.

China
In Beijing a water quota and high rates for exceeding it led to a 37 percent reduction in industrial water use in the 1980s. During the same period, the industrial sector was able to expand rapidly.

India
A fertilizer plant at Goa reduced water consumption by 50 percent in response to higher water prices. The Goa plant now uses 10.3 m³ to produce 1 tonne of nutrient, paying $0.12 per m³. In contrast, a similar plant at Kanpur pays $0.01 per m³ but uses 24.35 m³ per tonne of nutrient.

Indonesia
In Bogor a water tariff increase ranging from 200 to 300 percent (from $0.15 to $0.42 for the first 30 m³ per month) decreased monthly consumption by around 30 percent for domestic and commercial connections.

Source: R. Bhatia and M. Falkenmark. 1992. *Water resource policies and the urban poor: innovative approaches and policy imperatives.* Background paper for the ICWE, Dublin, Ireland.

as willingness to pay (demand) exceeds the incremental costs. In theory, marginal cost pricing yields the most economically efficient allocation.

A number of obstacles are encountered in the application of marginal cost pricing. One problem is the variety of definitions of the appropriate marginal cost concept, particularly whether to use a short-run (variable cost) concept or a long-run,

full-cost approach. A long debate ensued from the "short-run marginal cost" pricing proposal which emerged from welfare economists' work in the 1930s. For example, Coase [44] strongly objected to setting utility prices at

_____

[44] R. Coase. 1971. The theory of public utility pricing and its applications. *Bell J. Econ.,* 1: 113-128.

short-run marginal costs, especially where marginal costs are below average costs (thereby incurring a deficit and requiring a public subsidy). Coase also criticized the absence of a market test to determine whether users are willing to pay the full cost of supplying the commodity; the redistribution of income to favour users of decreasing-cost industrial products; and the impetus towards centralization of the economy.

Most of these criticisms can be dealt with by a multipart pricing system: the first part sets marginal price equal to marginal cost while the second part levies an assessment to recover those costs that exceed marginal costs. Even so, multipart schedules often fail to reflect the economic concept of opportunity costs correctly, focusing instead on recovering historical or embedded costs. The relevant opportunity costs include both the cost of securing incremental supplies of water and the value of water in alternative uses.[45] Opportunity costs should be determined after adjusting prices to allow for distortions brought about by government interventions in pursuit of other objectives. In economic jargon, "shadow prices" must be used.[46]

The *average cost pricing* principle calls for recovering all costs by charging for each unit according to the average cost of providing all units. It is simple and easy to understand, as well as fair and equitable. Beneficiaries pay only the resource costs incurred on their behalf. The desired signals to users are provided, although not in as precise a way as with multipart pricing. Here, too, often only historical costs, not opportunity costs, serve as the basis for calculating average costs.

The *ability-to-pay* principle rests heavily on the equity criterion. Water charges are dependent on income or wealth rather than on costs. This principle is the most common basis for setting irrigation rates throughout the world and is also regularly applied to village water supplies in developing countries. Economists who view water as a commodity tend to be critical of the ability-to-pay approach. Since charges bear little relation to costs, no allocative test of willingness to pay is provided. This ability-to-pay concept is inherently subjective and political pressures frequently influence the formula in ways that distribute wealth from taxpayers to water users.

In many places throughout the world, water is scarce enough to justify the tangible and intangible costs of establishing formal pricing systems. Flat rates could satisfy cost repayment requirements in the absence of serious shortages. However, when the signals of water scarcity are absent, pressures arise for structural solutions (more construction to capture, store and deliver water) to satisfy incorrectly perceived water "needs".

The inevitability of scarce water supplies suggests the eventual adoption of multipart rate schemes that reflect the real or opportunity costs of water and other resources required for service provision. The literature describing the most desirable form for

[45] G.M. Meier. 1983. *Pricing policy for development management.* EDI Series in Economic Development. Baltimore, The Johns Hopkins University Press.
[46] L. Small and I. Carruthers. 1991. *Farmer-financed irrigation.* Cambridge, UK, Cambridge University Press.

water markets and the literature dealing with water pricing have converged on the notion of a pricing system that reflects the opportunity cost of water via the mechanism of transferable water entitlements.[47]

Coordinating groundwater extraction
Groundwater is an extremely important resource for many developing countries, including Bangladesh, India, Pakistan and the entire Near East region. In India, tube wells accounted for nearly one-half of the net irrigated area by the late 1980s.[48] Because it deals with the complex interaction between society and the physical environment, aquifer management presents a formidable problem of policy design. Two types of collective policy decisions must be addressed in the management or regulation of overexploited aquifers. For one type, termed "managing the water", decisions are based on: *i)* the appropriate annual rate of pumping; *ii)* the geographic distribution of pumping; and *iii)* whether water supplies are augmented and/or the aquifer artificially recharged. The other type of policy decision, "coordinating the pumpers", determines: *i)* the institutions and policies that divide the extraction rate among potential

individual users and user classes and that influence pumper behaviour; and *ii)* how rules for limiting pumping are monitored and enforced.

The three broad types of institutional arrangement for managing aquifers are prices and charges, quantity-based controls and exchangeable permits.

Prices and charges to control pumping. Charging pumpers is one potential method of achieving economically efficient extraction rates. An appropriately scaled charge or tax confronts pumpers with both the foregone user cost and the external cost (from increased pumping costs) imposed on neighbouring pumpers. This type of water charge internalizes user costs and external costs and achieves an optimal extraction rate.

In aquifer management, this approach takes care of one important difficulty – pumpers impose costs on themselves (that is, the external costs are reciprocal). The reduction in water use resulting from a tax would be at the expense of redistributing rents to the taxing authority, thus lowering the net income of the aquifer exploiters.

Quantity-based controls. Quantity-based control mechanisms range from simple well permits to exchangeable pumping entitlements. Well and pump permits grant the right to install and operate a well of a particular capacity. Irrigation permits frequently specify the lands on which well water can be used, thereby restricting the transport of water to other sites.

To protect existing pumpers, permits for new wells may restrict locations. For example, the state of Colorado in the United States identifies "designated groundwater basins" (for aquifers with

---

[47] See, for example, R.K. Sampath. 1992. Issues in irrigation pricing in developing countries. *World Dev.,* 20(7): 967-977; and A. Randall. 1981. Property entitlements and pricing policies for a maturing water economy. *Aust. J. Agric. Econ.,* 25: 195-212.
[48] P. Crosson and J.R. Anderson. 1992. *Resources and global food prospects.* World Bank Technical Paper No. 184. Washington, DC, World Bank.

limited natural recharge) in which new well permits must meet specific criteria – no more than 40 percent of stocks may be exhausted within a three-mile radius over a 25-year period. In most cases, well permits do not set limits on the quantity of water pumped. The economic limitations imposed by pumping costs and crop prices are assumed to be sufficient to inhibit excessive withdrawals.

Permits with appropriate size and spacing specifications can slow extraction rates. They are relatively easy to monitor and are reasonably palatable to pumpers who strongly reject more stringent regulatory devices. On the other hand, permits are most effective before problems have become severe and complex – in cases when preventing new wells and pumps solves the problem or when pumped water is not exported away from the area overlying the aquifer. In more serious cases, where all existing users must reduce annual extractions, regulating rates of withdrawals must be considered.

A pumping "quota" is a more precise quantity control mechanism. The quota specifies a fixed annual rate of extraction for each water user. The initial quantity might be assigned in proportion to use in a base period (although such an approach might set off a pumping race to establish initial rights) or be based on the proportion of land that is owned overlying the aquifer. The technology for metering withdrawals is neither complex nor expensive so, if the pumpers are willing to be metered, regulatory monitoring and enforcement need not be difficult. In principle, pumping quotas are no different from conventional surface water rights,

which entitle owners to fixed shares of each year's available flow.

Anecdotal evidence suggests that farmers who have previously enjoyed an unregulated aquifer believe they are entitled to unlimited withdrawals for use on lands overlying the aquifer. They are frequently reluctant to submit to metering and the meters, once installed, are reportedly subject to high rates of unexplained "breakdowns".

Very small wells for livestock or individual households could be exempted from the permit and quota system. At moderate levels of overdraft, the cost of monitoring every small pump set might outweigh gains from reduced pumping. Also, for income distribution reasons, policy-makers may not want to restrain smallholders.

Transferable pumping entitlements.
When a fixed quota is too inflexible in the face of changing water stocks and demand conditions, transferable pumping entitlements are an alternative. The pumping entitlement can be divided into two parts: one component may provide a claim to the stock of water and the other to the annual recharge. Both claims may vary from year to year, with allotments set by the groundwater authority. Annual rights to the basic stock would vary according to current and anticipated economic and hydrological conditions (including energy and commodity prices, interest rates and the remaining stock of groundwater). Rights to the natural recharge and return flows from human uses could be set to reflect a moving average of estimated recharge in recent years.

The transferability of entitlements promotes economic efficiency over the long term, permitting a reallocation to higher-valued uses as economic conditions change. Transferable rights are also consistent with local control criteria and require minimal interference with individual freedom to operate a farm or business enterprise.

One recent study suggests that tradeable rights and water markets for groundwater appear to be increasing in India, where as much as one-half of the gross area irrigated by tube wells involves purchased water.[49] Box 17 provides an additional example, explaining how agricultural water sellers operate in Bangladesh.

In groundwater management, the quantity-based approaches appear to be preferable to pumping charges. They can yield economically efficient solutions with simpler monitoring and enforcement burdens, while avoiding the redistributive implications of taxes or subsidies. While some new outside controls on pumping are required, they need not be any more repressive than property rights for other resources or commodities.

Conjunctive groundwater and surface water management

Joint management of interrelated stream-aquifer systems is called *conjunctive ground-surface water management*. Aquifers interrelated with flowing streams frequently present both distinct management opportunities and problems. Unrestricted access to groundwater may reduce the water available to those holding rights to streamflows.

In the state of Colorado in the United States, a problem arose two decades ago for irrigators in the South Platte

basin. Groundwater exploitation reduced streamflow, but by only a small fraction of the amount pumped. The most obvious option – placing the pumpers into the existing surface water rights system while protecting those holding existing rights to surface water – would have sacrificed most of the substantial economic benefits of exploiting the aquifer.

After several methods had been experimented, a solution was found based on markets for existing rights to surface water. In the event of a shortage, groundwater users could replace the portion of streamflows taken by pumping the aquifer. They could also replace water by purchasing and delivering rights to reservoir water. Young, Daubert and Morel-Seytoux [50] demonstrated that this decentralized approach is economically superior to the alternative of forcing pumpers into the surface water rights system. The ready availability of substitute water supplies and the existence of flexible water transfer institutions are necessary to implement a solution of this type. Numerous opportunities for this market-based approach do exist, however, in the large alluvial basins of the Indus and Ganges-Brahmaputra.

_____

[49] See footnote 35, p. 269.

_____

[50] R.A. Young, J.T. Daubert and H.J. Morel-Seytoux. 1986. Evaluating institutional alternatives for managing an interrelated stream-aquifer system. *Am. J. Agric. Econ.*, 68: 787-791.

PRESERVING WATER QUALITY

Human production and consumption activities generate pollution by extracting and processing raw materials into consumer goods. Some wastes (residuals) from the production process are returned to the environment (e.g. waste chemicals from petroleum refineries discharged to rivers). Similarly, households return unwanted by-products of consumption activities to the environment – to sewers, to the air or to sites receiving solid waste. The *materials balance* principle, derived from basic laws of physics regarding the conservation of matter, asserts that, over the long term, the mass of residuals discharged to the

---

BOX 17

THE WATER SELLERS

One does not have to be a landowner or even a farmer to benefit from irrigation. Irrigation increases employment and provides the landless with opportunities to work on farms or in upstream or downstream activities. In Bangladesh irrigation has also opened profitable new avenues for the landless by enabling them to exploit and sell water. The "water sellers" are organized with the help of PROSHIKA, one of a number of NGOs that aim to develop an irrigation service for farmers by tapping the abundant groundwater which underlies much of Bangladesh.

Fresh groundwater is a widespread resource but is usually present in small amounts, only sufficient to service household needs. However, in the great alluvial basins such as the Nile, the Indus and the Ganges-Brahmaputra, the alluvium may be 100 m or more deep and 10 or even 20 percent of its volume may be freshwater. The vast reserve of groundwater is recharged annually by floods, canal and field seepage and rainfall infiltration.

Groundwater is particularly valuable because it is available consistently and, unlike surface reservoirs, evaporation losses are minimal. Where surface canal supplies are also available, and provide a more or less constant base supply, groundwater can be used conjunctively to satisfy the peak demands of crops. In addition, groundwater is usually available close to farms and is more under the control of farmers.

In rural Bangladesh more than 50 percent of the population is landless or has less than 1.2 ha of land. Providing the poor access to productive resources such as water is clearly important. The PROSHIKA experience was based on organizing landless groups, using credit effectively to purchase mobile pumping equipment and providing a reliable service to farmers and share-tenants.

The water sellers targeted their service in areas where

environment must equal the mass of materials originally extracted from the environment to make consumption goods. The environment's importance as an assimilator of residuals is equal to its importance as a source of materials.[51]

One important policy implication of the materials balance principle is that

residuals must end up somewhere, either as mass or energy. The management of discharges into

_____

[51] For further discussion see D.W. Pearce and R.K. Turner. 1990. *Economics of natural resources and the environment*, Chapter 2. Baltimore, The Johns Hopkins University Press.

---

farmers had very small scattered plots of land and irrigated their fields from shallow low-cost boreholes, using portable diesel pump sets. The farmers pay the sellers in crop share, cash or, occasionally, a fixed amount in kind.

The success of the PROSHIKA mission depended primarily on access to credit (which PROSHIKA helped to organize) as well as skills training and technical support relating to agriculture, management,

literacy, health and group solidarity.

The water sellers: improved water-use efficiency and equity by improving the direct access of small farmers who are usually tail-enders in other systems of irrigation; benefited from the more equitable distribution of productive assets between those with and those without landholdings; created additional employment within and outside the group as a consequence of more productive agriculture;

obtained cash to buy more food and promote commercial agriculture; participated in the developing water market, which has prevented richer peasants or landlords becoming monopoly "waterlords"; and showed that the poor can be creditworthy without land as collateral.

The PROSHIKA experience is being replicated throughout Bangladesh and has many lessons that may serve for other developing countries.

_____

Source: G.E. Wood, R. Palmer-Jones, Q.F. Ahmed, M.A.S. Mandal and S.C. Dutta. 1990. *The water sellers: a cooperative venture by the rural poor.* West Hartford, Connecticut, Kumarian Press.

watercourses must be integrated with waste disposal into the atmosphere and landfills. Reducing the amount of waste discharged into water may not solve society's overall problem if the waste is sent elsewhere, such as into the atmosphere by burning or to a land site by dumping.

There are two types of water pollution: *point source* and *non-point source*. Point source pollution refers to cases where a readily identifiable source, such as a pipe or ditch, transports the pollutant to a water body. Regulation and monitoring focus on the point of discharge. In non-point source pollution, no single source of pollutant discharge is easily identifiable but the collective effect of numerous sources results in a significant impact. Non-point pollution problems pose a difficult and costly management challenge.

Non-point pollution control options

Policy options to control non-point water pollution present special difficulties because of the great variety of sources and pollutants. The primary source of non-point pollutants is the agricultural sector. Fertilizers and pesticides are carried off the soil surface into lakes and streams or percolate into groundwater deposits. Aquifers become polluted by nitrates from fertilizer application and livestock wastes. Timber harvesting, land clearing for urban development and mining also originate non-point pollution of waters. Urban storm drainage, leakage from buried fuel tanks and subsurface and surface mining are other contributors.

Runoff from farms and forests may carry suspended solids and sediments, dissolved solids and chemicals (mineral fertilizers, particularly nitrogen and phosphorous, and pesticides). Other substances that often occur in diffuse source runoff are oxygen-demanding organic matter, petroleum products, heavy metals and faecal bacteria. Non-point source pollution is also characterized by its episodic nature. Occasional heavy rainfall or snowmelt is typically the trigger, in contrast to the more even flows of discharge from point sources. These characteristics of source type and timing imply that a variety of control technologies may be required for effective abatement.

Non-point pollution control may also be determined by the nature of human activities causing the problem. For example, the pollution resulting from a farmer's land depends not only on the rainfall patterns and the land characteristics (slope and soil texture), but on numerous prior land-use and production decisions, including choice of crops, tillage practices and pesticide and fertilizer use. The farmers' production choices are, in turn, influenced by market prices for inputs and products as well as by government price and income support programmes. In fact, pollution from the farm sector is exacerbated by government policies that make certain crops overly attractive. Successful policy interventions must change those aspects of farmers' decisions that are the source of pollutants.

Policy options for non-point pollution control are classed as *cognitive, regulatory* and *incentive-based.* Cognitive (voluntary) approaches use education, moral persuasion and technical assistance to influence the behaviour of polluters. Cognitive approaches are attractive because of their low economic and political costs. They have been tried in some countries but have had limited success. Several factors account for this; for example, private costs incurred to change land-use practices can be substantial while private gains may not be obvious. Because of the uncertain linkage between changing production decisions and improving water quality (often at distant locations), individuals have little incentive to try new approaches.

Regulatory policies call for specific actions or prohibitions against those responsible for water quality degradation. One approach is to use "design standards" that specify actions to be taken (such as a management plan for sediment control) or actions prohibited (such as certain cropping practices on highly erodible lands).[52] "Performance standards", in contrast, place limits on the rate of pollution discharge to a water body. In this case, interference with land-use practices is only in response to observed violations.[53]

Neither technique is without limitations. Design standard regulations are easier to enforce; however, they may be unnecessarily costly because their general application may impose costs on those

who contribute little to the problem. Performance standards, in principle at least, focus more directly on the pollutant source but are difficult to monitor and enforce. Because an accurate measurement of discharges (particularly from small farms) is nearly impossible, disputes over actual sources of pollutants are unending.

The alternatives to regulatory policies include various incentive methods such as taxes, subsidies and emission trading policies.[54] Taxes or fees can be levied on either inputs or pollution outputs. For example, extra charges have been imposed on agricultural fertilizers in Sweden, with proceeds used to fund water quality monitoring. Higher costs are expected to reduce fertilizer application rates and, therefore, water pollution. However, taxes are unlikely to be set high enough to affect land use significantly because of the adverse effects on income.

Alternatively, charges may be levied for pollution by imposing an "effluent charge". However, the technical and administrative complexity of setting fees and linking numerous farmers precisely to the damages caused by their effluent is mind-boggling. No successful example of this type of taxation of non-point source pollution is presented in the literature.

Subsidies could encourage farmers to reduce pollution, adopt more appropriate land-use practices or make environment-friendly investments. Subsidies to prevent soil erosion (and

---

[52] W. Harrington, A.J. Krupnick and H.M. Peskin. 1985. Policies for non-point source pollution control. *J. Soil Water Conserv.*, 40: 27-33.

[53] G. Anderson, A. De Bossu and P. Rush. 1990. Control of agricultural pollution by regulation. *In* I.B. Braden and S.B. Lovejoy, eds. *Agriculture and water quality: international perspectives.* Boulder, Colorado, Reiner.

[54] K. Segerson. 1990. Incentive policies. *In* J.B. Braden and S.B. Lovejoy, eds. *Agriculture and water quality: international perspectives.* Boulder, Colorado-London, Reiner.

the associated productivity losses) have a long history in many countries and are the most politically attractive of the available options. In contrast to other approaches, which impose costs on the emitting source and spread benefits over the entire society, subsidy costs are spread over the general population and gains are offered to the land user. Nonetheless, paying polluters to avoid polluting activities remains objectionable to some groups. Moreover, payments may be made to individuals who would adopt proper practices anyway.

Finally, the outright purchase of water rights and/or land-use rights is another approach. For instance, a public agency could acquire rights to part or all of the polluting lands and manage them to safeguard water quality. The purchase of tropical forest lands by either public or private agencies has been undertaken to preserve first-growth forests, with water quality improvements as a side-benefit. Again, costs are borne primarily by beneficiaries rather than by the land users whose practices are actually responsible for the pollution.

WATER POLICIES AND AGRICULTURE
IV. Policy issues in irrigated agriculture

Irrigation is an essential component of sustainable agricultural development but it is not a unique sector, since it faces challenges similar to those confronting other public and private sector economic activities. The previous two sections (II and III) of this report examine how various demand-side policy measures can help shape decisions that encourage water-use efficiency. However, while appropriate policies and regulations are necessary for improved water productivity, a variety of additional water-saving measures are required in the irrigation sector.

Some water-saving measures involve taking more advantage of the scientific, engineering and technological advances in soils, plants and irrigation. Other measures focus on administrative and managerial reforms to improve efficiency, including the decentralization of public irrigation agencies and a greater reliance on farmer-owned and farmer-operated irrigation.

This final section highlights three key irrigation issues: declining growth and investment trends in irrigation; the difficulties imposed by irrigation-induced environmental degradation; and efforts to reform managerial and administrative systems. Many of today's irrigation-related problems appear imposing and even overwhelming. The purpose of this section is not to present a discouraging overview of irrigation's future but to focus on important issues that will shape its future. When scarce water is under human control in irrigation systems, there are many opportunities to use it optimally. Understanding the problems associated with improper irrigation as well as the potential for efficient irrigation is a first step in the search for these opportunities.

IRRIGATION IN THE 1990s AND BEYOND

Many pressing irrigation issues reflect the various economic, social and political influences affecting society in this period of changing economic conditions and environmental concerns. At times, irrigation-related problems are the result of a distorted macroeconomy which, despite providing operating subsidies, renders farming unprofitable and results in repeated underinvestments on farms over long periods. If the macroeconomy is performing poorly and if prices in the economy are markedly distorted from their real value to society, then it is inevitable that irrigation will suffer.

In other cases, irrigation itself is the problem. The overall performance of many irrigation projects is disappointing. Evaluations document a wide range of problems, including: cost and time overruns; poor management; the non-realization of full, planned benefits; adverse environmental and health impacts; and the exacerbation of inequities in the existing social and economic distribution of assets among farmers.[55] Box 18 summarizes the major irrigation policy issues identified by FAO and the actions the Organization is undertaking to improve water use in agriculture.

Trends in irrigated area
In 1800, approximately 8 million ha of farmland were irrigated around the world. By the end of the nineteenth century, the irrigated area had

---

[55] A.K. Biswas. 1990. Monitoring and evaluation of irrigation projects. *J. Irrig. Drain. Eng.*, 116(2): 227-242.

expanded to 48 million ha, mostly as a result of large water projects in India and what is now Pakistan.[56] By 1990, net irrigated area reached 237 million ha, of which nearly three-fourths were in the developing countries. China, India and Pakistan alone now account for about 45 percent of the world's irrigated area and 60 percent of the developing country total.

On a global basis, irrigated area expanded by an average of 1 percent per year during the early 1960s, reaching a maximum annual rate of 2.3 percent from 1972 to 1975. The rate of expansion began decreasing after 1975 and is now less than 1 percent per year. At current levels of population growth, the slower expansion in irrigated areas is resulting in an unprecedented decline in the per caput amount of irrigated land.[57]

Among the reasons for the decrease are increased construction costs, falling real prices for wheat and rice, a growing awareness of environmental and social costs and poor irrigation performance at the farm and project levels.[58]

Crop prices and construction costs
Construction and operation costs for irrigation projects have risen steadily over the past four decades as the world's best land and most of the readily available water supplies have been developed. Over the same time period, world cereal prices fell sharply.

For example, the real price of rice fell by 40 percent between the mid-1960s and the late 1980s.

In Indonesia and India, the real costs of irrigation have doubled since the early 1970s. In the Philippines and Thailand, irrigation construction costs have increased by 50 percent and in Sri Lanka, costs have tripled.[59] After reviewing various recent reports and evaluations, including many from the World Bank and FAO, Postel[60] reports that: "Today, capital costs for new irrigation capacity run between $1 500 and $4 000 per ha for large projects in China, India, Indonesia, Pakistan, the Philippines and Thailand. They climb toward $6 000 per ha in Mexico. In Africa, where roads and other infrastructure are often lacking and parcels that can be irrigated are relatively small, per hectare costs have climbed to $10 000-$20 000, and sometimes even higher. Not even double-cropping of higher-valued crops can make irrigation systems at the top end of this spectrum economical." It is not just large-scale projects that have become so expensive; FAO estimates that even medium-sized irrigation construction costs range from $2 400 per ha in Asia to $7 200 in Africa.

Likewise, the modernization of existing irrigation projects is becoming increasingly expensive. Many old projects designed for monocropping have produced gradually declining yields. These systems need to be

---

[56] S. Postel. 1989. *Water for agriculture: facing the limits.* Worldwatch Paper 93, December.

[57] See footnote 7, p. 236.

[58] M.W. Rosegrant and M. Svendsen. 1993. Asian food production in the 1990s. *Food Policy*, 18(2): 13-32.

---

[59] M. Svendsen and M.W. Rosegrant. 1992. Will the future be like the past? In *Irrigated agriculture in Southeast Asia beyond 2000.* Colombo, Sri Lanka, IIMI.

[60] See footnote 7, p. 236.

**FAO AND
SUSTAINABLE
WATER USE**

The International Action Programme on Water and Sustainable Agricultural Development (IAP-WASAD) was created by FAO with the cooperation of other UN organizations as part of a strategy to implement the Mar del Plata Action Plan for the 1990s.

IAP-WASAD identified five priority areas of action and some common measures requiring concerted action to realize sustainable agricultural development. It pointed out that scarcity of water is a major constraint for the further agricultural development of arid and semi-arid countries. Without renewable water supplies and appropriate and reliable water control and management, sustainable agricultural development is simply not possible.

The five priority areas of action identified by IAP-WASAD include: efficient water use at the farm level; waterlogging, salinity and drainage; water quality management; small-scale water programmes; and scarce water resources management.

Efficient water use at the farm level
The current and potential roles of rain-fed and irrigated agriculture need to be quantified, taking into account the probabilities of rainfall, the available irrigation water supplies and

their cost. Small-scale irrigation, including supplementary water for rain-fed agriculture, and a variety of water harvesting and water spreading techniques have considerable potential and should be developed further.

The proposed priority action plan points out that increases in developing country production in the 1990s must come first from increases on existing irrigated lands and second from increases on rain-fed lands. In order to improve performance and control groundwater levels in irrigated agriculture, it is necessary to establish monitoring, evaluation and feedback systems. Appropriate irrigation management training must be available and irrigation extension services must be strengthened and developed further. Information must be shared among farmers, extension workers, design engineers and researchers for a better understanding of various approaches and techniques. Measures should also be taken to review, develop and implement water pricing policies, establish effective demand and supply management procedures as well as cost recovery mechanisms for the operation and maintenance of irrigation projects.

In order to increase production on rain-fed lands,

it will be necessary to employ existing soil and water management knowledge to help increase the efficient use of agricultural water. Additional research in the areas of rain-fed water and soil management is also necessary and examples of successful and effective rain-fed practices must be collected and disseminated.

Waterlogging, salinity and drainage

Waterlogging and salinity are among the principal causes of decreasing production on many irrigated projects. Waterlogging is due to an excessive input of water into systems that have finite natural drainage capacities. After waterlogging has occurred, soil salinity increases because the irrigation water leaves dissolved solids in the soil. It is essential to monitor the water table levels from the beginning of a project in order to implement corrective measures before soil damage has occurred.

The action plan notes that, in rain-fed agriculture, surface drainage is required to prevent any temporary waterlogging and flooding of lowlands. In irrigated agriculture, artificial drainage is essential under most conditions. It is vital to minimize drainage requirements and costs by

reducing the sources of excess water through improved system design and on-farm water practices. The implementation of groundwater monitoring and water balance studies will help predict drainage requirements. Soil salinity monitoring in problem areas should also be started in order to adopt practices to overcome the problems. In addition, pilot drainage projects should be established in waterlogged and salinized areas to verify the design and effectiveness of materials.

Water quality management

In sustainable agricultural development, there are two significant aspects of water quality: the quality of water used in irrigated agriculture should not cause crop damage; and agricultural activities should not adversely affect the quality of surface or groundwater in such a way that their subsequent use is limited.

The action plan suggests that groundwater quality monitoring programmes to assess agricultural water quality and its impact be developed and that strategies be implemented to minimize the extent of water pollution inflicted by agricultural activities. In addition, national strategies and plans should be prepared, outlining the rational use of treated waste

water and drainage water for agriculture.

Small-scale water programmes

Small-scale projects are normally undertaken by communities or individuals who develop and operate most activities of the projects themselves, although some technical assistance is often necessary. Small-scale programmes include a diversity of technologies such as water harvesting, well development, river offtakes and use of wetlands.

The action plan submits that small-scale water programmes can assist sustainable agricultural development. However, further expansion must be founded on adequate technical advice and support, improved institutional collaboration and greater involvement of the local communities. National policies and programmes should be developed for implementing small-scale water projects for rural development. Accordingly, it will be necessary to enhance the capability of farmers to implement, operate and maintain small-scale water programmes.

The monitoring and evaluation of the small-scale water project will help identify the failures as well as the successes.

Scarce water resources management

Many countries face constraints to their development, as available water resources are insufficient to meet demand. The action plan notes that water scarcity conditions require long-term strategies and practical implementation programmes in order to ensure that agricultural water is used in ways consistent with limited water resources.

A strategy must be formulated for the management of land and water for sustainable agricultural development under water-scarce conditions.

At the same time, these policies must remain compatible with the prevailing socio-economic conditions as well as the environment. In addition, measures should be implemented to deal with drought situations and to improve community resilience during such times.

Supporting action

The five areas outlined above require common supporting actions, i.e. the development of adequate databases, adaptive research, institutional strengthening, human resource development, improvements in socio-economic analysis, environmental protection, technology transfer and infrastructure development.

redesigned to permit crop diversity, increase yields, conserve water and reduce environmental hazards. Modernization involves canal lining, improved hydraulic control structures, better land development and appropriate irrigation techniques.

Increasing real investment costs (including recognition of environmental costs) and falling crop prices have resulted in a substantial reduction in new irrigation projects. Aggregate lending for irrigation by both international donors and the major cereal-producing countries in the 1980s was only half what it was in the 1970s.[61] This reduced investment has, in turn, resulted in falling growth rates in irrigated area.

Irrigation and land degradation

Escalating demand pressure on water resources during the past decade is only one of the concerns for policy-makers. Both watersheds supporting water resources and the land base supporting irrigated agriculture are becoming degraded. Industrial and domestic pollution are affecting irrigated agriculture, while sedimentation washed from denuded hillsides is filling up irrigation reservoirs and small tanks. At the same time, improper irrigation practices are causing waterlogging, salinization, soil erosion and water pollution which directly affects other irrigators.

FAO estimates that of the 237 million ha currently irrigated, about 30 million ha are severely affected by salinity and an additional 60 million to 80 million ha are affected to some extent. UNEP recently reported that the rate of loss of irrigated land from waterlogging and salinity is 1.5 million ha per year.[62] Millions of hectares of irrigated land, from Morocco to Bangladesh and from northwestern China to central Asia, suffer from this progressive condition. Salinity-affected areas as a percentage of total irrigated area is estimated to be 10 percent in Mexico, 11 percent in India, 21 percent in Pakistan, 23 percent in China and 28 percent in the United States.[63]

Salinity is caused by a combination of poor drainage and high evaporation rates which concentrate salts on irrigated land; it mainly occurs in arid and semi-arid regions. Even good-quality irrigation water contains some dissolved salt and can leave behind tonnes of salt per hectare each year. Unless this salt is washed down below the root level, soil salinity will result. A number of factors influence salinity, including the water table depth, the capillary characteristics of the soil and management practices regarding the amount of water applied in excess of plant evapotranspiration to leach the salts.[64]

A related concern is the rapid rise in groundwater levels, leading to waterlogging and depressed crop

---

[61] See footnote 59, p. 285.

[62] UNEP. 1992. *Saving our planet*. Nairobi, UNEP.

[63] D.L. Umale. 1993. *Irrigation-induced salinity: a growing problem for development and the environment*. World Bank Technical Paper No. 215. Washington, DC, World Bank.

[64] R.A. Young and G.H. Horner. 1986. Irrigated agriculture and mineralized water. *In* T.T. Phipps, P.R. Crosson and K.A. Price, eds. *Agriculture and the environment*. Washington, DC, Resources for the Future.

yields. Waterlogging is not an inevitable result of irrigation. It occurs when excessive water is used in systems with finite natural drainage capacities. Seepage occurs if: soils are very light; canals and watercourses are not lined or maintained; farmers near the head of a system withdraw or apply excessive amounts of water; fields are not levelled; and/or the delivery system cannot respond to rainfall by closing inflows.

Irrigation can raise groundwater levels to within a metre or so of the surface, which results in secondary salinization when the groundwater brings to the surface dissolved salts from the aquifer, subsoil and root zone. If seepage and horizontal recharge exceed evaporation and natural drainage, then groundwater levels rise, eventually causing waterlogging. In arid areas where the upward movement of water and evaporation exceeds downward percolation and where the groundwater, soil or irrigation water contains some salt, the buildup of salt in the soil surface layers will eventually reach toxic levels.

Countries suffering from water-logging and salinity face a dilemma. They cannot force abandonment of affected lands because of the growing populations that depend on them, but neither can they afford to drain the lands. The cure for rising water tables is drainage and improved water management to reduce percolation, but drainage is expensive and improved water management requires both on-farm investment and the training of extension personnel and farmers.

At the end of the 1950s, Pakistan began to sink wells to pump out salt-laden water. The initial capital costs were high and operating costs have been increasing constantly. Between 1971 and 1985 the cost of managing the wells and drains rose fivefold. Today, Pakistan spends more on reclaiming land than on irrigation. The cost of maintaining drains is five times the recurrent costs of supplying water and most farmers pay only half the costs of delivering irrigation.

Some policy-makers argue that, as the value of water rises, management will improve and much of the wastage (which creates unhealthy conditions as well as increased drainage requirements) will be reduced. Farmers may then be willing to pay for a drainage service that makes their investments sustainable.

Irrigation: good government and good management

Political pressures often prevent the implementation of apparently sensible and fair reforms for water services. Where water is regarded as a special commodity or has emotional or religious importance, governments are reluctant to charge farmers for irrigation. Policy-makers often find it extremely difficult to raise sufficient revenue to match even their priority needs. The practical effects on traditional public service activities may be harsh. Water has been one of the first sectors to feel the effects of budget-saving efforts and changing resource availability. However, it is unlikely to be treated more austerely than other areas. Box 19 discusses the relationship between good government and irrigation performance.

A prime opportunity for irrigation advancement – and indeed for development in general – lies in the enormous potential of the 237 million ha already operating. While the total

BOX 19

GOOD GOVERNMENT AND IRRIGATION PERFORMANCE

Improvement in irrigation performance depends on good government, or *governance*. This may be an obvious assertion, but what exactly does the term mean for irrigation? There are four main elements of governance which can be considered at the national or the local level: the *legitimacy* of government; its *accountability*; its *competence*; and its respect for human rights and the *rule of law*.[1]

Legitimacy refers to the way in which a population gives consent to be governed, how they are consulted and whether the consent can be withdrawn. *Accountability* of politicians and officials is tested by how they explain their role and decisions, provide information and can be held responsible for their behaviour. A government demonstrates *competence* in formulating policies and translating them into action in a timely and effective way. Governments who respect human rights establish a framework of known *laws*, applicable to

all, without bias or corruption, with limits on and protection against the exercise of arbitrary power. We can illustrate how these four elements of governance might affect irrigation with simple examples.

Legitimacy. When a new project is planned, are those living in the area consulted about the design of the scheme? Are there recognized representative groups of farmers, including women? Are the office holders elected and accountable to the members? Do these groups participate in decisions that affect them? For example, if a groundwater irrigation project threatens the availability of drinking-water from hand pumps, are self-help groups informed and invited to make representations?

Accountability. Are the financial plans of the irrigation scheme made public and arrangements made to explain them to farmers? Are there performance criteria with audit arrangements to ensure that officials adhere to the rules and, if they fail to perform satisfactorily, call them to account? Are officials responsive?

Competence. Can the professional staff prepare accurate budgets and effectively deliver services such as timely canal maintenance? Are there arrangements for training them or replacing them with competent officers if they fall short of their duties?

Rule of law. Is there a clear legal framework to regulate groundwater abstraction to prevent overpumping of the aquifers? Is it enforced? Can pollution by industry or by saline water from upstream drainage projects be regulated? Are illegal extractions by farmers at the head of canals monitored and offenders charged by legal processes that are fair, timely, objective and without discrimination on grounds of race, gender or minority status?

---

[1] World Bank. 1992. *Governments and development.* Washington, DC, World Bank.

value of irrigation investment in the developing world today is about $1 000 billion, the returns are well below the known potential. Many irrigation schemes need substantial investment to be completed, modernized or expanded. Although it is increasingly expensive, rehabilitation can yield high returns.

Beyond capital investment, investment in human resources is needed to improve economy, efficiency and effectiveness in management.

Investment in irrigation management can be an integral component of a productive rural employment policy and resource management can be improved to match developments in engineering and science. Those concerned with irrigation development and the welfare of farmers and their families are beginning to take a broader view of their responsibilities, paying as much attention to management and development as to engineering.

A review of recent literature on public sector policy and management suggests the need for transforming the typical irrigation authority from a technical, engineering and construction culture to an organization that is focused more on people (farmers) and that is more autonomous and more responsive to customers, i.e. a strategic management service agency.

In the developing world, many water subsector groups recognize their role in the management of valuable water and other complementary resources for economic growth and poverty alleviation.

Irrigation management does not generally have a good record, but the full extent of the problems has been obscured by a lack of performance assessment criteria and a variety of hidden subsidies. It has often been assumed that, if farmers are not complaining, then management must be good. A lack of complaints in a highly subsidized system is not a good indicator of efficiency. Similarly, managers with obvious problems have sometimes had to cope as best they could with a range of exogenous factors that limit their effectiveness, for instance overvalued exchange rates.

One example of a remarkably successful administrative reform is found in the Philippines, where irrigation operating expenses have been reduced, revenue has matched operating costs and operational performance has improved in the process. Box 20 details the Philippines' experience, demonstrating what can be achieved with good planning, dedication, determined technical staff and political support.

Irrigation management: water user associations and NGOs

An increasing number of private sector groups, including water user associations and other NGOs, are taking over some public sector irrigation responsibilities. The inclusion of water users in irrigation planning, management and ownership is proving to be an effective method for increasing irrigation system efficiency in many cases.

Studies throughout the world demonstrate that user participation in irrigation services improves access to information, reduces monitoring costs, establishes a sense of ownership among farmers and increases transparency as well as accountability in decision-making.[65]

Water user associations are expected to increase in number and importance over the next decade as the stress on self-reliance increases. Already, governments are turning many aspects of public irrigation systems over to water user associations. Well-documented examples can be seen in Argentina, Colombia, Indonesia, Mexico, Nepal, the Philippines, Sri Lanka and Tunisia. In Indonesia, for example, the government had transferred more than 400 irrigation systems, covering 34 000 ha, to water user associations by 1992.[66] In the future, as farmer financing becomes more commonplace, user groups will become even more powerful.

Other NGOs undertake a wide range of water-related functions, from developing projects for rural water supplies and minor irrigation to fostering water user associations for water management purposes. Some NGOs encourage farmers to try new technologies, for example the catchment protection and sprinkler irrigation techniques introduced by the Aga Khan Rural Support Programme in Gujarat, India.

Many NGOs stem from local initiatives and operate as independently funded and self-managed groups. These organizations bring fresh views, new ideas and participatory working methods to other areas of development policy and practice. Much of their success is attributed to their local knowledge as well as their interest in and experience of regional conditions. They have been particularly active in promoting the interests of poor and disadvantaged groups through articulate and forceful advocacy and service provision. In addition, the local base of NGOs may allow them to reach vulnerable or remote groups which are exceptionally difficult to reach with conventional public schemes.

Water is not an easy sector in which to promote cooperation, but the potential gains are high, which makes renewed efforts worthwhile. Resolution of many water allocation and development problems requires a common willingness to forego personal benefit for the social good. Government efforts to promote personal sacrifice through economic policies, laws and regulations that require self-restraint, such as water rationing or optimum groundwater pumping regimes, have seldom proved effective. On the other hand, with their close local contacts and skills in group mobilization and cohesion, NGOs can provide the institutional leadership required to bring about socially optimum solutions.[67]

___

[65] K.W. Easter and R.R. Hearne. *Decentralizing water resources management: economic incentives, accountability and assurance.* World Bank Technical Paper. Washington, DC, World Bank. (In press)

[66] Ibid.

___

[67] For further information on NGOs, see M. Cernea. 1985. *Putting people first: sociological variables in development.* Baltimore, The Johns Hopkins University Press; or M. Cernea. 1988. *Nongovernment organisations and local development.* World Bank Discussion Paper No. 40; or S. Paul and A. Israel. 1991. *Nongovernment organisations and the World Bank: cooperation for development.* World Bank Regional and Sectoral Studies.

BOX 20
SELF-FINANCED OPERATIONS:
THE PHILIPPINES' BUREAUCRATIC REFORM

The National Irrigation Administration (NIA) of the Philippines is a good example of how a bureaucracy can, over time, transform its strategy and operating style. Since the mid-1970s, the NIA has evolved from an agency that focused primarily on the design and construction of irrigation systems and told farmers about its key decisions into an agency that gives priority to the management and maintenance of irrigation systems, and that gives farmers, through their membership in irrigators' associations, the opportunity to participate in irrigation system management and to make key decisions about maintenance. How did this transformation come about and what have been its effects?

Commitment from the top. In the early 1970s, the NIA's top management diagnosed correctly that farmer organizations were crucial to effective irrigation management and, therefore, committed the NIA to developing and extending the responsibilities of irrigators' associations. The NIA's willingness to renounce its traditional authority was a key factor in this process.

Legal and financial status of the NIA. In 1974, the NIA was established as a public corporation and ceased to be part of a government ministry. It was given a five-year lead-in period in which to become financially self-sufficient in terms of its operating budget. The NIA's semi-independent status set the scene for farmer-financed irrigation and the devolvement of management tasks to farmers.

A gradual approach. The NIA did not transform itself overnight. The participative approach was first tried in the mid-1970s with smaller-scale "communal" irrigation systems that were traditionally managed by farmers. The end of the 1970s saw the development of a methodology to maximize farmer participation based on two pilot projects. Lessons learned were then incorporated into plans to manage the large-scale "national" irrigation systems jointly. Almost 20 years on, the transformation of the NIA from a top-down bureaucracy continues.

Future directions in water management policy
Sustainable agricultural development depends on sustainable water use. Governments today recognize that the search for sustainable economic growth requires, in part, both economy-wide and sector-specific policy reforms. Economy-wide policies attempt to create a favourable macroeconomic environment while water sector policies, for example, seek to encourage resource efficiency among water users.

Understanding farmers. How has the NIA motivated farmers to participate in and pay for irrigation, to commit time to maintenance, to liaise with the NIA and to plan for the future? The NIA experience illustrates some important preconditions for farmer participation: teaming community organizers and engineers in order to integrate social and technical activities into one process; involving farmers in all project activities from the very beginning, thereby building up their organizational skills; modifying NIA policies and procedures that obstruct farmer participation; allowing enough time for farmers to mobilize and organize themselves before new construction activity.

The quality of the irrigation service provided by and for farmers has undoubtedly improved, system operating expenses have been reduced and the recurrent cost burden of the scheme on the national budget has been eliminated. But what about the impact on irrigation performance? Recent research suggests that the reforms have made water supply more equitable.

On five schemes surveyed five years following the cessation of subsidies, the main impact was the increased equitability of supply. For reasons unconnected with the management reforms, water supplies fell by 13 percent but crop area held constant and yields remained the same. This confirmed the connection between equity of supply and financial viability. To appreciate the value of the reform we need to consider what would have happened to the deteriorating service if the impoverished state bureaucracy had continued to run the schemes.

The current emphasis on macroeconomic policy reforms and economic liberalization has several important implications for irrigation. One of the most important is that the era of large direct and indirect subsidies is nearly over. Moreover, recognition of the value of water (and the high cost of turning a water source into a service delivered to a farm) makes the water sector a prime target for further policy reforms. Nonetheless, irrigation remains a resource-hungry sector in this transitional period. Even successful irrigation consumes large quantities of capital and foreign exchange and ties up scarce skilled personnel.

Like many public sector personnel, irrigation managers must walk a fine line between a tighter control of finance, the need for more positive active leadership and better planning of resource allocations, on the one side, and the contradictory need for more ideas from below (farmer customers), on the other. Financial pressures are likely to be the dominant influence. Irrigation as a public sector agency still relies on budget allocations to obtain financing. Many argue that this gives little incentive to save money and may, in fact, have the reverse effect.

As private sector disciplines are applied in irrigation, policy-makers are finding that: agencies become more supportive of farmers' own efforts and less inclined to make all key decisions before informing farmers accordingly; management seeks more consensus on priorities, more information about the basis of decisions and a common view of external factors affecting management; irrigation schemes seek and receive more autonomy; the financial responsibilities and accountability of managers increases; and managers shift focus from their ministries and governments, depending on the amount of finance generated by service fees.

At present, water engineering feeds off mathematics, physics, chemistry and biology; management feeds off economics, psychology, political science, history and philosophy and also has a high requirement for personal skills in communication, negotiation and teamwork. However, as changes occur in irrigation in many countries, managers find they must acquire new knowledge and a new set of skills.

Following are some of the issues emerging:

- National water politics are shifting from *projects* to *policies* – this trend is likely to continue and even accelerate.
- Water may become a test-bed for economic reform, liberalization and accountability.
- Given water's scarcity and its value to cities and industry, the water subsector will be less dominated by irrigation and its multipurpose uses will be more widely acknowledged.
- Irrigation is a *service* with customers and users; it is not a production industry.
- At the level of the irrigation scheme, the process of water policy formulation, assessment and appraisal needs to include more open groups that are representative of political, technical, managerial and (most important) water user associations.
- These policy groups would be consulted before policy selection and then provide feedback and adjustment in the light of experience.
- The policy groups would identify options consistent with the national policy framework, as opposed to measures to protect and satisfy special irrigation interests.
- The goal is to identify a broader range of water policy options, to have less "policy by crisis" management and more resilience in the face of outside pressures.

Irrigation allows for better and more diversified choices in cropping patterns and the cultivation of high-value crops. Successful irrigation is a crucial determinant of the world's future development because of its influence on the supply and price of food. As the debate over water policies sharpens, it is increasingly important that agricultural policy-makers help shape the nature of the debate and influence policy decisions.

Special chapters

In addition to the usual review of the recent world food and agricultural situation, each issue of this report since 1957 has included one or more special studies on problems of longer-term interest. Special chapters in earlier issues have covered the following subjects:

1957
Factors influencing the trend of food consumption
Postwar changes in some institutional factors affecting agriculture

1958
Food and agricultural developments in Africa south of the Sahara
The growth of forest industries and their impact on the world's forests

1959
Agricultural incomes and levels of living in countries at different stages of economic development
Some general problems of agricultural development in less-developed countries in the light of postwar experience

1960
Programming for agricultural development

1961
Land reform and institutional change
Agricultural extension, education and research in Africa, Asia and Latin America

1962
The role of forest industries in the attack on economic underdevelopment
The livestock industry in less-developed countries

1963
Basic factors affecting the growth of productivity in agriculture
Fertilizer use: spearhead of agricultural development

1964
Protein nutrition: needs and prospects
Synthetics and their effects on agricultural trade

1966
Agriculture and industrialization
Rice in the world food economy

1967
Incentives and disincentives for farmers in developing countries
The management of fishery resources

1968
Raising agricultural productivity in developing countries through technological improvement
Improved storage and its contribution to world food supplies

1969
Agricultural marketing improvement programmes: some lessons from recent experience
Modernizing institutions to promote forestry development

1970
Agriculture at the threshold of the Second Development Decade

1971
Water pollution and its effects on living aquatic resources and fisheries

1972
Education and training for development
Accelerating agricultural research in the developing countries

1973
Agricultural employment in developing countries

1974
Population, food supply and agricultural development

1975
The Second United Nations Development Decade: mid-term review and appraisal

1976
Energy and agriculture

1977
The state of natural resources and the human environment for food and agriculture

1978
Problems and strategies in developing regions

1979
Forestry and rural development

1980
Marine fisheries in the new era of national jurisdiction

1981
Rural poverty in developing countries and means of poverty alleviation

1982
Livestock production: a world perspective

1983
Women in developing agriculture

1984
Urbanization, agriculture and food systems

1985
Energy use in agricultural production
Environmental trends in food and agriculture
Agricultural marketing and development

1986
Financing agricultural development

1987-88
Changing priorities for agricultural science and technology in developing countries

1989
Sustainable development and natural resource management

1990
Structural adjustment and agriculture

1991
Agricultural policies and issues: lessons from the 1980s and prospects for the 1990s

1992
Marine fisheries and the law of the sea: a decade of change

FAO Economic and Social Development Papers

84 Measures of protection: methodology, economic interpretation and policy relevance (1989)

90 The impact of stabilization and structural adjustment policies on the rural sector – case-studies of Côte d'Ivoire, Senegal, Liberia, Zambia and Morocco (1991)

95 Guidelines for monitoring the impact of structural adjustment programmes on the agricultural sector (1990)

96 The effects of trade and exchange rate policies on production incentives in agriculture (1990)

98 Institutional changes in agricultural product and input markets and their impact on agricultural performance (1991)

99 Agricultural labour markets and structural adjustment in sub-Saharan Africa (1991)

103 The impact of structural adjustment on smallholders (1992)

104 Structural adjustment policy sequencing in sub-Saharan Africa (1991)

105 The role of public and private agents in the food and agricultural sectors of developing countries (1991)

107 Land reform and structural adjustment in sub-Saharan Africa: controversies and guidelines (1992) *(French translation in preparation)*

110 Agricultural sustainability: definition and implications for agricultural and trade policy (1992)

115 Design of poverty alleviation strategy in rural areas (1993)

In preparation:

- International agreements for the protection of environmental and agricultural resources: an economics perspective
- Structural adjustment and agriculture: a comparative analysis of African and Asian experience
- A multidisciplinary analysis of local-level management of environmental resources
- Analysing the effects of liberalization scenarios in North-South production and trade patterns using the computable general equilibrium model
- Growth theories, old and new, and the role of agriculture in economic development

TIME SERIES FOR SOFA'93
Instructions for use

The State of Food and Agriculture 1993 is supplemented by a computer diskette, presented in English only on an experimental basis. If, as expected, there is a favourable response, starting with the 1994 issue the publication will also include an improved version of the diskette in French and Spanish.

The diskette, which contains a comprehensive set of annual statistical information on the agricultural, forestry and fishery sector, covers 153 countries and 12 country groups. The data stretch from the year 1961 to 1992 and, in addition to the information used in this publication, include most of the statistics published by FAO as "Country Tables". The diskette provides a program called TIME SERIES, which may be used for reading, displaying and manipulating the data. This program has been developed by Karl Gudmunds and Alan Webb of the Economic Research Service, United States Department of Agriculture, and FAO has been authorized use rights for the distribution of the country tables accompanying *The State of Food and Agriculture 1993*.

Technical information and installation of TIME SERIES for SOFA'93

TIME SERIES is a fast and easy-to-use tool for displaying and analysing large time series data sets. Data can be displayed in the form of charts and tables. The program supports basic statistical analysis and allows time trend projections and cross-sectional comparisons of data to be made. For further analysis, data can be exported into standard formats that are readable by commonly used database and spreadsheet programs or, alternatively, it can be directly exported to an ASCII file format. The program is fully menu-driven, offers an online help facility and can thus be used even by very inexperienced users.

• To use TIME SERIES for SOFA'93, you need:
– a DOS-based minicomputer with a graphic display
– a hard disk with at least 3.8 megabytes free
• If you are using MS-Windows, you can use TIME SERIES as a DOS application.
• TIME SERIES can also be installed on most Local Area Networks.

The program and data files are distributed on your TIME SERIES for SOFA'93 diskette in a compressed form and need to be decompressed before use.

The file containing the program (TSPROG.EXE) and the file containing the data (SOFA.EXE) are both self-extracting.
• For a standard installation from floppy disk drive A to a drive C:\SOFA93 directory:
– insert your TIME SERIES for SOFA'93 diskette in drive A
– type: *A:INSTALL* [press ENTER]

A small batch file on the diskette creates a C:\SOFA93 directory and does the copying and decompression for you.
• Alternatively, for installation on other drives or directories:
– copy the files TSPROG.EXE and SOFA.EXE from your diskette to the drive of your choice
– type TSPROG [press ENTER] ... then SOFA [press ENTER] in order to decompress them

• After installation, to start working with the program:
– type: *SOFATS* [press ENTER]

If you are short of space after successful installation, you may delete the files SOFA.EXE and TSPROG.EXE from your hard disk. You will save 1.4 megabytes, keeping the total space used by TIME SERIES for SOFA'93 to 2.4 megabytes.

Data on SOFA'93 diskette

When you start SOFATS, a list of 11 data files will appear in a central window on your screen. The files include the following data:

AGRFOOD.TS* – contains agricultural and food production indices for 149 countries from 1961 to 1993 (*Source:* AGROSTAT)

AGRFOODA.TS* – contains agricultural and food production indices for 12 regional groups from 1961 to 1993 (*Source:* AGROSTAT)

DEMOGR.TS – contains demographic information for 153 countries from 1961 to 1992 (*Source:* AGROSTAT)

DEMOGRA.TS – demographic information for 12 regional groups from 1961 to 1992 (*Source:* AGROSTAT)

NACCOUNT.TS – national account data for 133 countries covering the years 1961 to 1991; these national account data are expressed in constant 1980 US dollars (*Source:* UN/DESIPA)

PRODUCT.TS – agricultural, fishery and forestry production data for 153 countries from 1961 to 1992 (*Source:* AGROSTAT)

PRODUCTA.TS – agricultural, fishery and forestry production data for 12 regional groups from 1961 to 1992 (*Source:* AGROSTAT)

SUPPLY.TS* – food supply data for 149 countries from 1961 to 1990 (*Source:* AGROSTAT)

SUPPLYA.TS* – food supply data for 12 regional FAO groups from 1961 to 1990 (*Source:* AGROSTAT)

TRADE.TS – trade data for 153 countries from 1961 to 1992 for total merchandise and agricultural trade, from 1961 to 1991 for trade in forestry products and from 1961 to 1990 for trade in fishery products; all trade data are expressed in current US dollars (*Source:* AGROSTAT)

TRADEA.TS – trade data for regional groups covering the same periods as TRADE.TS (*Source:* AGROSTAT)

All data are stored and displayed in units of thousands except for the agricultural and food production indices and the food supply data (*) which are stored in single units. For a correct display of these data, you have to change the default setting of the TIME SERIES (this is explained below). The AGROSTAT-based data have been updated as of mid-1992.

The program does not allow specific handling of missing values. Missing information within the range of country and time coverage is represented by a zero. Zeros can therefore have three different meanings: *i)* a value of zero; *ii)* a very small value not displayed within the range of magnitude; or *iii)* missing information. *Caution:* a zero in the last year of a time series may produce misleading projection results.

• Check the time series in the BROWSE menu and truncate both the data year and the trend year in the SET LIMITS function.

• Select one of the data files listed above with your cursor key and press ENTER.

Data-use caution

Users are cautioned that, when data are not available, FAO estimates are provided. Note that linear or stepwise plotting in graphs may be a sign that the data are estimated, although this is not a foolproof method to detect estimates. For a detailed explanation of data sources and reliability, see the appropriate *FAO Production Yearbook* or *FAO Trade Yearbook.*

Some useful hints for working with TIME SERIES for SOFA'93
Your work with TIME SERIES for SOFA'93 is fully guided by pull-down menus with additional short instructions at the top and bottom of your screen.
• If you need more help:
– press the F1 key, which gives you full online instructions regarding your specific problem
– press the F1 key twice for help according to a list of subjects

After selecting your file, you will normally start by selecting a country and an item from the DATA menu. Then you have a range of five options to display and analyse your data in the GRAPH menu:
• The first choice (DISPLAY) will provide you with an immediate chart display of your data (always return with the ESC key).
• The second choice (TREND LINE) allows you to enrich your data display with a regression line. You have the choice of forcing the program for a linear, parabolic or exponential regression line, or leaving it for the program to determine the "best fit". Returning to the display will now give you a chart containing the data line, the trend line and R-square information.
• The third item (LIMITS) allows you to restrict the display of the time span of your data (DATA DISPLAY) and/or the years for the TREND LINE calculation. A third item (PROJECTION YEAR) allows you to make a time trend projection up to a target year of your choice.
• With the fourth item (STYLE) on the GRAPH menu you can change the shape of your chart (line, bars or scatter).
• The fifth item (VIEWPOINT) lets you switch from a time series display (TIME TREND) of your data to a cross-sectional comparison between countries (COUNTRY PROFILE) or items (ITEM PROFILE). When selecting ITEM or COUNTRY PROFILE, you will be asked to select either a number of

countries/items of your choice or select the TOP MEMBERS, which can be a number up to 50 (if available). The TOP MEMBERS will always be ranked when you display them as a chart. In addition, it is possible to remove a range of members from the top for display. (Hint: If you want to see only the last 20 countries out of 153, just remove 133 countries from the top.)

While you are displaying a graph on your screen
• You can call for help as usual by pressing the F1 key. In TIME TREND display you can scroll through different items and countries by pressing the ↑ and ↓ or the PAGEUP and PAGEDOWN keys. On ITEM and COUNTRY PROFILES, there are similar functions (press F1 for the HELP window).
• You will also see that you can print your graph on a printer by pressing P on your keyboard. Before printing, you can add any text of your choice to the graph (e.g. the REGRESSION function) by pressing the INSERT key. This text can be written in a horizontal or vertical mode and in large or small letters; for help while you are inserting text, press F1.
• You can add up to five different items/countries on one chart in the TIME TREND display. By pressing the + key you will be asked whether you want to add other items or countries or other items from different countries to your chart for a cross-country and/or cross-item comparison. To remove these items/countries again, press the – key.
• If you want to see the underlying numbers of your chart, press: *i)* the letter A and you will see the annual data with some statistics; or *ii)* the letter T and you will see the regression information, including the functional type (the latter will only work if you have opted for a TREND LINE).

Viewing data in the form of tables
• Go to the TABLE menu.
• Select BROWSE and browse through your data with the PAGEUP and PAGEDOWN (countrywise) and Arrow keys (item- and year-wise). Pressing F2 will transpose your table and display the years in

columns, which looks much better in most cases.

• If you need your data in any other program you can compose a table for exporting by selecting CREATE TABLE. Select the countries and items you want to export with the + key and SAVE the table in the format of your choice. Before saving, you may check the data with the VIEW function.

Options from the PROGRAM menu

• With the FILE option, you can select a different data file from your list of 11 files.

• You can write and store your own NOTES with the data file and view them whenever you work with your data. These notes are stored in a separate file with a different extension on your hard disk (no change is made or harm done to your data files).

• With the UNITS option you can change your data display from real figures to INDEX numbers. If you do so you have to determine the PIVOT YEAR, which will be the reference year with a value set to one.

• Changing the MAGNITUDE becomes necessary for the agricultural and food production indices and the food supply data (see above), because these data are not stored in units of thousands. Therefore, when you select data from the AGRFOOD.TS or AGRFOODA.TS files:

  – go to the PROGRAM menu
  – select UNITS and MAGNITUDE
  – place the cursor on 1s and press ENTER

• For SUPPLY.TS or SUPPLYA.TS files:
  – go to the PROGRAM menu

  – select UNITS and MAGNITUDE
  – place the cursor on 1s and press ENTER

You have to change back to 1,000s when working with other data. However, when you start your work with TIME SERIES, the setting will always be for 1,000s (default setting).

• The SCALAR option allows you to apply a factor to your current data set temporarily (valid only for this session). You can thus change the display of the population figures from thousands to millions, for example.

Warranty and conditions

All copyright and intellectual property rights are reserved. The Food and Agricultural Organization (FAO) declines all responsibility for errors or deficiencies in the database, for maintenance, for upgrading and for any damage that may arise from use of the database. FAO also declines any responsibility for updating the data. However, users are kindly asked to report to FAO any errors or deficiencies found in this product.

Note: Data and/or program files may be damaged during shipping. If you discover any damage to your diskette, please return it to:

ESP

FAO

Viale delle Terme di Caracalla

00100 Rome, Italy

You will be sent a replacement diskette as soon as possible.